RHODRI DAV

HOW PHILANTH
SHAPES BRITA

PUBLIC GOOD BY PRIVATE MEANS

Published by Alliance Publishing Trust

Copyright © 2015 Rhodri Davies

ISBN 978-1-907376-24-5

Alliance Publishing Trust
15 Prescott Place, London SW4 6BS

publishing@alliancemagazine.org
www.alliancemagazine.org

Registered charity number: 1116744
Company registration number: 5935154

A catalogue record for this book is available from the British Library.

Typeset in Akzidenz Grotesk and New Century Schoolbook
Cover and text design by Graphicacy

Printed and bound by Hobbs the Printers, Totton, Hampshire, UK

This book is printed on FSC approved paper.

Contents

Introduction

Philanthropy is slowly creeping back into the limelight in the UK, following many years hidden in the background. Levels of awareness and participation have risen significantly, and the number of donors willing to talk about their giving in public continues to grow. Articles in newspapers have even suggested that we may be on the cusp of a new 'golden age' of philanthropy in our country that could rival the famed charitable exploits of the Victorians.

Philanthropy has also, for better or worse, been dragged into the mainstream of political debate. The Conservative party's 'Big Society' agenda,[1] first unveiled in the 2010 election, made a valiant – if not entirely successful – attempt to place voluntary action at the heart of public policy. Meanwhile, increasing awareness of growing inequality between rich and poor in our society has brought questions of wealth and social responsibility to the fore. More worryingly, the attempt in the 2012 Budget to introduce a cap on tax relief on charitable donations, the ongoing criticism of campaigning and advocacy by charities which led to the introduction of the 'Lobbying Act', and controversy over charity fundraising practices have made it clear that despite the long history of philanthropy in the UK, we cannot assume there will always be a consensus that it is a positive thing.

Although philanthropy is growing in prominence, there is still a real lack of clarity about its overall role in our society. In a welfare state that uses our tax money to meet our basic social needs, alongside a commercial sector that enables us to buy pretty much anything else we want, does money voluntarily given away to help others still have a meaningful role to play? And if so, what is that role? This is the point of this book: to take a step back and ask why philanthropy is important in the UK today and how we ensure that it is an effective force for good.

Philanthropy is not a particularly well-defined term and this book does not attempt to give a strict definition. Rather, it considers the characteristics that typify philanthropy in its modern form and where they have come from.

A key feature of philanthropy is that it has a sense of purpose. Philanthropy requires there to be a clear goal in mind – a problem to be solved or an idea to be shared – and so the focus is not on the act of giving itself but rather on what it achieves. So one of the key factors in the birth of what we might call modern philanthropy was the shift from religious almsgiving, where the focus was primarily on what it meant for the donor and their immortal soul, towards giving that was focused on addressing the problems of society. Although this is not the full story, this central distinction had far-reaching consequences and played a vital role in the eventual development of the charitable sector as we know it today.

At the same time as philanthropy was developing into its modern form, both the state and the commercial sector were also slowly evolving into something like we understand them today. Philanthropy was shaped by its relationship with both of these, and helped to mould them in turn. The evolution of the modern state, in particular, is inextricably linked to the evolution of philanthropy. Initially, the welfare needs of society were not seen as the responsibility of government, and were instead left to philanthropy to deal with in a piecemeal fashion. Then, at around the same time as modern philanthropy began to develop, the state took a major step towards accepting responsibility for welfare with the introduction of the first Poor Laws at the turn of the 17th century. The line between state action and voluntary action was blurred at this point, but the Poor Laws played a key role in clarifying the appropriate role for philanthropy in addressing the quintessential social problem: poverty.

Over time, as the nature and scale of society's problems gradually changed, spurred on by the agricultural revolution and then the industrial revolution, it became increasingly clear that the Poor Laws alone were not sufficient to meet the needs of society. Many, indeed, had begun to worry that they actually exacerbated poverty. This led to an increased focus on the role that philanthropy and voluntary action should play in addressing such issues, which reached its pinnacle in the mid-Victorian era, when society effectively undertook a grand experiment to determine whether philanthropy could replace state provision in meeting many needs. Ultimately, this experiment proved a failure (if a noble one in many ways), and in almost all areas of welfare the state, often reluctantly, began to take a much larger share of responsibility. This led eventually to the development of the modern welfare state. Almost all elements of this welfare state, both in terms of the needs it addresses and how it addresses them, have their roots in earlier philanthropic endeavours.

As the welfare state grew and developed, many thought it would spell the end for philanthropy. But instead of disappearing, the role of philanthropy changed. Although it no longer had primary responsibility for meeting many welfare needs, philanthropy continued to play a crucial role in challenging state provision, either through innovations that demonstrated better ways of meeting need, or through campaigning to get the state to improve its own approach. The introduction of outsourcing and markets in public service delivery in the last 30 years has also opened up new opportunities for charities to deliver services on behalf of the state. This development has had a major impact on the nature of the relationship between philanthropy and the state.

But, of course, philanthropy has never just been about service provision. Philanthropy has always aimed to improve our society and our democracy, and while it achieves this partly through delivering services that directly meet needs, it also does it through campaigning and advocating for change. The ability to speak out, often on behalf of those who have been marginalised by society or the market, has always been a vital part of the role of philanthropy. It is at least as important as the provision of services, and remains critical even today.

Nor has philanthropy always been benign and motivated purely by altruism, or always a positive force. Many valid criticisms have been levelled over the years, and need to be addressed if the legitimacy of philanthropy is to be maintained. Some are directed at the practice of philanthropy – questioning whether it is an effective or efficient way to achieve social goals, or whether the element of individual choice at the heart of philanthropy makes it too fickle and subject to ideology. Others challenge the role of philanthropy within society; for instance, highlighting the potentially distorting effect that private philanthropy by wealthy individuals can have on public policy and the democratic process, or questioning whether philanthropy, with its inherent reliance on there being rich and poor, will always be a net contributor to inequality rather than a solution to it.

These are difficult and challenging questions that cannot be ignored. Philanthropy exists within the wider fabric of society, so people have a right to question its role and the way it is practised, in the same way as they question the role of the state or the private sector. Furthermore, both donors and the organisations they support receive tax relief from the government. Hence we all have a right, as citizens, to ask whether this is a justifiable use of public money – much as we might query any other use of our taxes. This book explores the question of whether philanthropic tax breaks can be justified and discovers that – as with a surprising number of other aspects of the UK charity landscape – the whole system may have arisen as the result of a mistake, rather than careful planning.

Philanthropy in the future

It is clear that philanthropy can play a role in our society, and an important one at that. It can meet needs that lie outside the responsibility of the state, or it can deliver services that supplement state provision by bridging gaps or adding value to existing public services. It can also offer challenge: to public service provision, government policy and legislation, and even to our democratic system.

If we face up to the criticisms that have been levelled at philanthropy over the years and find ways to answer them, we can reach an understanding of the role of philanthropy that recognises both its unique strengths and its limitations. Having such a shared understanding among policymakers, charities and donors is vital if we are to make the most of the value that philanthropy can bring to society. Only if we agree on what role philanthropy should play and what we can reasonably expect of it will we be able to realise its true potential as a force for progress in our society. To that end, the conclusion of this book proposes eight 'key principles' of philanthropy suggested by analysis of the history of philanthropy in the UK over the last 400 years, and reflecting the key factors that have led to successful examples of philanthropy having an impact on society.

These principles are not policy prescriptions in themselves, but are intended to provide a starting point for anyone proposing public policy that affects or relies on philanthropy in some way. If these principles are followed, the hope is that philanthropy can once again become a powerful tool for meeting the needs of society, but this time in a way that complements and strengthens both the state and the market. Finding a way to combine these forces, rather than having them act against one another, is vital if we are to overcome some of the most complex and deeply entrenched challenges facing our society.

Key principles of philanthropy

Philanthropy is about people and their choices

The freedom for individuals to choose where they direct their gifts lies at the heart of philanthropy and gives it much of its strength. But this also means that it is not good at providing consistency or equality at a systemic level. Rather than trying to overcome this by forcing philanthropy to be something it isn't, we should respect and cherish the importance of donor choice and tailor our expectations accordingly.

Philanthropic choices are about both head and heart

Not only is philanthropy about individual choice, but those choices are informed by a wide range of considerations, both rational and emotional. On the rational side there is a demand for evidence – of where need lies and how best to address it. On the emotional side is a complex mixture of factors – some are personal or cultural (which lie outside the remit of this book), and some are societal, such as prevailing attitudes towards wealth and need (as considered in Chapter 4). Philanthropy is therefore a product of both head and heart, and the balance between the two varies between donors.

Philanthropy is not the same as public spending and cannot replace it

Philanthropic giving is nowhere near the same order of magnitude as public spending, and the profile of giving does not match the profile of need at a societal level. The element of voluntary choice and the influence of emotional factors also make philanthropy ill-suited to meeting needs at a systemic level. Hence it is not a feasible or appropriate replacement for public spending.

Philanthropy is often 'political' (and that is a good thing)

A key distinguishing feature of philanthropy is that it has a purpose or goal. In most cases this can be framed as a problem that needs to be overcome or a change that needs to be made in society. By giving to a particular cause, a philanthropist is expressing a view about a way in which our society, our laws or government policies need to be different. This is an inherently political act. It is only if we incorrectly conflate 'political' and 'party political' that there is a problem. If we instead reclaim the proper understanding of what the sphere of politics includes, then it is clear that philanthropy is, and always has been, a valuable tool for people to express their beliefs within that sphere.

Philanthropy should be progressive

Philanthropy, properly understood, is about trying to improve society by tackling the root causes of problems, rather than just addressing their symptoms. Philanthropy should therefore be progressive, not regressive or conservative.[2] Philanthropy is not about maintaining the status quo or turning back the clock, but about moving society forward by overcoming failings in existing government, welfare provision or legislation.

Philanthropy should be prepared to take risks

Philanthropy is often aimed at intractable problems that have proved resistant to the efforts of government and the market to solve them. To succeed where these other actors have failed, philanthropy needs to try new and different approaches, and this means taking risks. The voluntary nature of philanthropy and its basis in the social motivations of individuals mean that philanthropy is able to take risks that would not be possible either for public sector organisations, which are accountable to taxpayers, or for private sector organisations, which are accountable to shareholders. This tolerance for risk is one of philanthropy's greatest assets.

Philanthropy can enable a long-term view

Philanthropy is not beholden to the political cycle or to the short-term demands of the market. That means that it should be able to take a longer-term approach to dealing with social problems than either businesses or government. This is a great strength of philanthropy, as there are many issues that clearly require long-term solutions and philanthropic organisations may be the only bodies capable of identifying and delivering them.

Tax relief on philanthropic donations is not a subsidy for services the state would otherwise have to provide

Offering tax relief for individuals on their charitable donations is a valuable tool for governments to support a philanthropic culture. It is not a given that donations should not be taxed, so the relief does count as a subsidy by government. But it should not be seen as a subsidy for the provision of particular services that the state would otherwise have to provide. The tax relief only makes sense when seen as a generalised subsidy reflecting a government view that a healthy civil society is important (including its role in advocacy and campaigning), and that supporting individuals to make voluntary donations is an effective way of ensuring this health.

A note on sources

The historical and philosophical underpinnings of philanthropy have attracted remarkably little attention in proportion to its importance in shaping the nation we live in today. A lot has been written about philanthropy (although far more of it in the US than in the UK), but the majority of this material has been concerned with practice rather than theory (or when it has been concerned with theory, it has been the theory of how to do philanthropy rather than the theory of what it is and what it is for). Where there has been academic research on the theory or history of philanthropy, it is often narrow in scope, or only touches on philanthropy as one aspect of a wider issue. And in practical terms, a lot of the most interesting research is in journals that are not easily accessible, or in books that are difficult to locate or even out of print, so the work does not reach a wide audience.

Researching this book involved spending a great deal of time hunting down interesting sources from a wide range of books, academic papers and newspaper and magazine articles to provide insights into some of the questions raised. Many of these sources would be barely known outside narrow academic circles, and few, if any, practitioners are likely to have come across them. This is a great shame, as they provide a huge amount of valuable insight. I hope that if this book achieves nothing else, it will draw attention to some of these under-appreciated gems.

Where quoted extracts are emboldened, the emphasis is mine.

CHAPTER ONE

The emergence of modern philanthropy

What are we talking about?

In any book about philanthropy, it seems obvious to begin by defining what 'philanthropy' actually means. This often involves pointing out that the etymology of the word 'philanthropy' shows that it derives from the ancient Greek for 'love of humanity' and then attempting to draw the distinction between 'charity' and 'philanthropy'. But that is not how this book is going to start. There are a lot of unavoidable grey areas that make it almost impossible to define 'philanthropy' exactly. Instead, this book adopts a working definition, with the acceptance that there may be occasional arguments over the boundaries.

Key points about 'philanthropy' form part of my working definition. The first is that it denotes an activity that is in some way aimed at achieving a particular goal, rather than simply being an indiscriminate act of doing good. One of the key developments in the emergence of philanthropy in the UK was the change from traditional religious almsgiving to the poor towards more secular (although often still religiously-driven) approaches to combating social issues. These more secular approaches are characteristic of philanthropy because they attempt to identify and deal with the causes of problems, rather than simply addressing the symptoms.

The second point is that while philanthropy often involves a significant commitment of time as well as money on the part of the donor, the money *is* crucial. For the purposes of this book, it is the use of one's own money

The *Selling of Indulgences* by Hans Holbein the Younger, *circa* 1529.
A classic example of Protestant criticism of Catholicism.

(at whatever level of wealth you happen to be) to achieve social aims that is distinctive about philanthropy. Social campaigners and charity workers who use other people's money to effect change, while obviously admirable in their own right, are not the focus of attention. Likewise, philanthropy involves the use of money to support groups of which one is not a member and causes that one does not directly benefit from. This distinguishes it from the tradition of self-help and mutualism – another important strand in the history of the voluntary sector in the UK, but one which is for another book.

Finally, for the purposes of this book, support for campaigning and advocacy is counted as philanthropy. Some argue that philanthropy must be about actions on the ground to address social ills or to protect culture or heritage, rather than trying to achieve social change through reform of the law or changes in social attitudes. It is not clear that this distinction works. There is always a choice in philanthropy between depth and breadth: do you focus on working with a small section of society and have a major impact on the lives of those involved, or do you try to achieve change that would affect society as a whole but have a smaller impact on each of the individuals within it? Campaigning is typical of the latter approach, and so is at one end of a spectrum rather than being qualitatively different to 'front-line' work.

Religion and secularisation – the impact of the Reformation

Philanthropy today is very different to the traditional notion of almsgiving prevalent in medieval times, where giving *'was a religious exercise. The gift was made for the sake of giving: the act was beneficial in itself and not in its results'*.[3] A major defining characteristic of modern philanthropy is that it is not done solely for the spiritual betterment of the donor, but rather is driven by a wider purpose that relates to the material world. Of course, a desire for absolution might still be part of the motivation for giving, but not its sole ambition – some appeal to the notion of social or public good must be employed.

By this criterion, we first see philanthropy emerging in its modern incarnation during and after the Reformation in the 16th century. Henry VIII's decision to break ties with the Catholic church had many far-reaching consequences that shaped Britain and Europe for centuries to come. Among these was a significant change in the nature and understanding of charitable giving, which was eventually to lead to the notion of philanthropy we have today. Protestant doctrine changed perceptions of poverty and the responsibilities that come with wealth in ways that laid the groundwork for a new, secular approach to giving. As Gareth Jones, author of a seminal book on the development of charity law in the UK, puts it: *'The Reformation statutes were the legal culmination of a complex social and religious revolution which affected all aspects of English life. The overthrow of papal supremacy and the decline of the authority of organised religion was paralleled by . . . a change of viewpoint concerning the nature and functions of religion, both in the individual and in society. One manifestation of such a change was in the character of man's philanthropy. The objects of charity were to become more secular as the majority of Englishmen reflected less on the fate of their souls and became more concerned with the worldly needs of their fellow men.'*[4]

While the introduction of Protestantism made the secularisation possible, it was not until much later that the shift in the nature of giving became decisive. Religion continued to be the backdrop for philanthropy for a long time, and *'through the first five decades of the 18th century . . . clerics continued to insist that almsgiving, directed by the spirit of sacrifice, was essentially a self-regarding religious act'.*[5] Slowly, however, things began to change and *'clerics also mentioned other, more mundane reasons for encouraging benevolence'.*[6] As time went on *'the advice of religious leaders was increasingly pragmatic in nature, and though still concerned about benefits in the hereafter, was more worldly and present-minded in its demands for an active, discerning, and effective charitable community'.*[7]

But even the introduction of these new, secular strains into the narrative about charitable giving did not signal a distinct shift away from a religious conception of altruism, because *'the new themes did not displace the older ones, but rather reinforced and reinterpreted them. [The clerics] did not deny the religious value of almsgiving, but added the social and practical value, the private- and public-interest aspects'.*[8]

So, it was not that charitable giving necessarily became less religious; it was simply that Protestant teaching lent itself more easily to social schemes designed to address poverty. Traditional Catholic doctrine taught that poverty was part of God's design: some were destined to be poor and others to be rich, and the poor provided the opportunity for the rich to celebrate God and secure their own immortal soul through acts of charity. This meant that *'giving to the poor, in whatever form, was encouraged, even if it was not possible, or desirable, to make an accurate assessment of the worthiness of the object of the aid . . . In God's eye, the intention of the giver, not the worth of the recipient, was the salient feature'.*[9]

Protestant doctrine, however, suggested that poverty was in fact a sin that went against God's plan. Combined with the rejection of Catholic notions of redemption in the afterlife, this meant that for Protestants the appropriate focus of giving was no longer making donations to the church in order to secure absolution for one's immortal soul, but rather giving in order to try to relieve the poverty of others in the society of the day. Over a long period of time, *'a wholesale transformation in the conception of good works occurred as religion was dissociated from charity, and a shift from religious to public charity – marked by the secularisation, institutionalisation and bureaucratisation of charitable giving – came to pass'.*[10]

The historian WK Jordan, author of one of the seminal works on the history of philanthropy in England, identified the schism between Catholicism and Protestantism as the key factor in the development of modern philanthropy, arguing that *'although it perhaps simplifies a process of social change far too much to say that men of the Middle Ages gave alms as an act of piety while men of the 16th century gave, and much more generously, under the dictate of social need, it still seems very much as though the evidence runs most persuasively with the statement'.*[11] He used a detailed analysis of charitable bequests between 1480 and 1660 to support his case, and highlighted the secularisation of giving by contrasting the decade 1480 to 1490 – in which around two-thirds of all charitable donations in England were for religious purposes – and the whole of the Elizabethan era, when less than 7% of donations were religious.[12] He also used his figures to argue that there had been a massive overall increase in donations as a result of this secularisation.

Although most historians agree that '*it is clear that both the purposes and mechanisms of philanthropy altered substantially between 1530 and 1780*',[13] not everyone believes that the shift from Catholicism to Protestantism was as crucial a factor as Jordan claimed. Some have pointed out that it can't be as simple as that because '*change had begun before Protestantism was firmly established, and it was visible in Catholic countries as well as those which became Protestant*'.[14] Others have criticised the figures Jordan used to support his arguments, arguing that his failure to take the effect of inflation adequately into account in his analysis led him to massively overstate the growth of charitable giving in the post-Reformation period. It has also been argued that Jordan's narrow focus on legacy gifts gives a skewed impression of a huge boom in giving, and that '*a broader assessment of all forms of private gifts that were given at the time of death or during the individual's lifetime – perpetually endowed gifts, but also non-recurring gifts and one-time contributions – indicates that a wide amalgam of gifts and donations, among which the lavishly endowed testamentary bequest was one, persisted and became more vigorous as the period progressed*'.[15] Despite all this criticism, more recently it has been admitted that Jordan's central point might not be so far off the mark, and that '*for all the faults in a methodology that resulted in exaggerating the scope of the increase, [his] assessment of a growth in charitable giving during the period following the Reformation remains sound*'.[16]

It is perhaps unsurprising that Jordan concluded that the move towards Protestantism was such a decisive factor, given that this narrative was actively promoted by contemporary sources and became part of the foundation myth of later Protestant philanthropists. It is possible that Jordan's focus on legacy gifts may have distorted the reality: as he himself noted, it was common practice for men during his period of study to give lengthy explanations of their bequests, often involving detailed justifications for why money was being left for secular, rather than religious purposes. However, the evidence from these wills and eulogies may partly reflect the desire of Protestants to craft their own charitable image in response to significant criticism from Catholics, rather than a decisive change in levels of donation or attitudes toward giving.

Protestant v Catholic

The chief criticism levelled by Catholics was that the dissolution of the monasteries carried out under Henry VIII had destroyed much of the infrastructure of formal and informal giving, and the Protestants had nothing to put in its place, to the great detriment of the charitable health of the country. In response, Protestant preachers and pamphleteers expended enormous effort attempting to demonstrate that their new understanding of charitable giving was superior to the earlier Catholic idea of alms, not only in doctrinal superiority, but also in its effectiveness in raising money

Thomas Becon.

for good causes. They lampooned the Catholic approach as vain and self-interested, arguing that the Protestant view eschewed the idea of charity as a way of securing passage to heaven in favour of a focus on addressing the social ills of society. *'Catholic charity,'* they argued, *'was fabricated of stone, whereas the charity of men of true faith gives men bread . . . [And] these godly donors understood that holy works do not purchase our salvation.'*[17]

Influential Protestant preachers of the day such as Thomas Becon used their position in the pulpit to lambast the Catholic church, claiming that it *'perverted the charitable impulse'* and *'persuaded amiable but misguided men to pour funds into "great monasteries for the bellied hypocrites, great colleges, chantries, and free chapels for soul-carriers and purgatory-rakers"'.*[18] By contrast, men like Becon maintained, *'Protestant charity . . . was characterised by modesty and by the effective concentration of resources on pressing areas of human need.'*[19]

Prominent Protestants rarely missed an opportunity to score points over their Catholic rivals by claiming superiority in their approach to giving. They even utilised thoroughly modern tactics such as deploying statistics: John Stow's *The Survey of London*, a book first published in 1598 cataloguing the many good works financed by the charitable gifts of London's merchant class, became a go-to resource for those looking to criticise Catholicism. In 1614, the Puritan minister Andrew Willett published a survey of charitable bequests (not dissimilar to Jordan's more than 300 years later), which found a significant rise in donations following the Reformation. He used these figures to argue that good works by Protestants not only exceeded those of Catholics in quality because *'theirs were done in the pride of the heart, in opinion of merit to purchase remission of sinnes'*, whereas the gifts of Protestants were only intended to serve as *'testimonies of our faith'*,[20] but also that they exceeded them in quantity too. Although as historian Ian Archer has pointed out, Willett's conclusions rely on some fairly judicious use of the facts, and *'his stress on the contribution of the gospel to the charitable activities of Londoners reflects the acute sensitivity of Protestants to the criticisms of the "carping popelings"'*.[21] He was far from alone. The poet John Donne used a similar statistical approach in arguing that the claims of Catholic superiority in charity giving were undermined by the fact that *'there have been in this kingdome, since the blessed reformation of religion, more publick charitable works perform'd, more hospitals and colleges erected, and endowed in threescore, than in some hundreds of years of superstition before'*.[22]

At the same time as downplaying the charitable achievements of the Catholics, the Protestant establishment *'moved quickly to assert the godly credentials of key donors'*[23] so that it could establish the supremacy of

Thomas Sutton.

Protestant charity. Men such as Thomas Sutton, who left a vast endowment for the Charterhouse, were held as exemplars of Protestant generosity. Andrew Willett called this endowment *'the greatest gift that ever was given in England, no abbey at the first foundation thereof excepted'*.[24] In some cases, the deeds of these heroic 'Protestant donors' were lauded even though it was unclear to what extent those donors were truly sympathetic to the Protestant cause.[25] In any case, the tactic seems to have worked, and *'the cumulative effect of funeral and commemoration sermons, memorial tablets and monumental epitaphs celebrating the piety and charity of benefactors, the ritual distribution of charity within the parochial framework and the recitation of prayers for benefactors was to inscribe the association of charity and Protestantism'*.[26]

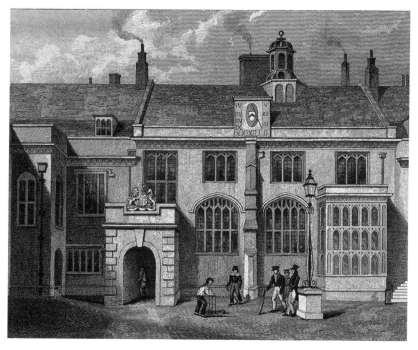

Charterhouse Hospital School, London: boys playing cricket.
Engraving by J Rogers after T H Shepherd, 1830.

Clearly, the struggle for supremacy between Catholics and Protestants was not primarily about philanthropy. But the fact that philanthropy was used as a significant pawn in this game of one-upmanship during such a major ideological struggle invites caution about unquestioningly accepting the narrative of Protestantism as the driving force behind the birth of modern philanthropy. As the historian Donna Andrew wryly notes: *'English men and women of the 18th century judged it to be a great age of benevolence. They were convinced that a new phase in England's care of the poor had been initiated, vindicating for all time the superiority of the Protestant faith, which, while not making good works the method of salvation, showed its true Christianity by its overflowing beneficence . . . This is an interesting though not entirely accurate assessment.'*[27]

Despite the many uncertainties and ambiguities, it is undoubtedly true that the Reformation had a significant impact on giving and is one of the key factors in the development of modern philanthropy. Firstly, it set precedents that made civic or government interference with religious and charitable institutions far easier than it would otherwise have been. This interaction between government and philanthropy was to be a constant and defining theme over the next few hundred years. Secondly, *'the Reformation destroyed much of the institutional fabric which had provided charity for the poor in the past: monasteries, guilds and fraternities.'* [28]

While the Reformation made positive contributions to the development of philanthropy in the form of new approaches to giving and a new understanding of the role of charity (albeit with caveats about the extent to which these things were truly 'new'), it also made a more negative contribution that may have been more influential in the long run. By decimating many of the religious institutions that had previously played a central role in meeting the needs of the poor, the Tudor government – either inadvertently or by design – also opened up a vast new space for charitable endeavour. Archer suggests that even now *'we have underestimated the damage done by the dissolutions, both because the scale of the alms distributed through monasteries and fraternities has been underestimated, and because the fraternities provided an institutional framework within which informal support could be offered'.* [29]

As the Catholic infrastructure of religious welfare came crashing down, there was an urgent need for something to take its place. It turned out to be two things, both of whose impact we continue to feel even today. The first was the introduction of systematic government-controlled welfare provision through the introduction of the Poor Laws. The second was the development of new forms of secular philanthropy focused on relieving poverty and trying to address its causes. The interaction between these two forces was instrumental in shaping the society we have today and in fashioning our modern understanding of philanthropy.

Legislation and a definition of charity
The 1601 Statute of Charitable Uses
There is more detail on the overall influence of the Poor Laws in Chapter 2, but one element of the package of Poor Law legislation played a fundamental role in the development of philanthropy: the Statute of Charitable Uses of 1601 (sometimes called the Statute of Elizabeth). Ostensibly, this was a fairly minor piece of legislation aimed at making trusts for charitable purposes more accountable, by introducing new procedures for the government to intervene when trusts were perceived to be mismanaged or used for purposes deemed not to be charitable. This was a necessary measure for the Tudor government, because even though it had taken the

radical step of introducing the first legislation allowing systematic state welfare in the form of the Poor Laws, it wanted as far as possible not to have to implement this legislation in practice. Instead, the government *'hoped to use charitable contributions to relieve poverty and thereby make unnecessary the unpopular imposition of taxes at the parish level'*. This meant that *'the legal stability of and accountability for charitable gifts became of great concern to the government'*.[30] So in effect, the Statute was part of an attempt to use a mixture of carrots and sticks to encourage and shape philanthropy to meet the political ends of the government. The Tudors realised that *'to create an effective system of philanthropy, donors needed to be exhorted in a theological sense, encouraged by government policies, and assured of protection that their sums would be appropriately spent. If a legal regime could be created to efficiently protect the use of charitable assets, and the ethos of society cultivated such giving, then the middle and upper middle classes, particularly the merchant gentry, might increase their support towards ends that the state approved. This was the rationale of the Statute of Charitable Uses'*.[31]

What makes the Statute such an important document in the history of philanthropy is that in the course of trying to tighten up the rules on the use of charitable assets, it clarified for the first time a legal definition of 'charity'. Or did it . . .? In fact, as a number of historians have subsequently noted, although *'the Preamble to the Statute of Charitable Uses is famous for providing a legal definition of charitable purpose and is the starting point for the modern law of charity'*, this was never its intention: *'It was not exclusive, but merely a listing of charities the state wished to encourage'*.[32] Jordan suggests that the lasting impact of the Preamble may have been a result of the quality of the language used (which was modelled heavily on the 14th century epic poem *Piers Plowman*),[33] and that although *'it was designed to be rather more hortatory than definitive . . . nonetheless the stamp of its eloquence upon law and aspirations has been such that the courts of the United States as well as of Britain have tended to be guided by its precepts'*.[34]

Whatever the explanation, over the course of time people lost sight of the fact that *'the Preamble was intended less as a definition of charitable purposes than as a statement of types of purposes that, to the late Tudor mind, were regarded as charitable'*, and by the time of the famous *Pemsel* case of 1891,[35] *'the Preamble was entrenched in judge-made charity law as a sort of index to be consulted when a question was raised as to whether or not some purposes were charitable'.*[36]

One of the distinctive features of the list of causes in the Preamble to the 1601 Statute is that religious purposes are excluded. Some historians have argued that this is a reflection of the secularisation of giving discussed in the previous section. Jordan, for instance, boldly asserts: *'The conception and definition of charitable purposes [advanced in the Statute] was starkly and coldly secular, just as were the benefactions of the age. The only religious purpose mentioned at all was the repair of churches ... This omission was flagrantly deliberate, because the whole temper of the age had grown so completely secular and because the preoccupations of men had fastened so tenaciously on the many and pressing needs of the world and the society which they saw about them.'*[37] Given the concerns mentioned earlier that Jordan may have overstated his case on the secularisation of giving, it is unwise to take this claim at face value. However, others have agreed that the omission of religious purposes from the Preamble, despite the fact that they had been the dominant focus of giving since medieval times, was an overtly political statement.[38]

It is possible that this deliberate omission of religious purposes was not so much a reflection of the government's desire to make philanthropy secular, but simply a smart piece of *realpolitik.* Religion in the newly-Protestant England was a politically-charged topic and charity was unavoidably drawn into the controversy because the Reformation had seen the seizure by the Crown of many 'charitable assets' previously held by the monasteries. Given that the government's primary motivation for introducing the Statute was to incentivise charitable donations for the purposes of poverty relief in order to avoid having to enact the local taxes that the Poor Laws required,[39] the inclusion of religious purposes in the Preamble would have opened a contentious debate that was extraneous to the central purpose of the Act itself. Furthermore, there was an ongoing controversy about the redefinition of many previously-valid Catholic purposes as 'superstitious', which made them forfeit and allowed the Crown to seize their assets. The *'fear that the religious use might infect by association other charitable uses',* and so allow the Crown to appropriate their assets too, *'encouraged the draftsmen of the Charitable Uses Act, 1601, to exclude it from the list of good and godly uses over which the charity commissioners had jurisdiction'.*[40]

Of course, this did not mean that religious causes were suddenly not charitable, but merely that they were subject to a different framework of regulation. *'The uses which were deemed to be within the equity of the statute were those whose endowments could materially contribute to the relief of poverty. Other charitable uses, such as those for the support of religious purposes, were outside the statute and had been enforced not by the charity commissioners but by an information brought by the Attorney-General at the relation of a private individual.'*[41]

The Statute of Mortmain

Two later historical developments also help to explain how the Statute of Charitable Uses came to be seen as the basis for a legal definition of charity. The first is the practical reality that *'[the system of] information ... proved to be such an attractive procedure that by the end of the 17th century it had come to be used to enforce all charitable trusts ... Thereafter the antithesis between charities enforceable by commission on the one hand and by information on the other gradually disappeared'.*[42] Once this distinction was eroded, *'no obstacle now remained to the formulation of a definition of legal charity'.*[43]

The other development was the introduction of the Statute of Mortmain in 1736. This was legislation that made gifts of land or money for the purchase of land for charitable purposes illegal unless they were signed well in advance of the individual's death and recorded on a written deed made in the presence of at least two witnesses. This was motivated by a growing atmosphere of distrust towards the clergy, and particularly by the concern that significant tracts of land would end up in the hands of ecclesiastical charities as a result of people being implored to make bequests on their deathbed.[44]

The fact that trusts for purposes deemed 'charitable' could be declared invalid recipients of legacies brought the definition of charity to the foreground. It also introduced multiple, competing incentives into the debate. On the one hand, the judiciary *'made little attempt to limit the class of objects which the law hitherto deemed to be charitable, for the terms of the Mortmain Act, 1736, enabled them to protect the interests of the family by characterising the object of the testator's bounty as charitable. This had the immediate effect of avoiding the devise and causing the property to result to the heir or the next-of-kin'.*[45] On the other, *'It was not surprising ...*

that objects which were in danger of being stigmatised as charitable often sought to divest themselves of this unwelcome status'.[46] This gave rise to the peculiar situation in which trusts whose purposes looked very much to be charitable tried to argue that they weren't, and that the definition of charity should be drawn more narrowly, while the government and the judiciary tried equally hard to interpret the definition of charitable purpose as broadly as possible. As Jones explains: '*It is paradoxical that the Mortmain Act, 1736, should have persuaded the courts to preserve for posterity a liberal definition of legal charity. But the general desire to protect the interests of the heir and the next-of-kin from the claims of rapacious charities could generally best be fulfilled by categorising the object of the testator's bounty as charitable. Consequently there was little judicial enthusiasm for any attempt to restrict the class of charitable objects which had been established in an age whose social aspirations and ideals were far removed from those of Hanoverian England.*'[47]

By the start of the 19th century, the blurring of the lines between charities regulated by information and those regulated by commission was complete, and in 1805 the Preamble to the Statue of Charitable Uses was officially equated with the legal definition of charitable purposes for the first time.[48] The perverse incentive introduced by the Statute of Mortmain also meant that the interpretation of these charitable purposes was as generous as possible, so engendering the broadly defined and highly varied charitable sector we have today.

Information and discrimination: research, advice and choosing charitable causes

Modern philanthropy was born when charity found a sense of social purpose in the years and centuries following the Reformation. However, for a long time this purpose was not always well directed: the efforts of donors were largely based on their own diagnoses of the root causes of social problems and their own prescriptions for dealing with them. This led to a small number of carefully thought-through, effective interventions but a much larger number of ill-conceived, ineffective or just downright wacky enterprises based on the whims and intuitions of wealthy individuals.

For instance, in 1580 a businessman named Robert Hitchcock proposed the creation of a vast national fishing fleet in which the poor could be given gainful employment. His plan was to give £1,000 to each of the principal UK ports, and £200 to each of 225 lesser or failing port towns – a vast sum of money for the time. The aim was to build a fleet of 400 fishing vessels, each of which would be manned by *'a professional master and twelve lusty beggars or poor men wanting employment'.*[49] Hitchcock reckoned that the social benefits of this approach would *'have the great merit of providing permanent work for a large number of unemployed persons, would greatly increase the diet of the realm, and would establish a sorely needed training school for deep-water mariners'.*[50] This was not an entirely altruistic enterprise, as Hitchcock felt that the £80,000 of capital required to implement his plan *'could be raised by loans from substantial men in all shires, from men fearful lest the worsening poverty of the realm lead to riotous outbreaks not easily suppressed'.*[51] His plan never found support and was left to founder on the rocks.

The architects of the Corporation of the Poor in London – responsible for a system of workhouses in the city – had a scheme that looks similarly quirky to modern eyes. They suggested that if times became particularly hard, the bells of London's churches – reckoned to be worth £9,660 – should be melted down to raise funds. They also proposed that money could be raised by curbing the fashionable instincts of Londoners and persuading them for *'one year to forebear altering their apparel into other fantastic fashions'*, with the saving paid into the stock of the Corporation.[52]

Slowly these grand visions settled down, and many philanthropists began to wonder whether handing out money based solely on their gut instincts was the best approach to solving society's problems. There was a growing recognition that philanthropic efforts to date had only managed to address symptoms, not causes. Eventually, however, *'a considerable number of rich, perceptive, and highly sophisticated donors, particularly among the merchant aristocracy, began to sense that the crux of the problem was not so much the outright relief of the poor as the prevention of poverty itself through the enlargement of the ambit of social and economic opportunity'.*[53] It led to a new focus on finding more effective ways to use philanthropy.

This took a number of forms. In part it was about developing a greater understanding of the causes of poverty and other social ills, in order to formulate and evaluate more effective responses to them. New methods of social research became important tools in the philanthropist's arsenal, and from very early on an industry sprang up offering advice to would-be philanthropists on how to give effectively. But for many philanthropists, although giving well was the ideal, it was at least as important not to give badly. The idea of 'discrimination' when it came to relieving poverty through philanthropy became a theme that was to remain for hundreds of years and would prove by turns influential and controversial.

The idea that philanthropic giving must be discriminating was almost always framed as being not about serving the interests of the donor, but of the poor themselves. As Andrew notes: *'The notion, that charity must be so directed that it would not only be of short-term benefit to the poor, but would also be to their long-term welfare, seems a growing sentiment . . . The sensible donor would not be indiscriminate; he would deny the requests of the poor or meet them only in such a way as to promote their real interests.'*[54] Indiscriminate charity was increasingly seen as not just bad practice, but as a major contributing factor to the continuation of poverty. As a result, *'by the late 18th century, the chorus of criticism of the consequences of indiscriminate giving was deafening'.*[55] Particularly vocal in this chorus were many Protestants, for whom *'disgust at continental Catholic "superstitious" giving combined with businesslike concern at the undercutting of the incentive to join the national labour market in order to condemn "indiscriminate charity" – charity which confirmed the donor's status at the expense of demoralising the receiver'.*[56]

This backlash against indiscriminate giving was driven partly by religion and partly by public policy. As stated earlier, Protestants sought to distance their own charitable giving from what they saw as the vainglorious, unfocused almsgiving that characterised Catholic charity; emphasising instead the importance of giving in order to address the material poverty around them. And at the same time, the government used the Poor Laws to try to influence charitable giving, because despite the introduction of a framework of state-provided welfare, philanthropic provision remained the preferred option. This meant, however, that the government had a keen interest in how philanthropy was practised, and specifically in whether it was effective in addressing the problems of poverty that were the government's prime concern. As such, *'the Poor Law set out to reform and remodel charity. It should be purposive and discriminatory. Begging and casual almsgiving were to be abolished. The generous instincts of donors should be disciplined by attention to recipients'.*[57] The lasting influence of this idea of indiscriminate charity is explored in more detail in Chapter 4.

Philanthropy in practice

The challenge facing early philanthropists who had accepted the need to be discriminating and to have a demonstrable impact on the problems of poverty was how to do this in practice. Understanding of many of the underlying causes of poverty was extremely limited, and methods of evaluating the effectiveness of interventions almost non-existent. This meant that at first the only real option for philanthropists seeking guidance on how to give more effectively was to ask those who had already engaged with the issues and developed some understanding of how they might be addressed. As a result, individuals who had enjoyed success in their own giving often became sought-after sources of knowledge. For instance, the 17th century businessman and philanthropist Thomas Firmin was so renowned for his understanding of the needs of the poor, and his prudent and discriminating approach to helping them, that he became the go-to middleman for other philanthropists wishing to give effectively. He has been called '*a kind of one-man council of social service*' and was dubbed the '*almoner general for the poor*' by his contemporary biographer.[58] And Firmin's fame suggests that he had tapped into something widespread: '*His ability to persuade individual private citizens to part with their money on the guarantee that it would be applied to the relief of distress by a competent, informed and personally connected intermediary was an indication of potential demand for specialist services waiting to be released across a growing segment of the propertied urban population of the early 18th century.*'[59]

Some of those who sought to position themselves as philanthropy advisers wrote down their thoughts on how to give effectively. Robert Nelson, a noted Protestant philanthropist, not only undertook a vast amount of charitable work himself but also included in his *Address to Persons of Quality and Estate* a section entitled 'Ways and methods of doing good'. This outlined for fellow members of the upper class where their charitable efforts could be best directed, by identifying what philanthropic initiatives already existed, where there were gaps in provision, and suggesting (with a surprising degree of prophetic accuracy) where new acute needs might develop in the future.[60]

Philanthropy advisers

The role of the informal or semi-formal philanthropy adviser continued to be relevant as philanthropy developed. In fact, it has been noted: '*The claim to be able to resolve the dilemma of the culturally sensitised yet apprehensive giver – a giver afraid of wasting resources on the relief of less needy (and often deceitful) supplicants – was to be a mainstay of charitable associational self-justification throughout the next 150 years.'*[61]

Some famous names tried their hands at offering philanthropy advice. No less a figure than Charles Dickens was – among his many other talents – a philanthropy adviser of some note. He worked with the renowned philanthropist Angela Burdett-Coutts (see case study below) to guide her in her giving and to act as an intermediary for the many requests for donations she received. Dickens was driven by a sense of outrage at the poverty and injustice he had seen in the working class areas of London while working as a reporter. As well as highlighting many of the issues through his hugely popular fictional works such as *Oliver Twist* (which remains the most vivid picture of the plight of workhouse children in Victorian London), Dickens was able to use his partnership with Burdett-Coutts to try to address some of the same issues through philanthropic means.

CASE STUDY

Angela Burdett-Coutts: The life philanthropic (with Charles Dickens)?

Angela Burdett-Coutts (1814–1906) is one of the true big hitters of philanthropy. She was the granddaughter of Thomas Coutts, the founder of Coutts' Bank (famously the bankers for the Queen). When Coutts' first wife died, he married the much younger actress Harriet Mellon with somewhat indecent haste, and to the disgust of his three daughters. They resented her bitterly, and were further enraged when Coutts died and left his entire fortune to her. Of Coutts' grandchildren, Angela was the only one to get along with her step-grandmother, but it was still a surprise when Harriet died in 1837 and left the whole of her fortune (including a large interest in Coutts Bank) to Angela. Even Angela's father, Sir Francis Burdett, was temporarily so enraged that his wife (Angela's mother) had been passed over that Angela had to leave home.

Burdett-Coutts proved herself adept at looking after her new-found fortune, but discovered that her real gift was in giving it away for the benefit of others. As mentioned above, she had help from no less a figure than Charles Dickens, and *'in guiding her benevolence [his] influence . . . was probably decisive . . . For some years [he] served as her almoner, screening applications and separating the worthy from the undeserving'.*[62] Burdett-Coutts, the young heiress steeped in the very male world of banking, and Dickens, the young reporter with a burning hatred of social injustice, made an unlikely but extremely effective pairing. She gave him a means, alongside his writing, of combating the scourge of poverty he saw all around him; while he was able to broaden her philanthropic horizons beyond the obvious Christian causes she initially favoured.

Angela Georgina Burdett-Coutts, Baroness Burdett-Coutts, by unknown artist, oil on panel, *circa* 1840.

The list of Burdett-Coutts' eventual charitable interests is vast. It encompassed education (support for the Ragged School movement), women's issues (the rehabilitation of prostitutes at the home for fallen women in Shepherd's Bush), children's welfare (she was heavily involved in the founding, in 1884, of the London Society for the Prevention of Cruelty to Children, which later became the NSPCC, the National Society for the Prevention of Cruelty to Children), and some more esoteric interests such as beekeeping (she was President of the British Beekeepers' Association for more than 25 years) and providing drinking fountains for dogs.[63]

But not all of her philanthropic ventures were successful. Most notably, she gave the vast sum of £200,000 to pay for the construction of Columbia Market in the East End of London, which turned out to be a massively costly white elephant. The intention was undoubtedly noble: Burdett-Coutts was concerned that the tolls collected at other London markets were pushing up the price of food and making it difficult for the poor to feed their families, and she wanted to find a way of supplying the inhabitants of poorer areas with cheaper food in the long term. Unfortunately, against opposition from the other London markets, Columbia Market struggled to get going. The sense that this was a grand philanthropic folly was not helped by the fact that, as a result of the desire to provide maximum employment during the construction of the market, the building itself was incredibly lavish. As *The Times* noted: *'The Halles of Paris and the central market of Brussels are as nothing when compared with the beauty of this almost cathedral pile.'*[64] Gradually the market declined, until it finally closed in 1886. The remnants of Burdett-Coutts' grand vision can still be seen today in the presence of Columbia Road flower market, which evolved from the street markets that had existed around the main market, and is now a popular tourist destination.

Burdett-Coutts had more philanthropic hits than misses though, and her interests spread beyond the UK. She supported various expeditions, including the African exploration of Livingstone and Stanley, and provided hospital equipment and nurses during the Zulu War of 1879. She even dabbled in social investment, making an advance of capital for the purchase of equipment by the Baltimore fishing fleet that resulted in a major turnaround in its fortunes and was almost entirely repaid over subsequent years.

This, along with other work in the city, led to her being hailed as the 'Queen of Baltimore'.[65]

She was widely feted in her homeland too, as a paragon of Victorian philanthropic virtues, and to many in Victorian Britain *'the name of Baroness Burdett-Coutts became almost synonymous with large-scale charity'*.[66] There are a number of reasons. In part it may be a reflection of the fact that *'more than with most of her wealthy contemporaries, she considered the practice of philanthropy to be almost a professional commitment'*.[67] It may also have been less about her philanthropy than about the woman herself, as it is clear that *'her contemporaries found her a fascinating figure, with the touch of eccentricity that adds colour – the fabulously wealthy heiress, strong-minded and shrewd, devoting her resources to improving the life of her time'*.[68] Whatever the case, she was widely renowned and appears to have been much-loved, and *'there is no reason to doubt the story that, when she died in her ninety-second year, some thirty thousand Londoners filed past her coffin as it lay in state at One Stratton Street'*.[69]

The Charity Organisation Society

As well as individuals, there were organisations that took on the role of intermediating between donors and beneficiaries and providing advice. For example, the Society for Bettering the Condition and Increasing the Comforts of the Poor was founded in 1796 *'to serve (in the modern idiom) as a "clearing house" for information about the condition of the poor and for helpful ideas for improving it – "useful and practical information derived from EXPERIENCE, and stated briefly and plainly"'*.[70] It was essentially an attempt to apply the scientific approach, so popular in many other fields at the time, to philanthropy, and *'to have done with vague benevolence and "deal with facts"'*.[71]

The new rigorous approach to philanthropy perhaps reached its zenith in the 19th century, in the form of the Charity Organisation Society (COS). This was founded in 1869 as the London Society for Organising Charitable Relief and Repressing Mendicity, and came to epitomise the idea of taking a 'scientific' approach to charity to overcome the problem of indiscriminate giving. The COS saw its roles as providing *'machinery for systematising, without unduly controlling, the benevolence of the public'*,[72] although many would argue that what it actually did was to pursue a *'crusade against mendacity, indiscriminate almsgiving, and laxity in Poor Law administration with enormous zeal'.*[73]

The legacy of the COS is somewhat controversial. Although it had many supporters at the time, it also had many critics and was from early-on the subject of much criticism and antipathy because its hard-line approach to philanthropy did not endear it to some in the charitable world of late Victorian London. However, even among its critics there were those who grudgingly admitted that the aims of the COS were laudable, even if its methods left a little to be desired. *The Guardian* newspaper, for instance, noted that while the organisation was sometimes guilty of *'disciplining philanthropy to death by their rules and principles'*, it was also true that *'by the impulse they have given to the duty of thoughtfulness in charity, and by their education of the rich as to the responsibility of how to give, rather than what – and by helping the poor out of their poverty, rather than merely relieving them in it, [COS] are doing work of vast and growing usefulness'.*[74]

In the long run, the positive aspects of the COS approach have been largely overshadowed by other aspects of the way it pursued its goals, and in particular its view of poverty as a failing of the individual, rather than something stemming from the wider failings of society. Although this belief had been widespread in the early Victorian period, by the time the COS was formed it was increasingly unfashionable. But the COS held this view with a ferocity that alienated many. It was *'little inclined to discover merit in criticisms of its philosophy or methods'* and its supporters described those who criticised it as *'featherbrained'*, *'perversely wrongheaded'*, or *'selfishly interested in perpetuating unsound philanthropy'*.[75] But the COS did make at least one unquestionably important contribution to society through its pioneering approach to casework, which set the template for modern social work. It eventually evolved from its origins as a proponent of scientific philanthropy into an organisation focusing largely on casework, becoming the Family Welfare Association in 1946 and eventually Family Action in 2008.[76]

There is also another, broader sense in which the COS succeeded – in promoting the need for a more 'scientific' approach to philanthropy. In the philanthropic world today concerns about 'measuring impact' and 'giving effectively' are riding high on the agenda.[77] The growing acceptance of tools like Social Return on Investment (SROI), which attempt to provide a meaningful measure of the value of philanthropic interventions, shows that for both donors and beneficiaries it is increasingly important to have evidence that their chosen approach is effective in delivering the outcomes they are trying to achieve.[78]

Implications for future philanthropy

The trend to measure impact in philanthropy is a positive thing: why would we not want to make sure that the things we are giving money to actually work? But perhaps the relevant lesson from the early years of the COS is that while a focus on effectiveness and efficiency is positive, it has to be done in the right way. Simply castigating people for giving in the 'wrong way' will always be counterproductive. It is true that giving driven solely by the heart without the engagement of the head can be ineffective, or perhaps even harmful. However, trying to remove the element of heart from philanthropy is just as wrong-headed. Even when it is guided by a scientific and rational approach, philanthropy is always underpinned by a personal and emotional link that motivates a person to give. It is when we forget this in our desire to sharpen philanthropy into a perfect tool that problems can arise because individuals and organisations push back against what they see as unreasonable demands that undermine the nature or ethos of philanthropy.[79] We should not stop attempting to make philanthropy as effective as possible, but we must be careful that we do not try to turn it into something it is not, and thereby damage the very thing we are trying to support.

We must also remember that impact is partly in the eye of the beholder: our choice of measurement system and metrics will determine whether we consider a particular approach to be 'effective' or not. And no system designed to date is perfect – there are still elements of philanthropy that many would argue are valuable and important, but that are not adequately captured by existing approaches to impact measurement. This is particularly true of longer-term philanthropic initiatives focusing on systemic change through advocacy and campaigning. The danger is that if we do not acknowledge the limitations of current impact measurement approaches, we fall into the trap of assuming that aspects of philanthropy that cannot be measured are not important. An article in *Forbes* magazine warned that the trend towards statistics-led 'Moneyball' philanthropy *'is dangerous because it leads donors to seek out only the most easily provable results. It pushes them towards interventions within the current system and beguiles them into thinking that the best charities must be able to produce simple cost-benefit figures'.* And, as the article points out, the problem is that *'this approach would have precluded some of philanthropy's greatest successes'.* Since *'many of us owe our liberty, our freedom of speech, and our education'* to the philanthropy of former days, *'we'd be crazy to sacrifice these kinds of achievements in pursuit of an immediate "return on investment"'.*[80]

Improving data – the census

A key part of the development of philanthropy advice and more 'strategic' or 'scientific' approaches to giving over the 19th century was the increasing availability of data and information on demographics and social phenomena, as this provided the means to develop a better understanding of the causes of poverty and the hope of designing more effective responses to it. A watershed moment in this new field of social research was the first census in 1801, which had major implications both for philanthropy and for society as a whole. It had been a long time coming: there had been calls for a census at various times in the preceding century, but these had always met with resistance. For instance, *'a census bill introduced in the House of Commons in 1753 had been opposed on the grounds that it would put heart into our enemies by revealing our numerical weakness'.*[81] However, the various objections were eventually overcome and the 1801 census now meant that, for the first time, there was detailed information on the demographic make-up of the country.

This was both a blessing and a curse for philanthropists: it provided a comprehensive source of information on the pressing social issues of the day, that could guide their efforts. But it also highlighted the extent of many of these problems and therefore the scale of the challenge of trying to address them using philanthropic means. As outlined in the next chapter, this eventually led to an increasingly widespread belief that the state had to play a role in tackling many social issues. This was perhaps inevitable because *'once the state had assumed the responsibility of knowing how the people lived it could not permanently ignore the general misery of their condition. Mischief was rampant everywhere. The spectre of destitution, both physical and mental, could not be denied, and would not be exorcised by the feeble conjuring of philanthropy'.*[82]

While the census undoubtedly had the most profound influence as a source of information due to its breadth, other data-gathering exercises also had a huge impact on philanthropic and government approaches in specific areas. For example, the pioneering work of Charles Booth was instrumental in refocusing efforts to meet the welfare needs in London at the end of the 19th century. The 17 volumes of Booth's *Life and Labour in London*, published between 1886 and 1903, provided a comprehensive and stark picture of the continuing extent of poverty and suffering in the capital. Most famously, the extraordinarily detailed maps showed, at a street-by-street level, the inequality that ran through the heart of London.[83] His studies particularly highlighted the plight of older people, and were an important part of the evidence base in the argument for introducing a state pension.

The precedent for harnessing the power of data had been set a century earlier, by the prison reform campaigner John Howard, who gives his name to the modern Howard League for Penal Reform. Howard was a remarkable figure, who seemingly paid little attention to his own welfare when conducting his studies. His uncompromising focus on obtaining an accurate picture of the state of England's prisons laid the foundations for the work of later reformers such as Elizabeth Fry (who should be familiar to anyone who has ever looked at the back of a £5 note).

CASE STUDY

John Howard: The curmudgeonly Indiana Jones of philanthropy

John Howard (1726–1790) was one of the most remarkable philanthropists of his – or indeed any other – age. Rarely can an individual have been so celebrated, both during and after his lifetime, for his good works, and yet seemingly cared so little for this adulation. He exemplified the contradictions and idiosyncrasies that make philanthropy both an incredibly potent force for change and a maddeningly difficult beast to harness.

The defining incident of Howard's life, which shaped his philanthropic work, was when he was captured by French pirates during a journey to Portugal in 1756, and thrown in jail. This experience of the inhumanity and depravity of prison life sparked his lifelong interest in prison reform in England. When he was elected High Sheriff of Bedford in 1773, he came into contact with the law court and prisons, which kick-started his real philanthropic efforts.

John Howard bringing water and fresh air into a prison in order to improve the conditions for the inmates. Watercolour, 1787.

Howard's approach to philanthropy was rigorously methodical: rather than leaping to conclusions, he set about carefully gathering information to get a complete picture. He had long been known to be a patient and stoical observer, and it was even said that '. . . *on the frost setting in, he used . . . to leave his bed at two every morning, for the purpose of observing the state of a thermometer which was placed in his garden at some distance from his house*'.[84] Howard brought the same slightly obsessive approach to his philanthropic research. He travelled extensively around the UK, visiting prisons to gather evidence on their failings, and also criss-crossed the Continent, visiting jails in other countries to get ideas for best practices and things to avoid.

While his detached scientific approach and his relentless pursuit of data might give the impression that Howard's philanthropic work was somewhat dry, the way he went about doing this work blows that assumption out of the water. His approach to rigorous data gathering seems to have been a decent approximation of Indiana Jones's approach to archaeology. To take one example: Howard developed an additional interest in plague treatment, and devised a plan to tour the continental plague quarantine stations (*lazarettos*) to learn more about disease prevention. He travelled without a servant because he thought it unfair to ask another man to accept the level of risk. He inquired of the French government if he could visit the lazaretto at Marseille, to be told that he would probably be thrown in the Bastille if he entered the country. Despite this, he sneaked into France and visited the site in Marseille; narrowly escaping the attentions of the authorities in Paris, who had been alerted by a spy among Howard's travelling companions. He then toured a number of other lazarettos around Europe, ending in Constantinople. Here, in 1786, he conceived an even bolder plan – to take passage from Smyrna to Venice on a ship carrying plague victims, so that he would himself be put into quarantine. His plan succeeded, although it was nearly scuppered when the ship he was sailing in was once again attacked by pirates (this time Tunisian), and he narrowly escaped capture.

These exploits in the name of philanthropy made Howard a heroic figure in the eyes of many, and a byword for how philanthropy should be done. Nearly a century later, *The Times* was still invoking his name to criticise the way that 'modern' philanthropists went about their business, arguing: '*John Howard, like an apostle of old, went to the places and mixed with the people that he wished to reform, and he had his reward in an early grave and the admiration of the world. But modern philanthropy does not run such dangers and will hardly excite such gratitude.*'[85]

However, there was a less appealing side to Howard's personality. Even those who lauded his charitable works sometimes acknowledged that the very traits that made him such a successful philanthropist made him a rather difficult person because *'he had many of those qualities and those vices which made for greatness: single-mindedness, unflinching tenacity, ruthlessness and even a streak of cruelty. He was not popular among the people he met, a certain coldness and inhumanity precluded affection, but he appealed to the public's imagination'.* [86]

A Sea View of the Lazaretto (or plague prison) at Genoa, taken from Howard's 1789 book, *An Account of the Principal Lazarettos in Europe.*

Some of these traits were present in his philanthropy too. We should not assume, for instance, that because Howard strived so hard for prison reform, he was some sort of humane liberal. He was a strict disciplinarian, and believed strongly in the use of manual labour and solitary confinement for inmates. Likewise, he was not shy to moralise on his own austere beliefs, and unafraid of enforcing these views in a distinctly authoritarian way. Like many middle-class philanthropists of his time, Howard *'disliked the fairs and the holidays, the dirt and the drunkenness, the squalor and the merriment of village life in England at that time'.* He was happy to help the poor, but thought that this was best done by telling them how to live. He gave generously to support the local community near where he lived, but stipulated that *'as well as having to attend places of worship, they had to refrain from going to public houses, or partaking in such amusements as*

Howard thought wrong'. And just to make sure they followed his advice, Howard threatened to evict any local residents who failed to meet these criteria. This resulted in an unsurprisingly mixed response: some viewed Howard with great affection for the help he had given them, but it is also reported that a group of locals plotted to kill him and were only foiled when on the given day he walked a different route.[87]

John Howard ('The triumph of benevolence') by James Gillray, published by Robert Wilkinson. Stipple and line engraving, 1788.

But while this unbending conviction in his own views made him a difficult man to like, it was also one of the characteristics that made him such a successful campaigning philanthropist. He disregarded the views of others, and this enabled him to speak truth to power in a way that few could match. He was able to do this precisely because *'he placed little value on the favours of kings or emperors; he would refuse to bend the knee to anyone, and he never hesitated to speak his mind plainly . . . Whether he was at home or abroad, he never hesitated to reprimand strangers if, as often happened, he disapproved of their behaviour, and many anecdotes are told of his forthrightness'.*[88]

Howard was not remotely interested in public acclaim. Ironically, he got more recognition and praise than many philanthropists who actively seek it could ever dream of. In fact, Howard had to go out of his way to avoid public honour. The University of Dublin conferred on him the honorary degree of Doctor of Laws, but he steadfastly refused to use the title. And when he heard of a proposal in the pages of *The Gentleman* magazine to raise funds for a statue of him, Howard disapproved strongly of the idea and most of the donated money was returned.

Although he shunned public profile in life, Howard could not escape the plaudits of others once he was gone, and this began almost immediately when *'his death was announced in the Gazette, an honour never before conferred on a private person. Articles in magazines, funeral odes and sermons from many pens praised "God-like Howard", "the consummate philanthropist" and "God's Minister of Good"'.*[89]

But despite the fantastic nature of his efforts and the admiration of his peers, Howard's work had little immediate impact on the prison system in England. It would have to wait until the next century, and the efforts of Elizabeth Fry and others, for true reform to take place. But those later campaigners all acknowledged that John Howard's work had paved the way for their own successes. And his name lives on today in the Howard League for Penal Reform, which continues to be one of the leading voices on prison reform issues.

Organisation and association: the birth of the charitable sector

Awareness of the scale of social problems, and the desire to address them effectively using knowledge and insight, led to the development of something we take for granted today: the charitable organisation. Initially, much of the visible charitable activity following the Reformation continued to be in the form of gifts left in wills, some of which resulted in the formation of charitable trusts. Slowly, philanthropists began to realise that the shift of focus toward the impact of giving rather than the act of giving meant that giving within one's lifetime made more sense as one could exert control over donations and judge their effectiveness. Yet despite the fact that these living philanthropists were at great pains to distinguish what they did from the almsgiving of their medieval forebears, they still followed broadly the same model, in that the focus was on individuals: individuals with money giving directly to other individuals in need.

In the 1700s, however, a new trend emerged. Although philanthropists *'continued to give or leave considerable sums of money as individuals',* they also *'discovered increasing merit in collective activity'*[90] and would come together to pool their expertise and philanthropic resources. As a result *'a new form of inter vivos charity developed . . . That was "associated philanthropy": the funding of charitable activity by subscriptions from a large number of benefactors'.*[91]

It is perhaps unsurprising that philanthropy went in this direction, as collectivism and association were shaping many other areas of life at the same time. For instance, the new model of the joint stock company was setting the template for modern business, while increasingly, prominent religious groups such as the Quakers were using subscriptions as a way of financing their activities. Furthermore, as some historians have pointed out, *'voluntary contributions and associative charity characterised much state and church welfare provision, and had done for centuries.'* However, in the same way that Protestants of the 17th and 18th centuries tried to craft for themselves a narrative that emphasised the value of their giving while denigrating that of their Catholic forerunners, philanthropists also tried to claim the idea of association as their own. As a result, *'the relatively free-floating, minimally religious, contribution-dependent charitable societies which proliferated in England during the 18th century and began to flourish on the continent from the 1780s were . . . hailed by contemporaries as something new, a new social phenomenon, manifestations of a new "associative spirit"'.*[92]

Even if, as with many other developments in the history of modern philanthropy, the idea of association was not in fact entirely new, the vastly increased prevalence of associational forms of charity throughout the 18th and 19th centuries marks an important conceptual turn. Previously, the only obvious option available to a philanthropist concerned about a particular problem was to go out and identify those suffering as a result of that problem and directly give them money and assistance to try to improve their lot. Now, however, a philanthropist could *'increasingly find his outlet by aiding, passively through his contributions, actively through his labour, or both, an organisation dedicated to a cause which he wished to further'.*[93]

These new charitable organisations would come into their own during the industrial revolution, when British society was transformed and social problems fundamentally changed in both nature and scale. While *'casual almsgiving and the visits of vicars and lady bountifuls [had] helped to ameliorate poverty and distress in pre-industrial England . . . they were inadequate to deal with the changing conditions'.*[94] It became *'out of the question for the philanthropist . . . to seek out for himself the cases of greatest need and become familiar with them'.*[95] This was partly a result of the urbanisation of poverty: whereas in the pre-industrial era poverty had largely existed at a comprehensible, parish level, it was now the case that *'in the rapidly growing cities, knowledge of hardship was not so easy to come by'.*[96] Furthermore, from the donor's point of view, it became *'more difficult to distinguish between real and feigned distress'.*[97] Voluntary associations sought to solve these problems by *'interven[ing] in the relationship between the benevolent and the needy',*[98] and they did this so successfully that *'the 19th century saw the charitable organisation come to full, indeed almost rankly luxuriant, bloom'.*[99]

Here lie the origins of the model that forms the bedrock of modern charitable giving: that of addressing a social issue by supporting dedicated, cause-driven organisations via donations. Philanthropists were no longer required to solve society's problems themselves, but instead could support a range of organisations already working to address those problems.

Founding new philanthropic organisations v supporting existing ones

This choice remains relevant for donors today – particularly those looking to donate significant amounts of money. They have to decide whether they want to go it alone, and set up their own operational entity aimed at combating a given problem, or whether they just want to support existing charities. The former obviously puts the onus very much on the philanthropist to find the right approach, and also has the cost implications of setting up a new organisation. The latter presents a different, but equally demanding challenge: how to pick the most effective and efficient organisations from the often vast range of charities working on a given cause.

Implications for future philanthropy

This need to choose between charities when one often has little or no personal experience of their work places a heavy emphasis on the organisations to provide information to help guide donors in their choices. Of course, that leaves open the question of what that information should actually be. We have already noted a growing industry in 'impact measurement', which seeks to develop objective measures to enable donors to compare the effectiveness of different organisations or the work they do, and also that there are risks in misapplying this approach (see earlier in this chapter).

However, there are also significant risks inherent in not facing up to these challenges: for one thing, if donors are not given the right information to make sensible choices, they will look for other bases on which to make their decisions, and this might be bad news for charities; witness the recurring suggestion that charities should publish their administration or fundraising costs as a way of demonstrating their effectiveness.[100] As many people have pointed out, these figures offer little or no indication of an organisation's effectiveness (or even efficiency),[101] but unless charities themselves take responsibility for providing more accurate metrics that also meet the needs of donors, we will almost certainly continue to hear calls for administration costs, fundraising costs or CEO salaries to be published as a measure of a charity's worth.[102] This should be a strong incentive for finding the right measures.

CHAPTER TWO

Philanthropy and welfare

A constantly evolving relationship

Chapter 1 detailed how modern philanthropy has undergone many changes since its birth in the late 16th century, as philanthropists slowly developed a greater sense of focus about what they were trying to achieve and clearer ideas about how best to make that happen. However, philanthropy has never existed in a vacuum. It has always been influenced by, and exerted influence upon, the wider world. In particular, the relationship between the state and philanthropy in the UK is a deep-rooted and complex one.

In the late 16th and early 17th centuries, at the same time as philanthropy began to emerge in the form we know it today, the role of public institutions was also evolving. The development of new modes of secular giving alongside an expansion of the role and responsibilities of government had a profound impact on the shape of society. Between individual and state there emerged a 'public sphere' of activity inhabited by organisations and institutions that were '*no longer directly regulated by state or ecclesiastical authority, [and which] . . . no longer relied on such authority either for the setting of policy goals or for funding*'.[103] Before this, '*there was no concept of the "public" as the core of civil society. There was the court, the Lords and an occasional Parliament, and then there were the people. No legitimate space existed for public associations of private individuals*'.[104] This changed ever more rapidly as the 17th century wore on and '*functional specialisation between the political, cultural and economic sectors created a public sphere. By the end of the 17th century, the contours of a public sphere were drawn by a greatly expanded associational life'.*[105]

The development of the public sphere really took flight in the 18th century. The philosopher and sociologist Jürgen Habermas, whose work has done much to clarify the notion of the public sphere, identifies this period as crucial in the development of our modern democratic structures. The flowering of free debate and discussion through the spread of coffee shops and debating societies, and the rise of pamphleteering, cemented the shift in power away from the state that had begun in the previous century. The growth in voluntary associations was another important element of this change, and the result was *'[the replacement of] a public sphere in which the ruler's power was merely represented before the people with a sphere in which state authority was publicly monitored through informed and critical discourse by the people'.*[106]

Philanthropy, and the blossoming of a 'sector' of dedicated charitable organisations, was a crucial factor in determining the sort of society we have today. The influence of philanthropy took two main forms: on the one hand charitable organisations (supported by philanthropists) helped to shape the state through the services they provided, by drawing attention to areas of need, and demonstrating which of those needs could be met by voluntary provision and which could not (and, therefore, those where the state was required to take greater responsibility). On the other hand, many philanthropists and charitable organisations sought to influence the nature of society more directly, by campaigning for social change and challenging policy and legislation in a wide range of areas.

These two approaches are not always easily disentangled, because in many cases campaigns for change designed to address the underlying causes of given social problems go hand-in-hand with delivering services to address their symptoms. However, this chapter will attempt to assess in turn: the service delivery and campaigning roles of philanthropy; how they have both played important parts in influencing the development of society in the UK; and how the balance between these two roles has changed over time. In this way, we can hopefully get a better idea of how philanthropists, charities and the government can best work together in the future.

The starting point: no role for the state in social welfare

For a long time there was no real question over whether particular needs would be met by public or by charitable provision: charitable provision (traditionally in the form of alms) was seen as the only option. Up to around the 16th century, the state viewed its responsibility as essentially that of *'the maintenance of power by means of the maximum of revenue'*, and *'had not yet accepted as its task the furthering of the welfare of the whole body of citizens'*.[107] Before 1500, *'assistance [for the poor] had been provided for by a miscellany of means: religious institutions – monasteries, fraternities and guilds; or village and parish resources – town "stocks", almshouses, church collections. There had been no co-ordination and little activity by the state, aside from legislation regulating labour and punishing beggars and vagrants'*.[108] Eventually, this situation started to change, and *'after 1530 . . . there was increasing government interference, centralisation and uniformity'*.[109]

The involvement of government in welfare provision developed slowly. At first, the only real sign of it was the introduction of a system of local levies designed to raise revenue that could be used to alleviate poverty in the local area. However, these levies were not mandatory or enforceable. At the same time, the Reformation had dismantled much of the existing structure of religious welfare provision controlled by the Catholic church, which meant that *'need . . . grew greater or at any rate more apparent'* as the 16th century wore on. As a result *'the levy which had not been forthcoming voluntarily was by degrees converted into the poor rate'*.[110] Furthermore, unforeseen events forced the pace of change to increase as the situation *'became more desperate in the last decade of the 16th century with a series of disastrous harvests and the increasing strain of the Spanish War'*.[111] This increased concern for the poor among the wealthier classes, and also a tangible element of fear, so that *'when Parliament met in 1597 members anxiously drew attention to [the] suffering [of the poor] and to the danger of violent upheaval if their misery was not immediately relieved'*.[112] This led, finally, to the Poor Laws of 1598 and 1601, which *'confirmed that the relief of poverty was a local as well as a national responsibility, and that the burden of assisting the poor should be borne by the parish and the county and financed by a compulsory rate levied on householders'*.[113]

While the introduction of the Poor Laws did give the state formal responsibility for alleviating poverty, this role was at first limited in practice and it was seen as preferable that as far as possible these needs be met through philanthropic efforts rather than through government activity. This probably had less to do with an ideological belief about whether state provision was more or less desirable than philanthropic provision, and rather more to do with pragmatics: in order to enact the legislation properly, compulsory local levies had to be enforced, and these were understandably unpopular. Far better, from the government's point of view, to encourage philanthropy so that needs could be met by voluntary means wherever possible and the imposition of new taxes could be avoided.

Jordan claims (in fairly florid terms) that this meant in practice that *'the state stood poised for intervention after 1597, if the need should arise, but because of the prodigal generosity of private men who had assumed for themselves an heroic burden of social responsibility that intervention was in fact to be long delayed'*, and that *'the Poor Laws were not invoked because they were not needed, because private charity bore almost the whole of the great burden of poor relief prior to 1660'*.[114] Others, however, have argued that this overstates the case somewhat, and that the state did have to take on a fair measure of the responsibilities outlined in the Poor Law legislation. In part, at least, this was precisely because voluntary means were no longer thought to be up to the job, hence *'the law was necessary, Tudor Englishmen felt, because some forms of charitable activity were in decline'*.[115]

Philanthropy leads state provision
Whatever the exact balance between state and philanthropy when it came to dealing with poverty, what seems clear is that from the early 17th century the responsibility was shared for the first time, and that philanthropy continued to shoulder the larger share of this responsibility. Thus, *'a partnership was established, in which the state filled in gaps left by charity rather than charity filling in gaps left by the state'*.[116]

The nature of this partnership changed over time. For a fairly long period the state was in the ascendant, as the Poor Laws came to be more rigidly enforced over the course of the 17th and 18th centuries, and the government became involved in a growing number of other areas of welfare provision. However, this eventually – and perhaps inevitably – led to a backlash against the idea of state-provided welfare, so that by the time the Napoleonic Wars came to a close in 1815, the *'crisis in social relations had*

convinced significant sections of propertied England that properly moni-
tored volunteer forms of relief were greatly to be preferred to involuntary,
impersonal, ratepayer-funded forms'.[117]

The idea that provision by voluntary means was always to be preferred
to state provision took firm hold in the early 19th century, and remained the
prevailing view for the next 100 years, so that *'throughout the 19th century*
and into the 20th the main responsibility for social welfare lay with volun-
tary agencies. The function of the state was largely supplementary, to fill
such urgent gaps as might be left by the network of private agencies and
to carry out its traditional obligation of relieving the genuinely destitute'.[118]

Writing in 1952, the Nathan Committee, taking a wide-ranging look at
the role of the voluntary sector shortly after the birth of the modern welfare
state, concluded: *'Until less than a hundred years ago, it would be broadly*
true to say that so far as personal needs were concerned, the activities of
the state were confined to a deterrent Poor Law and a harsh penal system.
All constructive action on behalf of individuals in need of help was under-
taken by voluntary agencies.'[119]

Although the state did slowly become involved in meeting more and
more of the welfare needs of its citizens, it did so with great reticence and
almost always took a back seat to philanthropic ventures. It was usually the
pioneering work of philanthropic initiatives – in highlighting the importance
of an issue, or demonstrating a better way of addressing it – that led to the
state rousing itself to action. Even once roused, the involvement was usually
reluctant and not intended to supplant existing philanthropic provision, but
merely to supplement it. Often this meant simply lending support to existing
initiatives, so that *'as the British state began cautiously to move into new*
areas of social action in the 19th century, it first subsidised the existing
pioneering work of voluntary organisations. From the 1830s, voluntary,
mainly faith-based, institutions providing schooling for the working classes
were funded, and increasingly regulated, by a state which was concerned
about the literacy and discipline of the population'.[120]

In education, philanthropy was very much the senior partner at the outset. Private philanthropists largely *'determined the conditions on which the*
state intervened', and when it did take action, it did so in a way that was not
supposed to displace charitable activity, but rather to act in a *'junior and*
supervisory' capacity.[121] The charitable school societies *'formed the chan-*
nel by which the state, with extreme timidity, entered the field of popular

education,' [122] and this balance of power took a long time to shift. It was only much later on that the state became unquestionably the senior partner.

This situation seems strange from our modern viewpoint, because *'an age that takes for granted large-scale public social services can appreciate only with difficulty the distinctive role assigned by the Victorians to charity'.* [123] Living in a country that now has a long-established welfare state, our expectations about the extent to which the government will meet our basic needs are high. However, in the 18th and 19th centuries, reticence by the state to get involved was certainly not deemed a problem. Rather, it was seen as the desirable state of affairs by all concerned, as *'neither public authorities nor philanthropists were disposed to demand a closer union of forces, save in special areas. They agreed, on the whole, that the proper concerns of the state lay within the ambit of "politics" and that matters of social betterment were best left to voluntary effort'.* [124]

In fact, it has been argued that the perceived purpose of the state with regard to welfare at that point was precisely to stay as far away as possible while ensuring the conditions for philanthropic endeavours to flourish, and that *'the essential quality of public life in Britain from the 17th century was its voluntarist disposition'.* The purpose of government was therefore *'to preserve the voluntarist complexion of the public sphere and, acting at the behest of private initiative, to secure and protect its territory'.* [125]

A classic statement of the Victorian view of the appropriate relationship between philanthropy and the state is given in a mid-19th century editorial from *The Times*, which argued that philanthropy must take the lead because it can identify solutions to social problems, and that the state should simply follow the example that has been set:

'Among the many considerations which make an Englishman proud of his country there is hardly one which can so justly excite his patriotic satisfaction as the contemplation of its vast, numerous and richly-endowed charities. Much of that which the church or the state has collectively done in other countries, the voluntary benevolence of individuals has done in this ... It is this spontaneity of action which distinguishes our social, as it distinguishes our legislative proceedings. We do not wait for the instigation of the Government or the dictation of a central bureau. The individual eye sees, the individual hand indicates, the social malady. Individuals' charity finds the remedy. If the experiment succeeds, Parliament and Government

follow in the wake, often after an interval of years. But it rarely, very rarely happens that in England any great scheme of comprehensive benevolence is initiated by the Government, which is only too happy to await the results of private enterprise and private experience.' [126]

In many ways, this attitude towards the limited role of role of government in welfare was reflective of the wider social and political views of the time, because it was a period *'in which the merits of voluntarism were highly prized: the ways in which it embodied individual choice and participation, personal independence and local control, freedom and flexibility. These were the political and cultural norms of the society of the time: ones which were able to embrace statutory initiatives of a localised kind – although here private initiatives were often preferred – but were highly suspicious of the compulsion and cost seen to go with the centralised state'.* [127]

Philanthropists themselves often *'had deep-seated views about the respective roles of government and charity which made accommodation difficult'.* This was mainly rooted in the common view of poverty at the time (detailed in Chapter 4), because this meant that they were *'inclined to attribute the source of social problems to individual failings'* and as a result *'they concluded that the remedy must be found in personal reformation, assisted by discretionary charity'.* [128] They could not countenance the idea of state responsibility for welfare because *'the individual, not as ratepayer but as fellow-sufferer, was responsible for the expiation of sin and the cares of the world. The law and the state were artificial contrivances, useful in punishing sinners, but incapable of redemptive action'.* [129]

Whatever the reasons for their preference for voluntary over state provision, the pride of the Victorians in their philanthropic culture is evident, and in some way they had good reason: the scale of donations in what many consider to be the 'golden age' of British philanthropy is certainly impressive. As historian Prochaska notes: *'The amount of money contributed each year to charity, not including donations at the altar and unremembered alms, far exceeded the gross expenditure on poor relief.* The Times *reported in 1885 that charitable receipts in London alone came to more than the national budgets of Denmark, Portugal, Sweden, or the Swiss Confederation.'* [130] Similarly, on a household level: *'A study of middle-class households in the 1890s established that on average they spent a larger share of their income on charity than on any item in their budget except food. A survey of working-class and artisan families in the same decade showed that half of them subscribed weekly to charity and about a quarter of them also made donations to church or chapel.'* [131]

To this day, there are those who latch on to these sorts of facts and continue to lionise the great donors of that period. However, other dissenting voices have argued that levels of charitable giving in the Victorian era may tell us more about the how bad the problems were than the generosity of the people at the time. As Brian Harrison notes: *'Victorians often congratulated themselves on the scale of their charities; Mayhew thought rather that they indicated the prevalence of misery.'* [132]

In the end it was the scale of the problems facing society that eventually put paid to the grand Victorian vision of a system of welfare based on philanthropy. The size of the challenges and the limitations of philanthropic endeavour became more widely appreciated, and consequently views on the appropriate balance of state and voluntary provision of welfare began to change. People increasingly believed that direct state action was necessary if any of these challenges were ever going to be overcome.

CASE STUDY

William Rathbone VI: Innovative angel of Mersey?

William Rathbone, 1906.

William Rathbone (1819–1902) is an interesting example of the many Victorian philanthropists with strong local affiliations who played such a major role in the public institutions we find today in cities and towns around the UK. Rathbone's city was Liverpool.

He was born into a wealthy family of merchants in the city, although the family firm was somewhat in decline by the time William took over, and he and his brother dedicated the early part of their careers to rebuilding it. They were comfortable in these early years, although not exceedingly wealthy, and had little spare time to devote to charitable deeds. However, one fascinating aspect of Rathbone's approach to philanthropy was that he firmly believed in the importance of developing a 'giving habit', even when he was not yet in a position to give on a large scale, because *'he thought it essential for the young man to form habits of saving and giving – not merely to do good to others but to improve his own character'.*[133] It would not do to leave philanthropy until one was rich, he claimed, because *'to postpone developing these habits until wealth had been acquired would be fatal and would produce a "pecuniary paralysis"'*. Instead, *'it was his formula, followed by himself and prescribed for others, to give "for the sake of practice" even while one's resources were scanty. Then when greater wealth came, it would be natural and relatively painless to increase not only the amount but the proportion of one's income used for social betterment'.*[134]

Rathbone certainly practised what he preached: he served as a voluntary worker for the District Provident Society, where he had the job of visiting some of the more unsavoury areas around Lime Street collecting savings (which the society paid favourable interest on) and offering advice where he could. The philanthropic habit he developed through this volunteer work stood him – and the city of Liverpool – in good stead in later years, when he was in a position to give on a much grander scale and did just that. He was instrumental, among other things, in the founding of the institution that later became the University of Liverpool.

Although Rathbone is inextricably linked to Liverpool, his most notable philanthropic achievement extended far beyond Merseyside: establishing the system of district nursing. As with so many philanthropic endeavours, this was born of personal experience. After

Florence Nightingale, 1872. She advised Rathbone on nurse training.

his first wife died in 1859, Rathbone was so impressed by the care offered to her by the skilled nurse who had tended her that he arranged for the same nurse to spend three months visiting the sick poor in their houses and seeing what impact this had. In his judgement, the results were obvious. The problem for Rathbone was that there simply weren't enough skilled nurses in the city at that time to scale up the approach. Undeterred, and like any good philanthropist, he sought expert help. Following discussions with Florence Nightingale, he decided to set up a nursing training school in Liverpool, and subsequently a district nursing system for the city. The success of the Liverpool District Nursing Society led to the model being replicated in Manchester, Leicester, Birmingham and London – and eventually all over the UK.

Cover of Liverpool Queen Victoria District Nursing Association booklet, *Queen's Nurses* (*circa* 1900), showing Queen presenting badges to a line of nurses in uniform.

Philanthropy finding its limits

It is clear that philanthropy played a major role in driving innovations in almost all areas of social welfare provision, and in doing so it often established the template for subsequent state involvement. But, despite the bullishness of many of the advocates of philanthropy during the Victorian era, it became clear as time wore on that state involvement was necessary in a wide range of welfare areas, because philanthropy could not by itself provide satisfactory answers to the problems facing society. As time went on, *'it became increasingly difficult to reconcile [the reliance on philanthropy] with the circumstances of the later 19th century, when the social problems associated with unemployment, over which the individual might have little control, became especially evident at certain times of "depression"'.*[135] This meant: *'For all their reservations about the state, more and more philanthropists came to recognise that on their own they were incapable of changing the conditions which bred many of the problems they sought to redress'.*[136] In the end, *'virtually all of the writers, some with reluctance, conceded the necessity for public provision for the poor...and none saw private charity as an adequate substitute for public provision'.*[137]

At first some saw this failure to adequately address social issues as a failing in the practice of philanthropy, rather than an inherent flaw in the concept. This led to the focus on increased efficiency outlined earlier in the previous chapter, which reached its strongest expression in the work of the Charity Organisation Society. Gradually, however, it became clear that no matter how efficiently philanthropy was practised, some problems would remain beyond its power to solve.

The issue that first highlighted in stark terms the unavoidable need for state intervention was the plight of the nation's older people, many of whom were living in conditions of dire poverty and ill-health. The pioneering work of Charles Booth and others played a key role in bringing the scale of this problem to light and provided a major impetus for the subsequent introduction of the state pension.[138]

Even starker than the plight of the elderly was the wider problem of unemployment, because *'if voluntary philanthropy could offer no comprehensive protection against the hazards of old age, its shortcomings were even more apparent with respect to unemployment'.*[139] In part as a result of the dogmatic views of poverty that persisted throughout the Victorian era, which maintained that *'to be out of work either implies spinelessness or incompetence on the part of the individual, or it marked him as the victim of abnormally depressed conditions of trade',*[140] it was clear that despite an enormous amount of effort being expended, *'private philanthropy could make relatively little contribution to a realistic handling of unemployment'.*[141]

The question in many areas of need was now *'whether the old synthesis of providence, paternalism, and philanthropy, of voluntarism and the minimal state, could any longer survive the strains to which it had always*

been subject, but which were now seen to be more severe. Could it cope
with the circumstances of the period, which seemed to call for "social
reconstruction"?' [142] The answer, many thought, was 'no' because '*the state*
now seemed to be the more appropriate agency, with its attributes of cen-
tralisation and uniformity, professionalism and expertise, resources and
capacity'. [143] The sense that the state might be not just pragmatically, but
also theoretically, better-placed to deliver welfare was also bolstered by the
spread of democracy throughout society, because '*as ever more individu-*
als became "citizens" in the sense of belonging to the political community,
the citizenship of entitlement from the state in matters of social welfare was
seen to be more correct and apposite than the citizenship of contribution
expressed through voluntary agencies outside of the state'. [144]

Blurred lines between philanthropy and state action

In this chapter so far, we have traced a rough narrative about the relationship between state and philanthropy with regard to welfare provision. This
has taken us from the pre-Reformation era, when the state assumed no
responsibility for welfare, through the beginnings of state-delivered welfare
in the form of the Poor Laws, and then to the backlash against this approach
that led to the dominance of the ideal of philanthropic welfare provision in
the Victorian era. While this narrative is broadly true, there is a danger that
it implies far too clear a distinction between 'state' provision and 'voluntary' provision. In fact, the line between these two has often been blurred
or even non-existent, because '*in the 17th to 19th centuries the terms*
"charity" and "philanthropy", like the modern term "welfare", designated
broad areas of concern, rather than particular modes of addressing those
concerns'. This meant that '*the polarity of charity and philanthropy on the*
one hand and state action on the other was unknown, for the former could
include the latter'. [145] The Poor Laws, for instance, were often referred to as
"legal charity", even though it was a state-administered system based on
taxation and redistribution. Furthermore, '*private charity was often distrib-*
uted through public institutions, but those public institutions often allowed
individuals considerable discretion in decisions about who got money, so
that the distinction between "face-to-face" giving and the new rational
philanthropy is somewhat blurred.' [146] All this means that '*the distinction,*
so fundamental to modern thinking, between private donations and state

funding, made little sense . . . No-one could say where the private ended and the public began.'[147]

There are numerous examples of this blurring of the lines between philanthropic and state funding in practice. For instance, at a crucial stage in the establishment of Thomas Coram's Foundling Hospital, the enterprise found itself facing financial difficulties, and those involved realised that *'an obvious expedient was to appeal to Parliament, for clearly the state was directly interested in the problem with which the Hospital was wrestling. Neither philanthropists nor public authorities accepted the view which to the 19th century seemed axiomatic, that private charity and the state each had their proper spheres and the less mixing of the two, the better for both'.*[148]

Likewise, the Philanthropic Society provides an example of a voluntary organisation that was essentially performing a public service function from the outset, sanctioned and supported by the state. The Philanthropic (as it became known) was founded in 1788 by a group of men who met in the St Paul's coffee house to discuss how to address the problem of the large numbers of homeless children in London who could be found begging on the streets or turning to petty theft.[149] What is intriguing about the Philanthropic is that it *'turned out to be something more than another voluntary charity. Almost from the beginning it took on semi-official status, as magistrates and judges committed certain juvenile offenders to the Society for discipline and training in useful trades'.*[150] This put it in the unusual situation of being *'a voluntary organisation receiving government support for performing what were essentially public police functions',*[151] although it is far from being the last voluntary organisation to take on this sort of quasi-official role.

In many ways it should not be surprising that philanthropy and the work of government were often so hard to differentiate, because *'what bound together state and voluntary bodies was that they were both concerned with formulating and implementing policies towards the poor'.*[152] This meant that something like the Poor Law could be *'distinguished from, but not sharply counterposed to, other forms of charity originated by religious and voluntary bodies'.*[153] Indeed, as the Nathan Committee pointed out in 1952: *'State action and voluntary action were not the antitheses of each other; rather they sprang from the same roots, were designed to meet the same needs and had the same motivating forces behind them'.* The

Committee even went so far as to posit that in general: *'State action is voluntary action crystallised and made universal'.*[154] This is a fairly Whiggish interpretation, as it clearly views the history of voluntary action as one of deliberate progress toward the eventual and inevitable establishment of the welfare state. Others have argued that the situation was more complicated, and that *'within the mixed economy of welfare, voluntary impinged on statutory, statutory on voluntary; and this was an enduring process. It was not so much a question of development from voluntarist activity to statutory agencies. That could happen; but more often, voluntarist and statutory agencies were in constant relationship within the mixed economy. This does not mean that the relationship remained the same; it changed over time, and such change brought with it a different distribution of emphasis and importance between voluntarism and the state in the delivery of social welfare'.*[155]

The next section examines how this situation came to a head in the 20th century, when the complex relationship between voluntary and state provision resulted in monumental changes such as the introduction of the welfare state, which had a profound impact on the nature of philanthropy in the UK that continues to this day.

CASE STUDY

General James Oglethorpe, 1913 (from an original engraving).

A grand philanthropic scheme: Georgia on my mind

Philanthropy in the 18th century was certainly not short of ambition, and one of the most ambitious of all philanthropic projects was the founding of the colony that eventually became the US state of Georgia. This was the result of a plan by a philanthropist named James Oglethorpe, a former general and Member of Parliament. He was concerned by the problem of men released from debtors' prison, who often had bleak prospects and faced an uphill

The Trustees of the colony of Georgia receiving the Indians, 1929.
(From a 1734 painting by Verelst).

struggle to put their lives back on track. His plan was to offer such men the opportunity of a fresh start in the New World, and he set about raising funds to get his project off the ground.

Fairly quickly, Oglethorpe's original plan of settling 100 debtors had ballooned into a scheme for founding an entire new colony. This meant that it needed significantly more money than originally envisaged, so Oglethorpe and his friends *'found themselves carrying on a vigorous and uncommonly well-publicised campaign for subscriptions'.*[156] Their fundraising was quite successful, and secured donations from some curious sources. For instance, City contacts were tapped, which led to the East India Company subscribing £600 and the Bank of England £300.

The government, spying a chance to deal with a difficult social problem in a relatively low-cost way, offered a grant of £10,000. This was a great help, but marked the beginning of the erosion of the original philanthropic nature and purpose of the Georgia colony enterprise. The project increasingly became reliant on government funding and, at the same time, slightly lost sight of its original aims of giving a second chance to those who wanted it, becoming instead a way for the government to dispose of vagrants and ne'er-do-wells who would otherwise be littering England's towns. This meant that that *'during the first eight years, 915 British emigrants went to Georgia, not all, by any means, worthy souls who lacked only a fair chance to become self-maintaining'.*[157]

> The Georgia project offers an interesting example of the blurred lines that existed between philanthropy and state between the 17th and the 19th centuries, and in particular of the way in which philanthropy often provided the lead for the state to follow because while *'the source of the Georgia settlement lay in a philanthropic imagination',* it is also true that *'its fulfilment would have been out of the question without the aid of the state'.*[158]

The 20th century: philanthropy, dead or alive?

By the end of the 19th century it was clear that, while philanthropists had made often-valiant efforts, in many areas of social need, the state had to step in to meet the needs of its citizens. The seemingly-infinite ambition of early Victorian philanthropists had given way to a pragmatic realisation of the limitations of philanthropy. Some were quick to pen its obituary. For example, writing in 1908, the socialist historian and economist Benjamin Kirkman Gray rather damningly wrote: *'The philanthropists firmly believed that it was theirs to heal the hurts of the people, and they only came by degrees to doubt their ability to do so. They were ready at any moment and without training to run the longest race . . . Private individuals were confident of their power to discharge a public function, and the government was willing to have it so. It was left to experience to determine that the work was ill done and was by no means equal to the need.'*[159]

In many ways, Kirkman Gray was ahead of his time in putting forward this argument. Although by the middle of the 20th century it became the case that *'the history of philanthropy was [now] written as a prelude to the history of the welfare state, a perhaps well-meaning but insufficient attempt to cope with social problems that were beyond its capacity',*[160] in the early decades of the century not many shared such a negative assessment of the value of philanthropy. While *'the period from 1884 to 1914 witnessed the emergence of issues and ideas which presented a challenge to a continuing role for voluntary social endeavour',*[161] that does not mean that all philanthropy simply ceased at the start of the 20th century and was absorbed by the state. In fact, prior to World War I, the state continued to *'rely on voluntary agencies to a considerable degree and could, indeed, still be said to have been filling in the gaps left by voluntary and local initiative of various kinds'.*[162]

The Liberal governments of the early 20th century, in particular, were careful to avoid any suggestion that philanthropy should be crowded out, because '*they . . . believed that voluntary action – people choosing to give their time and money to help others – was an essential component of a good society and should be encouraged not supplanted by the state. In their view, the role of the state was to supplement the limited resources of the voluntary sector and make the services pioneered by volunteers, such as sickness benefits, more widely available*'.[163] Even Winston Churchill, during his time as a Liberal, argued: '*It is not impossible to underpin the existing voluntary agencies by a comprehensive system – necessarily at a lower level – of state action.*'[164]

Despite the fact that the governments of the early 20th century remained positive about philanthropy and voluntary action, it was clear that few now believed that philanthropy was a viable solution to society's problems in its own right. This meant that '*philanthropy might pioneer new approaches for the state later to adopt, it might try to fill the gaps which the state did not cover, it might, and increasingly did, run services on behalf of and financed by the state, but it was not and no longer aspired to be the lead actor*'.[165] As a consequence, '*the public/private divide which is impossible to disentangle for most of philanthropy's centuries now came to be thought of central importance*'.[166] Once this distinction was clarified, the question of the appropriate relationship and balance of responsibility between state and philanthropy became more overt. And, as the century wore on, this relationship was '*perhaps best described as fitful*'.[167]

Shaping philanthropy and state

The development of philanthropy and its relationship with state welfare in the first half of the 20th century was shaped by a number of key factors and events – most notably the two World Wars, and the period of high economic turmoil and unemployment inbetween. As is often the case, the influence of these factors is not totally clear-cut and war, in particular, '*provided both a stimulus and a jolt to the voluntary sector*'.[168] On the one hand, the two World Wars and the intervening period may have provided a boost to philanthropy, because '*war . . . provided a focus for a profusion of philanthropic giving and effort. It may have weakened traditional charitable occupations; but it provided the opportunity for new ones*'.[169] But on the other hand this period may have weakened philanthropy's hand, as '*the circumstances of two World Wars and of the unemployment of the 1920s and 1930s further exposed the limitations of voluntarism – and further made the case for a planned and integrated approach to social welfare by means of the state'.*[170]

Poster promoting the work of the Salvation Army during WWI.

World War II, in particular, is often taken to be a decisive factor in the birth of the modern welfare state, because it accustomed people to the idea of central planning and the acceptance of a large degree of state involvement in the provision of services. Whether this state involvement necessarily had to come at the expense of philanthropic efforts, however, is discussed in the next section.

Theoretical objections

In addition to ongoing concerns about the limitations of philanthropy in addressing society's ills, others had more theoretical objections to the idea of philanthropy meeting welfare needs. As Finlayson puts it, there were those who thought that *'it **could** not cope adequately with the problems of war and want'* and others who believed *'it **should** not do so'*.[171] Many who thought it should not were in the Labour movement, where there was a high degree of antipathy to philanthropy and voluntary action because *'charitable activity, for all its efforts ... retained for Labour politicians and sympathisers elements of upper class condescension'*.[172] Also, levels of trust in charity had fallen even further because *'the efforts of volunteers to break the General Strike of 1926 hardened the feeling that voluntary activity among the propertied could as easily turn against the working classes as act on their behalf'*.[173] The class dimensions of this situation were not helped by the fact that the strike-breaking volunteers included *'enthusiastic bands of Oxbridge students'*.[174]

This erosion of trust was potentially a huge problem for philanthropy, because as soon as the Second World War was over, the landslide victory by the Labour Party in the 1945 general election brought many of the most vocal critics of charitable activity into prominent positions in government. For this reason, among others, the immediate post-war period was one of the most challenging times for philanthropists and voluntary organisations.

Creation of the welfare state: goodbye philanthropy?

The creation of a full-blown welfare state following the Second World War marked a moment of great significance and prompted something of an identity crisis for philanthropy. What was to be its role in this brave new world where the government aimed to meet all the welfare needs of its people? Of course, as already noted, many had been writing the obituaries for philanthropy since the start of the 20th century on the basis that the failure of the great Victorian project *'to create by private effort a series of universal social services'* was *'beyond doubt . . . a failure, however magnificent'.*[175] They argued that *'it grew obvious that the major social tasks lay well beyond the resources of private charity, however ambitious its aspirations and devoted its performance',* and concluded *'it became only a matter of time until the state would move, cautiously or decisively, into areas previously occupied by voluntary agencies'.*[176]

Most acknowledged the importance of the role that philanthropy had played in laying the groundwork for the welfare state. For example, in 1937, the think-tank Political and Economic Planning (PEP), which played a key role in the development of the ideas behind the NHS and the welfare state, said in a report on British Social Services: *'Practically every public social service in operation today has its roots in some form of voluntary provision'.*[177] But many thought that this would come to an end, and that the welfare state would 'crowd out' philanthropy. This view ranged across the political spectrum, as *'[both] laissez-faire libertarians and anarchist critics of social policy argue that the welfare state discourages private giving. They agree that state help replaces private help, and that the more the state helps people, the less people help one another'.*[178] There is reasonable evidence to suggest that this proved to be the case, and that philanthropy did suffer, because *'the growth of the welfare state caused uncertainty for established voluntary organisations, who wondered whether they were still needed. Donations began to dry up due to high taxes and as donors came to believe that the state had taken over responsibility for eliminating need'.*[179]

The key difference of opinion was between those who thought that this crowding out was a problem and philanthropy and voluntary action had a continuing role to play, and those who believed that this takeover by the state was an inevitable and desirable process. Those in favour of the takeover by the state believed that philanthropy was an anachronism, which had served its purpose in laying the foundations for the welfare state, but could be discarded now that the goal of a state-run system of universal welfare had been realised. At least at first, it seemed as though this view may have won the battle of ideas, and that philanthropy and voluntary action were to be consigned to the dustbin of history. In fact, *'a common expectation in those years at the end of the war was that the voluntary sector would just wither away'*.[180]

Statue of Aneurin Bevan, by Robert Thomas. Queen Street, Cardiff, UK.

As noted, this was largely due to the fact that major figures of left-wing politics had a distinctly negative attitude to philanthropy. For instance, Labour Prime Minister Aneurin Bevan *'diplomatically accepted that the Labour government should make full use of the voluntary organisations, but he was no friend to charity'.* He was far from alone, as *'many other Labour politicians, civil servants and students of social policy, transfixed by state social action and their part in its promotion, shared the view that charity was demeaning. As government would attend to everyone's needs from the cradle to the grave, what was the point of it? For those who took this view, Victorian traditions of parochial service and self-help were repugnant, remnants of a tribal past'.*[181] Bevan went so far as to paint philanthropy as not just irrelevant, but malign, claiming: *'a patch-quilt of local paternalisms is the enemy of intelligent planning'.*[182] It seems many in the grassroots Labour movement shared Bevan's distaste: one contributor to the 1947 Mass Observation Directive on voluntary work was recorded as saying: *'I detest charity . . . Being a socialist I simply feel that all the talk about "sweet charity" aside, pretty well all such work should be done by the state . . . I have no sympathy with the ramshackle condition of charity . . . and all the lazy, thoughtless humbug that takes the place of real socialism.'*[183]

William Henry Beveridge, 1st Baron Beveridge, by Howard Coster, 1940s.

The prominence of these sorts of views among senior figures in the post-war Labour government may give the impression that they were the accepted orthodoxy of the time, but that is not strictly true. Most notably, William Beveridge – seen by many as the intellectual father of the modern welfare state – strongly believed that philanthropy was still highly relevant. Despite the fact that his highly influential report of 1942 *'put forward universalist, statutory solutions to social problems'*, it was in fact the case that *'voluntarist assumptions about the desirability of individual effort in building on the still fairly minimal state provision permeated Beveridge's thinking'*.[184] He subsequently clarified his views in his 1948 book *Voluntary Action,* which makes it clear that *'to regard Beveridge as an arch-collectivist, responsible for sponsoring massive welfare state provision . . . is to misrepresent him, and to ignore the plea for a continuing role for voluntary social action which [he] made in 1948 in* Voluntary Action'.[185]

Unfortunately, much of Beveridge's original thought on the importance of philanthropy and voluntary action was lost in the process of implementing his vision of state-provided social security. There was resistance to his ideas within the wider Labour movement, where *'. . . there was a strong and understandable strain of hostility to what was seen as "charity", which many working people had experienced as demeaning, and a growing feeling that voluntary action belonged to the past, and was no part of the new, post-war world order'.*[186] In practical terms this meant that *'the post-1945 Labour government was less influenced by Beveridge than is often thought. It greatly expanded the welfare role of the state in some ways at the expense of voluntary action'.*[187]

Beveridge was not alone in maintaining that philanthropy had an important role to play in the new welfare state. Since the beginning of the 20th century, there had been a clear school of thought that believed greater state involvement in welfare would require philanthropy to adapt, but would not make it redundant. This was evident under the Liberal governments of the early century, and *'as the sphere of state welfare grew in the early years of the 20th century, the state and voluntary organisations worked closely together. Pioneering state measures, such as old age pensions (introduced in 1908 and long campaigned for by voluntary organisations), national health and unemployment insurance (introduced 1911) were administered mainly by voluntary organisations, the non-profit, working-class mutual associations: Friendly Societies and trade unions ... This was partly because it was cheaper for the state to build on their experience in these fields and on pre-existing administrative structures than to create a new bureaucracy, and it mollified the antagonism of some of them towards state action in these fields'.*[188]

Even as the state became involved in meeting more and more social needs, and the early incarnation of the welfare state was introduced, philanthropic organisations continued to play a vital role. The Nathan Committee, a parliamentary committee established ostensibly to consider 'the law and practice relating to charitable trusts', but which in reality took a far more wide-ranging look at the role of voluntary action within the nascent welfare state, acknowledged in its 1952 report that *'certain growing pains have been evident in the years during which this change [the introduction of the welfare state] has come about'.* The committee suggested that this might be because *'large claims to superior performance have been made by both statutory authorities and voluntary agencies and each has sometimes felt the other debarred by its very nature from doing a good job'.*[189] But it went on to declare that *'this immature attitude was ... far from universal and in its doctrinaire forms it is now virtually dead'*, and attributed this success to *'those wise provisions as to grant-aid and agency service in much modern legislation, which have in fact resulted in a statutory-voluntary partnership'.*[190]

Philanthropy in the new context

Despite the negativity of some within the Labour movement, the belief that greater involvement of the state need not mean a reduced role for voluntary organisations was fairly widespread in the first half of the 20th century. One might suppose that the introduction of the NHS and the wider elements of the welfare state in the middle of the century eventually put paid to this point of view as it became clear that the presumption of state provision had won out. However, this was not the case at all, and '*it would ... be quite mistaken to believe that the creation of the welfare state introduced a monopolistic statutory system of social welfare in all areas*'. In many spheres '*the mixed economy was still amply evident*', but it was still clear that '*the predominance of the statutory involvement within the mixed economy did pose problems of adjustment*'.[191] A number of individuals and organisations dedicated a great deal of thought to the role of philanthropy in this new context.

Interestingly, the idea that there was now a presumption in favour of state provision and that this meant a vastly reduced role for philanthropy was largely based on a misunderstanding of how the welfare state was supposed to function. In the case of the NHS, for example, the responsibility of government was not necessarily to provide services directly, but merely 'to secure the provision of services', which left open the possibility that voluntary agencies might deliver the relevant services. Furthermore, NHS provision was only ever intended to meet the core requirements of patients, and it was acknowledged that there would be many additional, desirable elements of service that could be added to this core, which therefore left ample room for the involvement of charities and philanthropists. As the Nathan Committee report explained: '*Under part I of the National Health Service Act, 1946, the Minister of Health has an obligation to provide hospital accommodation and services "to such an extent as he considers necessary to meet all reasonable requirements". Who can say that this obligation extends to providing everything which might conceivably make for the cure, comfort or happiness of a patient or that the Minister's obligation does not leave ample room for any other effort, whether by way of voluntary funds or voluntary services?*'[192]

The Nathan Committee concluded that the choice between state and philanthropy was a false one, and that '*while a society is alive and growing it will not make rigid choices between state action and voluntary action, but both alike will expand as the common expression of its vitality*'.[193] This, the committee believed, meant that '*the democratic state, as we know it, could hardly function effectively ... without such channels for, and demands upon, voluntary service*'.[194] Many were inclined to agree with this assessment and argued that philanthropic activity would continue to be a vital part of society despite the presence of a framework of universal state welfare.

These arguments more often than not rested on characterising the features that were claimed to be particular or unique to philanthropic endeavours, in order to identify ways in which voluntary action could supplement or add value to state provision, and hence carve itself a distinct niche. Broadly, these unique features crystallised into two distinct themes: the ability of philanthropic organisations to drive social progress through campaigning (considered further in the next chapter); and their ability to innovate.

Innovation, added value and participation

Although Beveridge was absolutely clear that society needed to move away from the Victorian-era reliance on philanthropy for welfare provision, arguing that *'the democracy can and should learn to do what used to be done for public good by the wealthy',* he acknowledged from the outset that innovation would present a significant challenge within a framework of state-provided services, where *'the problem is that of getting the democracy to give for new things, and unfamiliar needs'.*[195]

Many over the years have identified the ability to innovate as one of the defining characteristics of philanthropy and one of its key advantages over state provision, and therefore the crux of what philanthropy has to offer within the framework of a welfare state. Some have expressed this view in fairly strong terms. For instance, the historian Betsy Rodgers claimed: *'Voluntary societies can venture and experiment where a government department will only prevaricate and elude',* and this meant that *'[while] the early philanthropists had faults and weaknesses ... they were pioneers who often influenced the course of history'.*[196] The Nathan Committee took a more cautious view, arguing that although *'it is the duty and privilege of charity to pioneer',* this did not mean *'the whole of the voluntary movement should be continually marching ahead of public services'.* Rather, the committee explained, it would be the case that *'some elements in [the voluntary sector] may continue for a time to carry out services as parties to arrangements with local authorities so as to give them the benefit of their experience; and yet others may rightly remain in this field indefinitely – perhaps to continue some particularly valuable tradition of service*

– and thus provide some healthy competition between themselves and the public authority'.[197]

Beveridge agreed strongly with this assessment of the innovative power of philanthropy. He noted with approval the role that philanthropic initiatives had long played in driving social innovation and argued that this is a role philanthropy must continue to play. In his view:

> *'Time after time philanthropy is seen breaking in on official routine, unveiling evils, finding fresh channels for service, getting things done that would not be done for pay . . . In the face of [enormous] changes philanthropy has shown its strength of being able perpetually to take new forms . . . The capacity of Voluntary Action inspired by philanthropy to do new things is beyond question. Voluntary Action is needed to do things which the state should not do, in the giving of advice, or in organising the use of leisure. It is needed to do things which the state is most unlikely to do. It is needed to pioneer ahead of the state and make experiments. It is needed to get services rendered which cannot be got by paying for them.'*[198]

The idea that philanthropic organisations could not only match state provision, but could bring features to service delivery that public bodies would never be able to, proved compelling. In particular, *'the delivery of "personal social services" of a specialised nature for certain groups in society was a noted feature of voluntary sector activity in the period after the formal creation of the welfare state – and one much praised by Beveridge.'*[199]

For Beveridge, and other proponents of similar views, *'the sector's characteristics of flexibility, its specialist activity, and the considerable expertise which it could bring to bear made it well suited to deliver such services'.*[200] This additional value was thought incredibly important, because *'as material standards rise and security of subsistence income is achieved, the relatively simple task of meeting needs for money falls into the background. The new tasks of voluntary agencies then become more difficult, not less difficult: they are concerned with such tasks as the formation of the right outlook in youth, or helping to adjust personal relationships, or rescuing the handicapped physically or socially. All these things and many other things that have still to be done to make a good society need knowledge as well as goodwill in the doers'.*[201]

This notion that philanthropic organisations and voluntary action could bring 'added value' to service delivery gained traction over the second half of the 20th century. As people began to get to grips with the reality of universal state welfare, there was a growing realisation that perhaps it was no more valid as a standalone solution to the problems of society than the Victorians had supposed philanthropy to be. By as early as the 1960s there was '*a growing sense of frustration at the welfare state itself, which was felt to be too large, too impersonal, and too inaccessible to the ordinary citizen*'.[202] As a consequence, '*just as it had once been felt that voluntarism alone could not cope with all the problems of society, now it was increasingly recognised that the state could not cope alone*'.[203] For instance, the future Conservative Chancellor of the Exchequer Geoffrey Howe argued in 1975: '*The welfare state does not eliminate the need for private charity; it enhances it, it releases it for those purposes to which it, and it alone can make the vital contribution . . . the state can do a great deal that voluntary organisations by their nature are inadequate to perform . . . but voluntary organisations have the ability to provide a form of service which the state is ill-fitted to provide, however dedicated its administrators.*'[204]

At the same time as the limitations of state welfare were becoming clear, the social revolution taking place in the 1960s brought a renewed emphasis on the idea of 'participation'. Often we think of this simply in terms of the famous demonstrations of the time, such as the many anti-Vietnam war protests or the Aldermarston Marches in support of the Campaign for Nuclear Disarmament, but '*the voluntary sector could readily fit into this increased desire for participation; the involvement of "active citizens" was, after all, its very essence*'.[205] Their success in enabling participation not only gave philanthropic organisations renewed relevance in a climate where people were keen to get involved with causes, but also brought many of those causes into the mainstream for the first time. This further bolstered the role of the voluntary sector, because it was able to provide '*a counterpoint to the picture given in official reports*'[206] and so foster '*an increased, or heightened, social perception: a perception of needs which were not being met by the welfare state*'.[207] Many of those needs were ones that charities had been addressing for many years, so as a result '*the growth of voluntary organisations catering for different needs and disabilities – some medical, some social and some psychological – was a marked feature of the period after the formal creation of the welfare state: and the 1960s and 1970s were important decades in that respect*'.[208]

The rehabilitation of philanthropy

The resurgence in profile of philanthropy in the 1960s and 1970s was accompanied by a softening of political attitudes towards it, particularly on the left as '*the Labour Party increasingly made its peace with the voluntary sector*'.[209] Richard Crossman, who held various Cabinet positions in the governments of Harold Wilson in the 1960s, recalled in 1973 that in his younger days in the 1930s '*he and his fellow left-wing associates had derided voluntarism, and in particular charity and philanthropy, as an expression of elitist do-gooding*' and '*had looked forward to the replacement of the do-gooder by a socialist welfare state, in which trained professional administrators and experts held the key posts*'.[210] By the 1970s, however, Crossman had come to believe that this attitude towards philanthropy had been mistaken, and that '*the welfare state . . . had cut itself adrift from the altruistic motive which had inspired the old philanthropy at its best*'.[211]

It is wise to be cautious in accepting Crossman's view of things entirely at face value, as it is likely that he '*significantly overstated his case*'[212] about the degree of Labour antipathy to philanthropy for rhetorical purposes. However, as we have seen, despite the ameliorating influences of people like Bevan, there had been a clear thread of anti-philanthropic feeling in the Labour Party and it seems safe to conclude that '*[Crossman's] change of heart may be taken to some extent as the articulation of a wider evolution of opinion within the Labour Party*'.[213]

A combination of softening attitudes on the political left, dissatisfaction with some of the realities of monolithic state welfare provision, and increasing public demand for participation led to a revival in the idea of philanthropy and voluntary action. So '*the voluntary sector, after a period in the doldrums in the 1950s, came to life in the decades which followed*',[214] and in the 1960s a 'new, radical philanthropy' was born which '*gave birth to a new wave of campaigning, politicised organisations such as the Child Poverty Action Group and Shelter*'.[215] The voluntary sector in this period had a '*vibrancy and vigour that gained the attention of policymakers and won [it] a new place within the welfare state*'.[216] However, there were still significant differences of opinion about what that role should be and these came to a head in the last quarter of the 20th century.

Rediscovering philanthropy: the New Right and the challenge to state welfare

The resurgence of the Conservative Party under Margaret Thatcher at the end of the 1970s marked an important turning point for philanthropy and the voluntary sector in the UK: one that we are perhaps still coming to terms with even today. Unlike the Labour Party, which as discussed has not always had an easy relationship with philanthropy, *'support for charity and philanthropy as a principle of social action has a long history in the Conservative Party'.*[217] For much of its history, the Conservative Party's enthusiasm for voluntary action was part of a tradition of paternalism based on fairly strict adherence to class structures, but in the 1970s a new strain of right-wing ideology emerged under the influence of thinkers like Milton Friedman and Friedrich Hayek, which lionised the role of markets and began to mount a series of attacks on the welfare state. This school of thought found powerful advocates on both sides of the Atlantic in Margaret Thatcher and Ronald Reagan.

For adherents of this 'New Right', philanthropy and voluntary action were primarily of interest insofar as they could be part of an approach to reducing the size of the state. Whereas many traditional Tories believed that *'voluntary organisations were "not a substitute for state provision" but were additional to them'*,[218] under the influence of the New Right, *'this approach tended . . . to harden into a rather different kind of pluralism: one which wished to reduce the role of the state and advance the role of the voluntary sector – not as a supplement to the state but as an alternative to it'.*[219] At first this ideological division was somewhat hidden, because *'the common vocabulary, with its imprecisions and mystifications . . . managed to placate the noblesse oblige tradition with a positive accent on more voluntary social services, while appeasing the Right with its stress on the reduction of public expenditure'.*[220] Once the party came into government, however, it became obvious that *'the declared intention was to reduce public expenditure and, in the cant of the day, to "roll back the frontiers of the State"'*,[221] and that philanthropy was largely just a means of achieving this goal.

The era of Thatcherite politics had both short- and long-term consequences for the role of philanthropy and voluntary services. In the short term, one major challenge was that while New Right ideology was ostensibly positive about voluntary action, it was seen as preferable for this to be informal rather than organised. Patrick Jenkin, then Conservative Minister for Social Services, said: '*We should recognise that the informal sector lies at the centre with the statutory services and the organised voluntary sector providing backup, expertise and support.*'[222] Margaret Thatcher herself said in a speech to the WRVS that '*the volunteer movement is at the heart of all our social welfare provision; that the statutory services are the supportive ones underpinning where necessary, filling the gaps and helping the helpers*'.[223]

It was clear that philanthropy and charity had a central role to play in the thinking of the Thatcher government; but it was a version of philanthropy that harked back to a (perhaps fictional) time before the voluntary sector itself became organised and professional. It therefore did not represent quite such an opportunity for charities as it might have seemed at first glance.

Outsourcing public services

In the longer term, the most significant impact of the Thatcher government on philanthropy and the voluntary sector has almost certainly been the huge increase in the outsourcing of public services to non-state organisations to be delivered on a contractual basis. This began with the introduction of compulsory competitive tendering (CCT) for local authority services such as refuse collection and street cleaning. The idea was to use market mechanisms to drive down costs by opening services up to the private sector and getting the advantages of competition. Gradually, however, it became apparent that CCT was a blunt instrument, and that 'lowest cost' did not mean the same as 'best value'. In response to this realisation, the practice of public service commissioning has evolved significantly and has spread widely: there are now virtually no areas of public service in which markets or quasi-markets cannot be found.[224]

Although the voluntary sector may not have benefited from the earliest incarnations of public service outsourcing (perhaps due to the antipathy toward professionalised charities among those on the New Right), attitudes slowly softened and charities became an increasingly important part of the landscape of public service delivery. Since the mid-1990s, public service delivery has been one of the defining issues for the voluntary sector, and contracts to deliver services have grown enormously in importance as a source of income for charities. In 2000/2001, contractual funding made up less than half of overall government funding for the sector, yet by 2011/2012,

80% of statutory funding for charities came in the form of contracts to deliver services.[225]

Often the arguments in favour of involving charities in public service delivery have rested on the claim that they bring 'added value'. The exact nature of this added value has usually been ill-defined. In part this is because *'reference to the unique and special attributes of the voluntary sector is made most typically by politicians when they wish to anticipate accusations of looking for caring "on the cheap", and to demonstrate that theirs are loftier considerations than mere questions of economies and cuts in public expenditure'.*[226] Slightly less cynically, it is fair to say that views about the nature of 'value' have changed over the years, as the nature of the relationship between the state and charitable organisations has evolved.

Determining value

The move away from grant funding toward contractual relationships had a particular impact on the notion of value in public services. As relationships between the state and charities have become more formal and prescriptive, the balance in terms of defining what counts as 'value' has shifted decisively toward the state. Rather than the criteria of value emerging from discussion between all parties with a stake in public services, including charities and their beneficiaries, they came to be almost entirely dictated by the state's own priorities and policies. And, at least in the early days, 'value' was seen as primarily a monetary measure.

As highlighted above, outsourcing was originally introduced into public services as a way of cutting costs in the 1980s. Charities then found themselves trying to compete in a world of commercial public sector markets for which they were ill-equipped, because the focus was entirely on driving down costs regardless of wider concerns about the needs and experiences of service users. Slowly, however, policymakers began to realise that commissioning services solely on the basis of how cheap they were inevitably led to low-quality and high-profile failures. Attempts were subsequently made to reintroduce broader criteria of value, which looked a lot like the sort of considerations that people like Beveridge had identified back in the 1940s as being integral to the delivery of public services.[227]

This process is far from over. One noteworthy landmark, however, was the introduction in 2012 of the Social Value Act. This is legislation that requires, for the first time, those commissioning public services to take into account social and environmental factors when selecting organisations to deliver contracts.[228] The hope is that this will allow charities and social enterprises to compete more equally by highlighting the wider value they bring to service delivery, and that it might also change the way commercial organisations choose to deliver services. At the time of writing the Social Value Act has not been in force long enough to gauge its effectiveness, but it is generally regarded as a positive step.[229]

It is important to understand the changing nature of charities' role in public service delivery and its consequences for the notion of value, because this provides much of the context in which to understand the role of charities following the introduction of the welfare state. But what has been the impact of changes to the nature of public services on philanthropy?

The main hypothesis in answer to this question is that the increasing involvement of charities in public service delivery has a negative impact on their ability to attract philanthropic support. Those who support this argument may point to the fact that the introduction of the welfare state meant that '*in many voluntary organisations ... autonomy progressively dwindled: they became increasingly the agents and clients of the state, holders of state licences, beneficiaries of state tax concessions, recipients of and competitors for state financial aid – or simply pressure groups urging government to change its policies on some deserving cause*'.[230] One result of this loss of autonomy and independence was felt to be a reduced ability to attract voluntary donations. The Nathan Committee warned back in 1952 that '*if [voluntary bodies] allow themselves to fall into the position of securing the great bulk of their income by way of fees from local authorities, the charity may become little more than the agent of the authorities, may lose much of its freedom of action and may thus irretrievably forfeit the interest and enthusiasm of its subscribers*'.[231] This is still a valid concern, although many now accept that charities can, at least *in principle,* receive government funding for delivering services without harming their relationships with supporters. Rather, it is claimed, the problem is a pragmatic one, arising from the ways public service commissioners deal with charities in practice.

Some of the main practical concerns are that charities for whom service delivery contracts are an important source of income may fall victim to 'mission drift' if they end up going too far beyond their original purpose in order to secure funding,[232] and that charities receiving contractual statutory funding may no longer feel able or willing to speak out against government policy, even when that would be in the best interests of their beneficiaries. Stories about the introduction of 'gagging clauses' in service delivery contracts in an attempt to prevent charities speaking freely if they are contracted to deliver services make it clear that these sorts of concerns are certainly valid.[233]

From the point of view of charities, there are clearly issues with the way in which public services currently operate. The balance of power between the state and philanthropic organisations has shifted markedly from the situation prior to the First World War, when philanthropic organisations were leading the way and dragging the state (often reluctantly) with them. We now have a situation in which the nature of public services and the way they are delivered is almost entirely dictated by the state. And while this problem has been recognised, and various measures introduced in an effort to combat it, few would disagree that progress in improving the situation remains slow.

Implications for future philanthropy

This imbalance of power is a valid source of concern for philanthropists who want to support organisations that also receive money for delivering public service contracts. Why would a donor give to a charity if they felt its priorities were being dictated by the agenda of a public sector commissioner, or if they felt that an organisation was failing to speak up on behalf of its beneficiaries when they are victims of the failings of government policy?

In order to maximise the potential for philanthropy in modern Britain we need to understand these concerns, get a sense for how widespread they are and how significant a barrier to philanthropy they represent, and find ways in which charities can maintain the trust of their donors while also working effectively with the state. This may mean a rebalancing of the power dynamic between individual citizens, the charities that represent them, and the state. It will also require thinking about new ways in which we can bring public, private and philanthropic funding together effectively to address major social issues.

Delivering services v campaigning for policy change

It was highlighted above that involvement in public service delivery might have a negative impact on the relationship between an organisation and its philanthropic supporters, due to the perception that the organisation's independence of voice might be compromised. This draws our attention to a wider tension facing all philanthropic organisations: that between being deliverers of services and advocates for change. This has presented a challenge for hundreds of years, and continues to do so even today.

The tension is sometimes presented as between having a narrow but deep impact, or having a wide but shallow impact. By providing a service that addresses a specific social problem for a defined group, a charitable organisation can make a profound difference to a limited number of people; by campaigning for legislative change that would address the same issue, that organisation could make a smaller difference to a far greater number of people. This distinction does not stand much scrutiny, as many charitable organisations have delivered services at such a scale that they have had an impact on almost the entire population, and conversely, many successful instances of social reform through legislative change have had huge and immediate impacts on the lives of individuals.

The historian Joanna Innes notes that in the late 18th and early 19th centuries: *'contemporaries commonly conceived efforts to improve social conditions, and efforts to ameliorate the circumstances of individuals by making appropriate assistance available to them, as complementary rather than alternative strategies'.* Although she also acknowledges that *'not everyone was equally interested in both: radical socialists might scorn most charitable activity as so much bourgeois self-limitation, addressed, at best, to the symptoms rather than the causes of social evils. Conversely, not all charitable activists raised their sights much above the tasks of assisting and rehabilitating individual poor people'.*[234] Both approaches sit on a spectrum where impact can be measured in terms of how many lives are affected and to what degree, and both approaches are equally valid and important tools for achieving a philanthropic mission, even if neither is likely to work that well in isolation from the other.

Implications for future philanthropy

Although the choice between providing services directly and advocating for reform remains one that all philanthropic organisations have to take in particular instances, it should be obvious that there is no reason why, at an organisational level, the two approaches cannot be combined. It should be possible both to address the symptoms of a problem by delivering services and to address the root causes of the problem through campaigning for reform. Many charities successfully adopt such a twin strategy. The complicating factor, as we saw earlier, is often the involvement of government: while governments are enthusiastic about the potential for philanthropic organisations to help overcome the pressing challenges facing society by delivering services, they are usually less keen on the idea of those same organisations continuing to point out the failings of government policy that are contributing to the perpetuation of those problems. The temptation for governments, therefore, is to encourage and promote charities insofar as they are service providers, while at the same time finding ways to suppress their role as advocates on behalf of their beneficiaries. This is a dangerous road, because it risks creating a false view of the role of philanthropy and charitable organisations that ignores the clear historical importance of campaigning, and instead tries to characterise it as a 'modern development' that needs to be controlled or curbed.

The wider importance of philanthropic support for campaigning is covered in the next section. But even in the narrower context of welfare provision, it is clear that the ability of philanthropic organisations to challenge through advocacy and campaigning is just as important a part of their role within the welfare state as the actual delivery of services. The Nathan Committee argued back in the early days of widespread state welfare provision that: '*Some of the most valuable activities of voluntary societies consist . . . in the fact that they are able to stand aside from and criticise state action, or inaction, in the interests of the inarticulate man-in-the-street. This may take the form of helping individuals to know and obtain their rights. It also consists in a more general activity of collecting data about some point where the shoe seems to pinch or a need remains unmet. The general machinery of democratic agitation, deputations, letters to the Press, questions in the House, conferences and the rest of it, may then be put into operation in order to convince a wider public that action is necessary.*'[235]

In the second half of the 20th century the campaigning role of charities increasingly came to the fore. Faced with growing dissatisfaction with the welfare state and a new appetite for participation and radicalism, '*established voluntary organisations recovered and reconfigured their activities to fill the gaps and new ones were formed to campaign for improvements . . . The voluntary sector, reinvigorated, continued its role of innovation, pressing for and working with a bigger state'.*[236] Organisations like the NSPCC adapted their ways of working to combine service delivery and campaigning into a single approach, and *'many organisations . . . established a model for the future, by identifying a social problem, seeking viable ways to help the victims, then campaigning for government to adopt these methods, because only the state had the resources to deal on a national scale with challenges beyond the scope of unavoidably limited and localised voluntary action'.*[237]

This meant that charities found a new sense of purpose, as it became apparent that they still had an important role to play within the developing welfare state because *'far from the state seeking to crowd out voluntary action, it was, often reluctantly, persuaded into action by voluntary organisations'.*[238]

Case study

Doing well by doing good: the long (and sometimes rocky) history of social investment

As well as innnovating by highlighting new areas of social need and new interventions designed to address them, philanthropy has also led the way when it comes to new models for financing social outcomes. There has been growing interest in recent years in approaches such as 'social investment' and 'social enterprise', which combine philanthropic and commercial elements to offer innovative ways of addressing issues.[239] Many assume that this kind of hybridisation is a new phenomenon, but it is nothing of the sort. If anything, the 'discovery' that commercial and philanthropic approaches can be blended is more of a rediscovery of something our forebears took for granted.

For example, more than 300 years ago the London merchant philanthropist Thomas Firmin established a series of projects 'for the imploying of the poor' whereby he employed over 1600 spinners and weavers. These projects were run as loss-making social enterprises, and *'Firmin conceived of his enterprise as thrifty philanthropy rather than as an ordinary business'.*[240] He was clear that *'he could look upon a loss of twopence in the shilling*

as money well spent' [241] and contributed an annual investment of
between £2,000 and £4,000 to the businesses. Firmin's aim was
to convince the state of the merit of this approach so that it would
take over from him, but unfortunately, he proved to be too far
ahead of his time and that never happened.

Another attempt to introduce an early model of social investment
met with a similar lack of success, although in this case as a
result of human failing rather than government inertia. The
Charitable Corporation was founded in 1707, with the ambition
of bringing the European model of the 'mount of piety' to the UK
(variously known as *monte di pieta*, *mont de piété* or *monte de
piedad* in Italy, France and Spain respectively). These mounts
of piety were institutions that had arisen largely in Catholic
countries on the continent, and aimed to offer low-cost loans to
the poor as a solution to what was seen as the ungodly practice
of usurious lending and pawnbroking. The idea was that by
appealing to the charitable motivations of the moneyed classes
(and with more than a little exhortation from priests), it would be
possible to raise capital that could then be used to make loans at
rates appropriate to the financial needs and resources of the poor,
rather than at the extortionate rates lenders focused entirely on
profit were likely to impose.

The idea was evidently a good one, and the model spread across
large swathes of Europe. Unfortunately, its progress in the UK
was undermined by a simple case of human greed. A number of
the directors of the Charitable Corporation embezzled the money
they had raised, and the whole operation eventually collapsed
amid bitter recriminations and legal battles. As the historian
Benjamin Kirkman Gray noted: *'No doubt the[se] circumstances
... had a great deal to do in preventing the naturalisation in
England of the European institution, the mont de piété.'* [242]

A more successful attempt to blend philanthropic and financial
motivations came in the area of housing in the late 19th century
and early 20th century. A number of model housing schemes were
established, including the East End Dwellings Company, the Four

Per Cent Industrial Dwellings Company and the Metropolitan Association, which all sought to finance the building of new, affordable homes for the poor by raising capital from socially-motivated investors. This idea became known as '5% philanthropy' as the idea was that *'in order to provide decent homes at affordable rents in expensive areas, it was necessary to find investors who were prepared to accept a rate of return somewhat below the normal range of 7–10%'.*[243] Many big names of late Victorian philanthropy, such as Octavia Hill, Nathan Rothschild and Edward Guinness got involved in 5% philanthropy, and there was a lot of optimism that it could prove a real success because, as contemporary accounts report, *'it is considered that many investors will be found willing and even anxious to contribute their capital towards a scheme, which while yielding a moderate and safe return, will largely tend, not only to improve the dwellings of the poor, but also reduce the high rates now paid for the minimum of accommodation'.*[244]

Peabody Square Model Dwellings in Blackfriars Road, Southwark, London.
The Peabody Trust was one of the most prolific builders of model dwellings in London; like its contemporaries it sought to provide the working classes with good quality housing at affordable rents, while also offering investors an opportunity to make a modest financial return.

In this case, the optimism was largely vindicated, as the model dwellings companies proved successful on the whole – as evidenced by the fact that many of them survive to the present day. Of course, not all were able to meet their goal of paying a stated percentage to investors, and as with many other instances of philanthropy, there was scepticism about whether they made any real difference to the underlying problem they were trying to address. But they did set a definite precedent for the successful combination of philanthropic and social motivations, which is the same concept that underpins all of the social investment and impact investing initiatives we see today.

CHAPTER THREE

Philanthropy and government

The relationship between philanthropy and government is not simply about welfare provision and public services. There are broader issues involved in how private giving fits within a democracy that are crucial to understanding the role of philanthropy and the attitudes of governments towards it.

Philanthropy and democracy

Philanthropy poses a fundamental challenge to democracy: by offering individuals a way of furthering their own priorities outside the normal democratic process, it potentially subverts the authority of elected officials and allows a small minority of those with significant wealth to exert a disproportionate influence on the direction in which society is travelling.

This has been a recurring concern since philanthropy in its modern form first emerged. For example, George Washington used his farewell speech as US President to warn of the dangers of unchecked philanthropy, arguing: *'Combinations and Associations, under whatever plausible character, with the real design to direct, control, counteract, or awe the regular deliberation and action of the Constituted authorities . . . serve to organise faction, to give it an artificial and extraordinary force; to put in the place of the delegated will of the Nation, the will of a party; often a small but artful and enterprising minority of the Community.'*[245] Washington warned that these philanthropic enterprises would, over the course of time, *'become potent engines, by which cunning, ambitious and unprincipled men will be able to subvert the Power of the People, and to usurp for themselves the reins of Government; destroying afterwards the very engines which have lifted them to unjust domination'.*[246]

These concerns became even more pressing in the US with the enormous growth in the size and influence of private foundations in the first half of the 20th century. Many expressed a great unease as they saw large amounts of money being passed into the hands of institutions that were far from transparent and had no real need to act in a democratic fashion. Frank Walsh, the Chairman of the US Commission on Industrial Relations, which probed the activities of some of the major industrial philanthropists of the early 20th century such as Rockefeller and Carnegie, even declared that *'foundations appear to be a menace to the welfare of society.'*[247] Despite significant new requirements being placed on foundations in the US in an effort to minimise some of the risks they posed to democracy – such as the introduction of a minimum annual payout rule to ensure that funds were not allowed to sit dormant simply as a way of avoiding tax – concerns about the role of big-money private foundations continue to this day. For instance, David Nasaw, author of a biography of the celebrated philanthropist Andrew Carnegie, gives the following critical assessment of the role of 'big philanthropy':

'No one wants to criticise generosity or look a gift horse in the mouth. But there are large questions of social policy here that go unconfronted. Private foundations can do virtually anything they please with their billions, tax-free and with little regulation. I might applaud the work of the Rockefeller, Carnegie, and Gates Foundations. But I might be considerably less enthusiastic about a torrent of private money unleashed on educational campaigns to outlaw abortion and birth control, defund the public schools, abolish inheritance and income taxes, end gun control, and withdraw funding from the United Nations and international organisations. You might disagree; either way neither of us should be sanguine about a future in which billionaires play a larger and larger role in determining social policy without any say from the rest of us.'[248]

This sort of criticism has been heard often in recent years in response to the 'Giving Pledge' initiative led by Bill Gates and Warren Buffett. Despite the evident generosity of those who have signed the pledge, many remain deeply uncomfortable with the amount of power such wealthy individuals are able to wield through their philanthropy. The German billionaire Peter Kramer pointedly declined to sign the Giving Pledge, and explained that his reason for doing so was a concern that *'these guys have so much power through their wealth that they, instead of the government elected by the people, can decide what's good and what should be promoted and subsidised . . . That can be dangerous'.*[249]

An illustration of this point came in May 2014, when *Businessweek* magazine ran an in-depth profile on the philanthropy of three highly secretive hedge fund managers, who despite giving around $13 billion to charity via their private foundations were not even on most people's radars.[250] The article was not suggesting there was anything amiss, or that the philanthropy was not aimed at perfectly worthwhile causes, but it did make the point that this was an example where a sum of money sizeable enough to skew social spending priorities (and which, taken in total, would constitute the fourth largest charitable organisation in the US) was being put into the system with little or no transparency or accountability. This point was driven home by a startling infographic that detailed the incredibly complex web of foundations, corporations and trusts the three donors had established to keep their giving anonymous.[251]

Although there is clearly an issue of principle at stake here about the extent to which wealthy individuals should be able to influence the shape of public policy and welfare provision, there is also a pragmatic truth that the degree to which you believe any particular instance of philanthropy to be a concern will depend on whether you agree with the aims and political views of the donors behind it. For example, in the US, the philanthropy of the Koch brothers is criticised by many as a result of their support for conservative political causes.[252] Similarly, the donations of George Soros are disparaged by others because of his long-standing support for liberal causes.[253] In all such cases, the implication is that the philanthropy is just another part of an insidious attempt to further the donor's own world-view by circumventing the democratic process. Unsurprisingly, this sort of accusation is not often levelled at those philanthropists with whom the critic has political sympathies.

Partisan attacks like these are in danger of obscuring an important debate about the interaction of philanthropy and democracy. If we are able to put aside our own political beliefs and consider the matter in dispassionate terms, it is obvious that regardless of how we feel personally about any one instance of philanthropy, there are valid questions about the extent to which private wealth should be able to further the priorities of small groups of individuals, when that might run counter to the interests of society as a whole. This was highlighted in a 2013 study in the US, which concluded that the policy preferences of the top 1% of wealthy Americans differ markedly from those of the populace as a whole, suggesting there is good reason to be concerned about the impact on democracy if these individuals are exerting influence through their philanthropy.[254]

Defenders of philanthropy might argue that one of its key principles is donor choice: i.e. that individuals should be free to decide how to give away their own money, and that it is wrong to criticise philanthropists. However, philanthropy does not exist in a vacuum and it clearly needs to fit in with the other structures of democracy and society. Furthermore, in countries such as the UK, there are generous tax incentives available for charitable giving, which cloud the picture even further. If a donor is taking advantage of such incentives, then at least part of the money they are directing towards causes of their own choosing is money that would otherwise be available for redistribution by the government. Critics would therefore argue that we all have a right to question how philanthropic money is being used. We will look in more detail at the implications of the tax treatment of donations later in this chapter.

Philanthropy as political

It might seem from the preceding paragraphs as though philanthropy, even when done with honest motives and great propriety, is a force that runs counter to democracy and must therefore be kept under close watch and potentially curbed. However, this assumes that democracy is a perfect system that we must seek to maintain in its present form above all else. In fact, democracy is a constantly developing notion, and in a number of cases important challenges to the status quo have had to come largely or wholly via means that lie outside the existing democratic system.

This has been the case with many of the seminal stages in the development of democracy in the UK, such as the extension of the vote to the working class and universal suffrage for women. In both cases, the majority of those seeking change were denied a voice within the democratic system, so they had no choice but to resort to other means. For some this meant radical protest action, such as the Chartist Riots of the early 19th century or the militant tactics of the Suffragette movement in the early 20th century. For those who did not want to embrace extremism, voluntary action and philanthropy were high on the list of other options. In these cases, a simple truth about philanthropy becomes abundantly clear: almost all philanthropy is 'political'. The Rockefeller Foundation has made the same point, arguing that '*because most philanthropy seeks to change society, it is inherently political*'.[255]

While there are obvious concerns about the extent to which philanthropy can be used by those with wealth to exert a disproportionate influence on society, that does not necessarily mean that 'political' should be seen as a pejorative term when applied to philanthropy. Anyone who wants to change the society around them for the better (which is surely true of almost all philanthropists) is automatically straying into the realm of the 'political', and some would argue that is a wholly good thing, and that the political sphere should not be seen as the sole preserve of professional politicians and political parties. Intriguingly, a summit convened in the US in 2013, which brought together philanthropists, politicians and policymakers, came to precisely this conclusion, and highlighted the fact that government officials thought that philanthropy should be doing *more* to influence policy.[256]

One interesting thing to note is that philanthropy has not just been a means to achieve particular ends through campaigning; the process of philanthropy has itself brought significant benefits to those engaging in it. For instance, it has been argued that the driving force behind the huge rise in philanthropy in the Victorian era came from women, for whom philanthropy offered a means of agency in a society where they were not able to vote. According to the historian Frank Prochaska: '*If we are to isolate one profession that did more than any other to enlarge the horizon of women in 19th-century England, it would have to be the profession of charity . . . In an age when women found so many doors closed, they discovered a crack in the doors of charitable societies.*'[257] Through this philanthropic work, women laid the foundations for a different conception of their role, because '*charity work . . . was defined as a natural extension of the intimacy of the home. Philanthropy was domestic ideology writ large . . . But the opportunities that it provided for women to claim some public space were to contribute to the destabilisation of boundaries later in the century*'.[258] So the experience gained through involvement in charitable activities became for women '*a lever which they used to open the doors closed to them in all other spheres, for in its variety it was experience applicable to just about every profession in England'.*[259]

These women may not have been explicitly campaigning for greater rights for themselves (and in many cases actually disagreed with the idea of universal suffrage), but their philanthropic campaigning on unrelated issues had the effect not only of changing the thinking of some men about the role of women, but also of making many women reconsider their perceptions of themselves and their role in society. So *'the interest of philanthropic women in female suffrage emerged, not inevitably, but quite naturally out of certain of their activities, for as the more penetrating of them argued, there were limits to their freedom of action without political power'.*[260]

The empowerment of women through charitable activities was not limited to the Victorian era. It is something that has been seen again, for instance, in *'the experience of women during the British miners' strike of the 1980s'*, which showed *'the power of voluntary action as a politicising force'.*[261]

Philanthropy has also provided a means of overcoming class as well as gender barriers; offering a means of entry into society for the working classes at a time when they were denied the vote. In the same way as for middle-class women *'when the working classes cooperated with their wealthier neighbours, as in hospital provision, education, or foreign missions, their philanthropy acted as a springboard into the existing social system'.*[262] And in many cases, the philanthropic choices of individuals were a substitute for the political choices denied to them, so that *'when the poor contributed to unemployment funds, founded Chartist Sunday Schools, or passed the hat round for the Tolpuddle martyrs, their actions may be seen as an expression of radical politics through private benevolence. Such forms of self-expression were particularly important before the advent of universal suffrage'.*[263]

As well as offering working class people a route into society, these philanthropic endeavours also enabled them to develop skills that would stand them in good stead when they did finally secure the right to vote. Getting involved with charitable causes might well have been a ticket to greater social status, but it was also *'a part of the pattern of working-class education and leisure . . . [which] was as important as the training picked up in schools or mechanics' institutes'.*[264] Through charity work, working class people could develop their basic education and gain skills such as book-keeping, secretarial work and general administration. They could also experience, often for the first time, a sense of agency because *'in voluntary societies, unlike the wider world over which they had little control, working-class campaigners could make decisions that had meaning for their own lives and those around them'*.[265] This opportunity to learn new skills and to develop a sense of power and responsibility led the Nathan Committee to suggest in its 1952 report that charitable work represented a *'nursery school of democracy'*.[266]

It is clear that philanthropy offers the opportunity to influence society outside the bounds of the normal political framework. While this may be a concern for those who believe that philanthropy is being used by a small minority of the powerful to circumvent the democratic process and further their own priorities, it also means that philanthropy has proven at times to be a powerful tool for those who have been marginalised in a democracy, giving them a voice and a means to influence the society in which they live. And by doing this it can help to stem unrest, as without the opportunities for influence that philanthropy and voluntary action offer, these individuals and groups might otherwise resort to extremism or direct action to further their cause.

Campaigning

Philanthropy may be used to try to change the nature of a democracy, as in the examples above. However, it is more common for it to be used as a means of effecting change within existing structures. Chapter 2 highlighted the historical role that campaigning by philanthropists and voluntary organisations has played in shaping government provision of welfare services, but the importance of philanthropic campaigning goes much further than this. Some of the most important changes to UK society in modern times are a result of the work of philanthropists and voluntary organisations.

Charity reformer Thomas Hare, giving a speech to the Social Science Congress of 1869, noted the importance of philanthropy as a tool for effecting social change precisely because it allows people to work around existing structures without becoming trapped in them, and so enables them to overcome political and social inertia or antipathy. He said:

> *'I regard endowments as an important element in the experimental branches of political and social science. No doubt the nation at large may take on*

itself the cost of such tentative efforts, but this involves taxation; and the assent of the majority to increased taxes could not be justly demanded by philanthropists or projectors, and certainly would not be obtained until their speculations had taken such a hold upon the public mind as no longer to require an exceptional support or propagation. The most important steps in human progress may be opposed to the prejudices, not only of the multitude, but even of the learned and leaders of thought in a particular epoch.'[267]

The Anti-Slavery Society Convention, 1840, by Benjamin Robert Haydon. Oil on canvas, 1841.

One of the most famous campaigns for social change in the UK was the crusade against slavery in the late 18th and early 19th centuries. Figures such as William Wilberforce and Granville Sharpe are celebrated for their work on this issue, but the campaign involved many other people. Interestingly, it was not the preserve of wealthy donors. If anything it was one of the most democratic examples of philanthropy as it drew in people from all walks of life, many of whom were not wealthy at all. Looking at the *Anti-Slavery Reporter* newsletter, there is the distinct impression of '*a movement supported chiefly, at least in its later stages, by large numbers of people in moderate or modest circumstances*'.[268] The supporters of abolition were forced to rely largely on voluntary action and philanthropy, at least at first, because there was little political will to address the issue. They discovered, like many who followed them, that sometimes, '*appealing to the reason and benevolence of Parliament would accomplish little*',[269] and that instead (despite the reluctance of Wilberforce), the first step must be to mobilise public opinion in support of the cause.

In pursuing their campaign through voluntary action, it is fascinating to see how many of the tactics used by the anti-slavery campaigners seem very familiar to us today, such as:

- Fact finding and data collection
- Targeted letter-writing
- Protest songs/poetry (Cowper's poem *The Negro's Complaint* was set to music and acted as effective propaganda)
- Celebrity-designed products ('*Josiah Wedgwood . . . designed a seal portraying a kneeling negro, which as a cameo on snuffboxes and bracelets, became something of a rage.*'[270])
- Consumer boycotts (there was a boycott of slave-grown sugar)
- Petitions (519 petitions had been on the floor of the House of Parliament by the time Wilberforce proposed abolition).

Wedgwood Anti-Slavery medallion. Josiah Wedgwood (1730–1795), renowned potter and leading member of Great Britain's Society for the Abolition of the Slave Trade, created this design for reproduction on fashionable jasperware medallions and seals. It is inscribed with the Society's motto: '*Am I Not a Man and a Brother?*'.

Other campaigning organisations of the past also employed innovative approaches. For example, The Society for Superseding the Work of Climbing Boys, established in 1803, aimed to demonstrate that employing boys as chimney sweeps was neither right nor, crucially, even necessary. These boys endured often terrible working conditions and death rates were very high (their harsh way of life is depicted in fiction such as the Victorian fantasy novel *The Water Babies* by Reverend Charles Kingsley). Early on in its campaigning, the Society issued a challenge prize: £200 for the best design for a sweeping machine to remove the need to send boys up chimneys. This proved successful, and they built such a machine, but struggled to convince chimney sweeps to use it instead of climbing boys. Since they had no power to force people to use the machine, they cleverly decided to use more subtle methods, drawing up a 'white list' of employers who used the machine.[271] This can be seen as a forerunner of modern kite-marking schemes such as Fair Trade.

The members of the Society also attempted to use parliamentary means, putting forward a Bill to ban the use of child chimney sweeps. This passed the Commons, but came to an abrupt halt in the Lords. This was not a huge surprise, as at that point many Lords had large homes with many chimneys and were consequently among the most resistant to reform in this area. Undeterred, the Society instead established its own network of expert inspectors to watch the conduct of master sweepers. Even though these inspectors had no statutory authority, their presence alone had a positive impact on the treatment of boys.

Both of these examples demonstrate the vital role that philanthropic campaigning has often played in achieving social reform in Britain, where 'reform is often understood as something which is the outcome of public agitation against an at-best-reluctant government'.[272] By providing a means to develop a groundswell of support and build a firm evidence base, these sorts of campaigns make it possible to overcome inertia on the part of government and force it to face up to issues. In many cases 'it would be fair to say that the voluntary sector has "alerted people to numerous issues of public concern since Victorian times". These have often been controversial issues, to which government could not commit taxpayers' money owing to the fact that they could not command sufficient public acceptance'.[273]

It is easy when considering issues such as slavery or the plight of child labourers to assume that all philanthropic campaigning is a good thing and should be viewed positively. However, these are fairly uncontroversial examples where the campaigners were on the right side of history and we have the benefit of hindsight to tell us as much. There are other cases, though, where a philanthropic campaigner's zeal seems misguided to modern eyes. For example, Mary Augusta Ward, a well-known novelist and philanthropist, counted among her many other interests the establishment of the Women's Anti-Suffrage League, which encouraged women to campaign against the vote for themselves.[274] There was a rationale for her position, in that she believed it would be better if women had other means for bringing their views to bear on Parliament without the need to vote, but from a modern standpoint she certainly seems misguided.

Philanthropic campaigning has also come in for more than its fair share of criticism over the years. Unsurprisingly, those in power, who often speak in glowing terms about the great social reform campaigns of yesteryear, are sometimes far less keen on contemporary campaigning that brings into question their own policies and priorities. We have seen this played out recently in the UK with the growing criticism of the campaigning activities of charities. The accusation usually levelled at these activities is that they are 'political' and therefore not part of the appropriate role of charities. However, this not only ignores the distinction between being political and being partisan, it also ignores the fact that campaigning on 'political' issues on behalf of marginalised and oppressed groups has always been part of the role of philanthropy and charities, and is just as important as the provision of services.

Political purposes and charity law

Although one of the main points of this book is to argue that involvement in the 'political' arena through campaigning and advocacy has always been one of the most important aspects of philanthropy organisations, charity law in the UK prevents organisations from having 'political purposes'. They are allowed to engage in *activities* that are political in nature (campaigning, lobbying, public affairs etc), but this must be in pursuit of charitable aims that are demonstrably non-political. But is this right? Why should charities be prevented from having 'political' purposes? We might well assume that there is some deeply enshrined point of principle acting as a justification, but in fact, when we look at the historical development of charity law, it becomes clear that the inadmissibility of political purposes is yet another quirk that arose more by accident than design.

The origin of charity law's rule disqualifying political purposes is usually taken to be the judgment of Lord Parker in the case of *Bowman v Secular Society*.[275] The case concerned the legacy of a man named Charles Bowman, who died in 1908. He wanted to bequeath a portion of his estate to the Secular Society Ltd, an organisation set up to promote 'the principle that human conduct should be based upon natural knowledge, and not upon super-natural belief, and that human welfare in this world is the proper end of all thought and action', and which at that time was incorporated as an association under the Companies Act. His next of kin disputed the validity of the gift, on the grounds that the organisation's purposes were blasphemous and therefore unlawful. The claim of blasphemy was not upheld, but in the course of the judgement, Lord Parker made a series of assertions that were to have profound and lasting implications for charities.

One of his central contentions was that '*a trust for the attainment of political objects has always been held invalid*'.[276] However, many commentators have subsequently questioned this assertion, noting that '*when* Bowman v Secular Society *was decided, it was far from clear that trusts for political purposes had invariably or even mostly been regarded by decision-makers as invalid*' and that '*the history of Victorian Britain reveals a strong tradition of charities pursuing political purposes of different types, with no suggestion that such purposes were impeded or constrained by charity law*'.[277] It appears that Lord Parker's view in the case was largely based on a discussion of the question of political purposes in a late 19th century text that represented an '*idiosyncratic view of the extant case law*'.[278] It centred on the argument that such purposes had to be disqualified from being charitable because there was no way of applying the required public benefit test when one of the key aims was reform of the law, as '*the Court has no means of judging whether a proposed change in the law will or will not be for the public benefit*'.[279]

As scholars of charity law have noted, Lord Parker's assertion can be interpreted either as a claim that courts are pragmatically incapable of making such judgments; or as a claim that, for constitutional reasons, courts should not seek to make findings of fact as to the public benefit of law reform, even if they are in practice capable of doing so. The former interpretation doesn't hold much merit, as it is clear that there are many cases in which the courts have in practice made findings of fact as to the public benefit of law reform. The latter interpretation is more compelling, but even so it remains the case that '*in the common-law world it is a well-established practice for judges . . . to indicate that the public would benefit from a law reform of one type or another but at the same time state that any such reform is for the parliament to realise*'.[280] However, some may argue that perhaps the point of a rule against political purposes is precisely that it forces the involvement of the courts. And while we may be comfortable with the idea of judges making decisions about what is in the public benefit, they question if we would be so sanguine about other officials doing the same. Matthew Harding argues that '*it seems unlikely that the charity regulars and tax officials who might, in the absence of a rule against political purposes, be asked to assess the public benefit or otherwise of law reform in the setting of an inquiry into whether or not some political purpose is charitable could be constitutionally empowered to do so except with specific authorisation from the legislature*',[281] and that this suggests a rule against political purposes may make pragmatic sense if nothing else.

Although it is intriguing to note that the origin of the rule against political purposes is not quite as clear-cut as it may seem, and that '*there are reasons to think that Lord Parker's judgment in* Bowman v Secular Society '*did not carry the authority that has often been claimed for it*'; in the long run this doesn't really matter because '*the judgment, and the rule against political purposes that it recognised and endorsed, has been approved and applied many times since around the common law world*'.[282] However, in light of the increasing number of charitable organisations that have taken some sort of campaigning or advocacy stance since the revival of the voluntary sector in the 1960s and 1970s outlined in the previous chapter, the fact that the rule against political purposes has been accepted has had significant implications for the voluntary sector. Confusion over the distinction between 'political' and 'partisan', and between 'political activities' and 'political purposes', has led to accusations that charities have overstepped the mark by entering the political arena. Antipathy towards the idea of campaigning or lobbying for change by charities has grown among certain sections of the public and the political classes, who often claim that it undermines the 'traditional role of charities', which they see as providing services that directly address the needs of the poor and the needy.[283]

The Lobbying Act

In the UK the culmination of these anti-charitable campaigning sentiments (so far) has been the introduction of the Transparency of Lobbying, Non-party Campaigning and Trade Union Administration Act 2014 (commonly known as the Lobbying Act).[284] Among other things, this legislation has placed new restrictions on the political campaigning activities of charities and other not-for-profit groups. While these restrictions are not necessarily damaging in themselves (as few organisations will reach the minimum spending limits specified in the legislation), the uncertainty created in terms of which activities will or won't fall under the scope of the new law (which at the time of writing is still very unclear) and, perhaps most importantly, the message the Act sends out about the government's attitude towards the legitimate and long-standing campaigning role of charities has the potential to be very damaging.

Implications for future philanthropy

The UK is not alone in taking a less-than-positive attitude towards philanthropic campaigning. There is a wider global trend towards restricting the ability of non-profit organisations to speak out.[285] The danger is that, if it continues to take a regressive attitude on this issue, the UK will find itself in far from desirable international company. And not only that, we will also do a real disservice to our nation's rich tradition of social campaigning by philanthropists and charitable organisations. In the same way that we have invented and exported many sports over the years, only to find ourselves languishing in world rankings behind other nations who have followed our lead and subsequently overtaken us, we may find that the UK falls behind in terms of the way our government encourages and interacts with civil society, despite the fact that we developed many of the principles and approaches that define civil society in its modern form.

Although the rule against political purposes in the UK has its roots in a historical quirk, it has become established through usage and in many ways has a compelling logic to it. One has only to look at the situation in the US: although there is a similar rule which prohibits many of the organisations that we would think of as charities from engaging in partisan activity, there is a separate category of not-for-profit organisations (so-called 501(c)(4) organisations) which have far greater freedom to intervene in politics.[286] This has led to the rise of so called 'Super PACs' – organisations that use non-profit structures to avoid restrictions on campaign spending by political candidates during elections.[287] While there is no indication that there is any risk of super-PACs emerging in the UK, they offer a salutary lesson in the way in which philanthropy could become a distorting influence in electoral politics. But then, that is why UK charity law prohibits organisations from having political *purposes* and engaging in partisan activity.

What we must not do is try to restrict the ability of charities to engage in political *activities* in furtherance of their missions. This is an absolutely vital part of what charities do, and a crucial element of what makes our democracy work. As Harding explains: *'Democratic government flourishes only when government is as responsive to the marginalised voices of groups such as these as it is to the voices of the powerful. Thus, to the extent that 'not for profit' organisations facilitate government responsiveness to the marginalised by bringing their needs and interests to the attention of government and urging government to place due weight on those needs and interests, those organisations contribute to a democracy-promoting culture of free political expression in a way that might not be achieved in their absence.'*[288] So, far from undermining democracy, campaigning by charities actually strengthens it.

Philanthropy beyond the state? Arts, heritage and higher education

So far we have primarily been concerned with the overlap between charitable purposes and public purposes, and in particular with the question of welfare provision. Largely this is because there has been a consensus for more than 400 years that both philanthropy and the state have a role to play in this area, and so the debate about the appropriate balance of responsibility has been thrown into much sharper focus. However, there are other areas of charitable activity that were seen as outside the remit of the state for far longer, or are even still viewed as such to this day. Some, people might expect the state to be responsible for, such as the provision of lifeguard services or the end-of-life care provided by hospices. Others are things that no-one would suggest that the state should have a role in, such as the many voluntary organisations that support hobbies and activities like bee-keeping or model railways, which seem perfectly justifiable as charitable pursuits on the basis that they enhance civic life but could not be argued to constitute a public good that the state should provide or fund. Then there are also the many membership bodies such as the Women's Institute or the Scouts, whose voluntary nature is intrinsic to their identity and could therefore never be replaced by the state, even if the work they do sometime overlaps with public purposes that fall within the remit of government.

Other activities are far less clear-cut. In these marginal cases, there may be significant differences of opinion about the extent to which their purposes fall within the realm of pure philanthropy or should be the responsibility of the state. Two notable examples are arts and heritage, and higher education.

It makes sense to consider arts and heritage, as well as higher education, as special cases for a number of reasons. Firstly, there is the practical point that they are important areas of focus for philanthropy. Even philanthropists whose main interests lie elsewhere will often give to arts organisations or universities as part of their overall philanthropic portfolio. And this is disproportionately true of the wealthiest donors. While education and the arts make up only 3% and 1% respectively of the total amount of charitable donations in the UK,[289] they receive a far bigger proportion of the largest donations: higher education accounting for 41% of all donations over £1 million and the arts accounting for 7% of such donations.[290]

The appeal of arts, heritage and higher education stems from a number of factors. The first, and probably most important, is that since having a personal connection and being asked are two of the key motivations for making a donation,[291] then this puts arts, heritage and higher education at an advantage over other causes when it comes to attracting wealthy donors because those donors are likely to be beneficiaries themselves (i.e. through visiting galleries, museums and heritage sites, or as alumni of universities) and their peer networks may well consist largely of others with the same connections. They are more likely to be asked to donate to these causes; and more likely to respond positively because they have an existing personal connection.

The second consideration for very wealthy donors is that arts, heritage and higher education lend themselves particularly well to the use of philanthropy as a tool to enhance social status (considered in greater detail in Chapter 4). Organisations in these sectors often make capital appeals for large sums, linked to specific physical institutions, which offers wealthy donors the opportunity to make major gifts that pay for the entirety of something that they can then have their name attached to.[292]

Gifts to arts, heritage and higher education organisations arguably also represent an 'easier' or 'lower-risk' option for enhancing social status than other types of philanthropic gifts. The stakes are lower in some senses, because people's lives and livelihoods are not usually at risk when supporting these kinds of causes, so there is less pressure on the donor to maximise the effectiveness of their donation and less chance of damaging criticism if things go wrong. The power imbalance that is inherent in almost all philanthropy (since it involves the transfer of resources from those who 'have' to those who 'have-not'[293]) is also less pronounced when it comes to arts, heritage and higher education, both because the recipients of the donations are more likely to be of a similar social class to the donors, and because the donors themselves are receiving a more overt benefit from their donation. A donor giving money to support young musicians may well enjoy attending concerts by those they have supported and meeting them. A donor giving money for the relief of extreme poverty, however, might meet beneficiaries but is unlikely to mix with them socially in the same way. And while this donor might get pleasure from their donation in the sense of the 'warm glow' of altruism,[294] that seems qualitatively different from the enjoyment one might get from a cultural experience that one would otherwise be willing to pay for.

Whatever the reason, it is clear that arts, heritage and higher education represent an important part of the philanthropy landscape. These causes are also interesting because they are ones where the state has taken on some measure of responsibility, albeit more limited and far later in the day than in the area of welfare. There is a valid debate to be had, therefore, about the relative roles of state funding and philanthropy in each of these areas, but one that has different characteristics to the debate about welfare provision.

For a long time, arts, heritage and higher education did not really figure in the government's view of philanthropy. The Preamble to the Statute of Charitable Uses (1601), previously discussed as a crucial milestone in the development of modern philanthropy, was only really concerned with charitable uses relevant to poverty reduction and the administration of the Poor Laws. Hence the arts did not get a look in. And while higher education was mentioned, this was only to make it clear that the powers of the Charity Commissioners enshrined in the new law did not apply to endowments owned by the colleges of Oxford and Cambridge Universities (which were, effectively, the English higher education sector at the time).

It was only with the Pemsel case of 1891, and the 'four heads of charity' identified by the judge, Lord Macnaghten, that the position of arts, heritage and higher education as acceptable charitable purposes was cemented. One of the four heads was 'trusts for the advancement of education', so higher education was covered, while Macnaghten's fourth 'head' comprised 'trusts for other purposes beneficial to the community' which did not fall under the previous three allowable definitions. As long as arts causes could be said to be 'beneficial to the community', they would therefore be allowable. Interestingly, Macnaghten made it clear even at the time that the fact that wealthy people themselves benefited from the arts, in a way that they didn't from most other forms of charitable activity, was not a reason to discount them as a valid charitable purpose. He specified: *'The trusts last referred to are not the less charitable in the eye of the law, because incidentally they benefit the rich as well as the poor.'* [295]

The lack of clarity up to this point does not seem to have harmed cultural and higher education philanthropy. Some of the most notable gifts of the Victorian golden age of philanthropy were given to found universities, art galleries or museums. This was true in London, where many of the most obvious examples of the city's great philanthropic heritage are to be found in the form of museums and art galleries such as the Tate Gallery, the Wallace Collection and the Horniman Museum, but it was also true in many other cities around the UK. Major industrialists often used their philanthropy to fund cultural institutions and universities as a way of enhancing public life. Men like Andrew Barclay Walker and William Lever in Liverpool, Joseph Whitworth in Manchester, and William Armstrong in Newcastle, gave donations that helped to found galleries and museums that still bear their names and so became synonymous with the cities in which they made their fortunes and ensured their lasting legacy.

This astonishing physical legacy makes a strong case for the value of philanthropy, and would probably have been conclusive if philanthropy remained the only game in town, as it would have provided a clear rationale for its ongoing relevance. However, as in many areas of welfare provision, philanthropy gradually came to be seen as insufficient and the calls for state involvement grew louder. In the case of the arts, the turning point came in 1940 when the government-funded Committee for the Encouragement of Music and the Arts (CEMA) was set up, installing John Maynard Keynes as its Chairman in 1941. [296] This was renamed the Arts Council in 1946, and granted a Royal Charter. In the case of higher education, although there had been public funding of various kinds available for students from local authorities and the Board of Education, the big change came in 1962 with the introduction of mandatory maintenance grants for all students.

Government funding in these areas did not necessarily crowd out philanthropy, but it did complicate the picture. The argument for the continued relevance of philanthropy on the basis that it was necessary to support the arts, heritage and higher education was weakened if it was no longer the only funding option. Once the state had accepted that support for the arts and higher education did constitute a public good, it was open to opponents of philanthropy to argue that state funding in these areas was preferable and should be the default option, as they had in the case of welfare provision. The argument for philanthropy would therefore have to be more nuanced.

One obvious continuing benefit philanthropy provides is that through endowments it can offer a means of funding or ownership of assets over the long term (even theoretically in perpetuity). From the point of view of maintaining the cultural heritage of the nation, this is invaluable as it provides a means of securing art, cultural objects, land, buildings and institutions that is not subject to changing political priorities and views. The importance of this role can be seen in the many endowed museums and art galleries around the UK and in the work of charitable organisations like the National Trust and the Woodland Trust, which own and manage significant proportions of the UK's natural and cultural heritage so that it can be preserved for future generations.

It may be that the appropriate role of philanthropy versus that of the state in the arts, heritage and higher education is a moot question. Over the years government funding in all these areas has slowed down and even gone into reverse, for economic or policy reasons. The current environment of austerity and reduced public spending has meant significant cuts for the arts, from both central and local government. Likewise, the removal of grants and the introduction first of student loans, and then of university tuition fees, has radically changed the funding environment in higher education. Against this backdrop, there is an increased onus on philanthropy to provide sustainable funding for the arts; to secure the long-term future of our natural and cultural heritage; and to support world-class academic institutions and ensure that access is open to students from all backgrounds. There are current and vigorous debates in all these areas about how to boost philanthropy, as people come to accept the reality that government funding is on the wane and that securing voluntary donations is a crucial part of ensuring sustainable future funding. It may even be that philanthropy once again becomes the main player in all these areas, and the involvement of the state comes to be seen as a historical blip.

Taxing philanthropy

Philanthropy and taxation are inextricably linked. Since a fundamental part of philanthropy is about giving money away for the benefit of others, the obvious question is whether this money should be taxed. The answer is much more complex and goes right to the heart of issues about the role of philanthropy in our society and the treatment of private wealth. Many countries around the world offer some sort of tax incentive for individual giving, which might lead us to conclude that the rationale for offering these sorts of tax breaks is clear. But this is not the case: there are a number of potential theoretical justifications for offering charitable tax breaks, only one of which seems to withstand scrutiny, yet it is far from clear that most governments have thought this through.

This theoretical underpinning is important not only because it tells us what the incentives on offer are supposed to achieve, but also because it has a major bearing on how those incentives are structured, and that in turn will dictate how effective those incentives are at encouraging philanthropy. This may at times seem esoteric, and there are some aspects that are unavoidably slightly technical, but it will hopefully become clear that this is a question of profound importance for philanthropy and one that we must address.

The framework used here for categorising the possible justifications for tax breaks on charitable giving is devised by Stanford University philosopher Rob Reich.[297] He identifies three possible rationales:

- **Tax base rationale:** Tax incentives for charitable giving are not really tax 'breaks' at all, because you need to deduct any charitable gifts from an individual's income in order to properly define what that person should be taxed on. The reasoning is that people should only be taxed on personal consumption or wealth accumulation, and money given away to charity does not count as either.
- **Subsidy rationale:** It is appropriate for the state to offer tax breaks for people to be charitable because by doing so it stimulates greater social value than the state could have produced on its own. The underlying reasoning here is that the state collects taxes in order to pay for public or social goods, and charities and civil society organisations work to produce these same goods. Hence it is fair and efficient to allow people to choose to contribute to social good directly through charitable gifts rather than through paying their taxes.

- **Pluralism rationale:** Rather than justifying the tax break because
  of any specific social good produced by a particular charitable gift,
  it should be justified more broadly on the basis that there is inherent
  value to society in having a thriving charitable sector – i.e. the public
  good is civil society itself. Hence any decent liberal democracy
  should support the ongoing health of civil society by offering tax
  breaks to those who want to contribute to it.

Reich's argument is that the pluralism rationale is the only defensible justification for tax incentives. The tax base rationale does not work because
it does not take into account the purpose for which the money is given
away. This means that there is no basis on which to differentiate between
charitable giving and any other form of discretionary spending, so the tax
system should treat them in the same way. You could argue that there is an
inherent difference between money given away and money spent. However,
this is a difficult claim to back up: giving money away is still a discretionary
use of private wealth, and furthermore it cannot be said to be entirely selfless as there are often clear benefits to donors from making gifts – whether
concrete (i.e. having a hospital wing named after them) or more intangible
(i.e. increased happiness and wellbeing).

Without an internal justification for why gifts should be treated differently
from spending, the only option is to try to justify this on the basis of external
factors. This means clarifying the social good produced as a result of the
donation and contrasting this with forms of spending where the benefit
goes only to the individual. We are then free to argue that charitable giving
is different to spending because it produces public benefits, rather than
just private ones.

This is sound reasoning, but switching to a reliance on external factors
has fundamentally changed the nature of the argument. If we now believe
that the government should treat donations differently due to the social
value produced by them, that is very different to claiming that they should
be treated differently simply because it is definitional of the way tax works
that gifts should not be taxed. For one thing, it would now be possible for a
transaction to be unquestionably a gift but still not be eligible for tax relief,
if we could not feasibly claim that it was going to produce the required
social value.[298] In order to make a successful argument for philanthropic
tax breaks based on external factors, we need to go one step further and

explain why the state should value these externalities. We have two options for doing this, which automatically lead to the second and third rationales identified above.

The first option is to argue that the state should value the specific social goods produced by donations because they are things that would otherwise have to be provided by the state itself. This is the 'subsidy rationale'. It proposes that philanthropic tax breaks are justified on the basis that they are an effective way for the government to meet its own responsibilities by incentivising people to give voluntarily to produce public or social goods that would otherwise have to be achieved through direct government spending. This is the justification that is most commonly offered for why it is right for governments to give charitable tax breaks. Unfortunately, it doesn't work.

The problem with the subsidy rationale is partly theoretical and partly pragmatic. The theoretical problem is that there are features that we may consider vital to the delivery of public services that philanthropy is incapable of guaranteeing. Philanthropy is inherently based on the motivations and priorities of individuals, and while this means it has many advantages over monolithic state provision in terms of flexibility, risk-taking and innovation, it is a drawback when it comes to other criteria such as equality, consistency and fairness. At a macro level, if we look at the profiles of public spending and philanthropic giving, we can see how different the priorities are. Higher education and the arts, for example, are significant beneficiaries of major gift philanthropy, whereas they only make up a small proportion of public spending.[299] This problem is exacerbated by the fact that when incentives for giving come wholly or partly in the form of a deduction (rather than a credit) they are not progressive, in the sense that they are worth more to those in higher tax brackets. Hence it is the case that *'when power over the expenditure of revenue is distributed to citizens via the tax privileges of charity law, it is distributed unequally; this is most notably because of the regressive effect of those tax privileges, a regressive effect that is especially pronounced in the case of deductions for charitable donations, but that also characterises other forms of state support for charitable giving, as well as exemptions from income and other taxes for those with charitable purposes'.*[300]

Of course, not everyone believes that these problems are that important. For instance, some would argue that the introduction of 'postcode lotteries' into public services as a result of having them delivered by philanthropic means would be a price worth paying, on the basis that in at least some areas there would be an increase in the quality of services, even if this came at the expense of the overall consistency of the system. Likewise, some might argue that the existing profile of philanthropic spending is not an accurate benchmark because there is currently 'crowding out' by the state in many areas, which skews philanthropic giving towards areas that are not well served by the state. The argument concludes that we would only see the real benefit of tax breaks for charitable giving if the state was radically shrunk and there was room for philanthropy to expand to meet the needs of society.

However, there is little evidence to support these arguments, and the differing profiles of philanthropic and public spending as they are now provide a compelling reason to be very wary about seeing the former as a substitute for the latter. Commentators in the US who have noted the failings of American charitable giving to address poverty issues have concluded much the same thing, arguing: '*It's theoretically possible that if public programmes like food and nutrition assistance were cut, marginally reducing tax burdens, people would give some of the money they saved to charity. But given the small percentage of donations that go to poverty relief, poor people would undoubtedly be left even worse off by such a change.*'[301]

However, even if one does believe that philanthropic spending is an acceptable or desirable substitute for state spending, the major pragmatic problem is that the amounts of money involved simply do not stack up. The total value of voluntary donations in any one year in the UK tends to be around £10–11 billion, whereas Total Managed Expenditure by government in 2012/13 was an order of magnitude higher, at £675 billion.[302] The annual budget for the NHS alone, at over £95 billion,[303] is nearly 10 times higher than the total of voluntary donations. While some might again argue that philanthropic giving would increase if state spending were cut back, it seems unfeasible to suggest that any increase would be of sufficient size to even begin to bridge this gap.

Former New York Mayor Michael Bloomberg, one of the world's leading philanthropists over the last few decades, highlighted this disparity in an interview where he said: '*All the billionaires added together are, as they'd say, bupkis compared to the amount of money that government spends*

... *It's trillions of dollars. Private philanthropy can't do that.'* And to drive this point home, he recalled an anecdote about a chance meeting with a hedge fund manager early in his mayoralty in which *'he says he's going to raise $1 billion from the hedge fund community over the next five years to fix public education. When I explained to him that New York City's annual school budget was $22 billion a year, that was the last time we ever heard from him'.*[304]

It is clear that philanthropy should not be seen as a substitute for public spending, because both its nature and scale make it ill-suited to the task. Hence justifying charitable tax breaks on the basis that they are an effective subsidy for state-delivered services does not work.

The last of the rationales outlined above – the pluralism rationale – attempts to get away from this problem. Rather than interpreting charitable tax reliefs as a subsidy designed to stimulate the private funding of public goods that the state would otherwise have to provide, it is argued that we should interpret it as a generalised subsidy offered by the government to support a vibrant civil society. So the tax break is not justified on the basis of the specific social value delivered by each individual philanthropic donation and how much that saves the state, but rather on the basis of the overall value to the government of supporting a vibrant civil society. The assumption is that this is something a mature democracy should want to encourage, and that offering tax relief on donations is a cost-effective way of achieving this aim.

The additional benefit of the pluralism rationale is that, unlike the subsidy rationale, it is able to account for aspects of the value of charity that are not linked to delivery of services. In particular, it gives us a way of understanding why it is entirely justifiable for the campaigning work of charities to be supported by charitable tax breaks on donations, when that campaigning clearly does not replace something the state would otherwise do itself. It is justifiable, according to the subsidy rationale, because the government acknowledges the inherent value of a vibrant civil society, which includes its role in holding those in power to account through advocacy and campaigning. Of course, it is not always comfortable for governments to acknowledge this; particularly when they themselves are more often than not the targets of this campaigning. It requires politicians to take a mature, long-term view that is focused on ensuring the conditions for healthy democracy, rather than simply making life easier for themselves at that particular point in time.

The history of tax relief on donations

Charitable tax relief in the UK goes back a long way. There has been some sort of relief for charitable activities ever since the introduction of income tax in 1799. At first this was limited to charitable organisations, which were exempted from paying tax on their income and investments, but from 1842 individuals were able to get income tax relief on their donations by establishing a deed of covenant with a charitable organisation. This effectively allowed the individual to transfer their income tax liability on the amount donated to the charity, and since the charity itself was exempt, neither they nor the donor paid income tax on the donation.

This situation continued for 80 years or so, withstanding the occasional attack from critics such as Gladstone (see next section). It was only ever really a workaround though: the system of covenants in its original form was not designed with philanthropy in mind; it merely happened that there was a way of using the system to get tax relief on donations. Eventually this situation was rectified, and tax relief on donations was put on a surer footing. But intriguingly, there is some evidence to suggest that this was an unintended consequence of efforts to clamp down on other loopholes.

William Gladstone led something of a one-man crusade against charitable tax reliefs. In particular, his broader antipathy towards inherited wealth meant that he deplored the situation that gave endowed charities a tax advantage over those that relied on voluntary donations. Eventually, the government recognised this quirk in the law, and resolved it – but not in the way Gladstone intended. He thought the answer was to extend income tax to charitable trusts, but the government actually extended the tax relief to individual gifts, although this appears to have been an accident, because '*it was no part of the Government's intention to grant such a favour to donors. On the contrary, the concession was the wholly unforeseen result of a provision in the Revenue Act of 1922 designed to plug certain leaks in the flow of tax money*'.[305]

The provision in the 1922 Act had the effect of making the seven-year charitable deed of covenant –which had up until then had something of the air of a gentlemen's agreement – into a recognised and lawful means of getting tax relief on donations. The former Charities Aid Foundation CEO Dick Livingston-Booth explained this peculiar origin in a booklet written to mark the organisation's 25th anniversary, noting:

'The strange thing about deeds of covenant is that there is nothing in our laws which says "Let there be a deed of covenant". It all began by accident when, in 1922, the Government resented the fact that too many people were claiming that they should not have to pay tax on a part of their income which, they said, they had given away. Consequently, government set out to limit this growing leakage of tax revenue, and legislation that year then decreed that freedom from income tax could no longer be claimed for casual gifts. However, it also provided that if the giving was to be a regular annual payment of a like amount for a substantial period (at that time capable of exceeding six years), and if the payments were made as the result of a legally executed deed approved by the Revenue, then those payments would not form part of the donor's taxable income . . . And so, at last, donors had a recognised legal means of making tax-free gifts to charity, and the Deed of Covenant was born.'[306]

Interestingly, the origins of tax relief on donations in the US are quite different: there, the charitable deduction was introduced in 1917 as part of legislation designed to help raise money for US involvement in the First World War (the War Revenue Act). The exact motivation for offering the deduction is not certain: it was partly to incentivise philanthropy, but was also at least in part to compensate for the top rate of tax shooting up from 15% to 67%. Either way, what is certain is that the application of the tax break to charitable giving was entirely deliberate, as the legislation specified deductions for *'contributions or gifts actually made within the year to corporations or associations organised and operated exclusively for religious, charitable, scientific, or educational purposes, or to societies for the prevention of cruelty to children or animals'.*[307]

Although the introduction of charitable covenants in the UK was an accident, once the principle of offering tax relief on donations was established, it stuck firm. Almost immediately, people began to explore ways in which they could take advantage of the new incentive and expand its application. One notable innovation was the introduction of the 'discretionary deed of covenant', in which a charitable organisation would agree a covenant with a donor in order to secure the tax advantage but then allow them to make onward donations to other charitable organisations of their choosing. This was pioneered by the Liverpool Council for Social Service and subsequently adopted by The National Council for Social Service (NCS – later to become the National Council for Voluntary Organisations, or NCVO). The NCS established its 'Charities Department' in 1924, which specialised in allowing donors to set up generalised covenants. This underwent a number of changes, evolving into the Benevolent Fund in 1939 and then into the Charities Aid Fund of the National Council for Social Service in 1959.[308] When this organisation was eventually registered as a standalone charity in 1974, it became the Charities Aid Foundation and has continued to this day to support effective charitable giving, although with a far greater range of means at its disposal than were available to its forebears in the Charities Department.

Deeds of covenant remained the only method of tax-effective giving available to donors until 1986, when Payroll Giving was introduced. This allowed individuals to give directly from their salary prior to tax and so receive full tax relief on their donation. A few years later, in 1990, Gift Aid was introduced as a replacement for the system of covenants. This meant that there was now a tax incentive for cash donations designed with the specific intention of encouraging philanthropy. At first, there were quite demanding eligibility criteria (initially Gift Aid only applied to gifts of £600 or more) but over the years these were lowered and then eventually removed completely in 2000. For the first time there was a democratic system of charitable relief, as people making donations of all sizes were able to do so tax-effectively.

Given this history and the organic way in which charitable tax reliefs in the UK have evolved through a combination of accident and design, it is not surprising that the main failing of the system is complexity. The tax breaks on offer for giving in the UK are as generous as those available anywhere in the world, but the challenge for donors is to understand them and navigate the system to make use of them. The fact that still less than half of donors use Gift Aid suggests that there is a lot more work to do to overcome this challenge.[309]

Charitable tax relief under fire

The principle of exempting charitable organisations from income tax has been around for over 200 years, and the idea of official tax relief for charitable donations for nearly a century. However, both have come under attack at various times since their introduction.

Undoubtedly the most notable critic of charitable tax relief was William Gladstone, the famed Liberal politician who served as Prime Minister no less than four times during the late 1800s. While he was Chancellor of the Exchequer, Gladstone proposed reforms to the taxation of charities that would address what he saw as a number of issues. His arguments are interesting, as they bring together a number of ideas we have already explored.

William Ewart Gladstone by Harry Furniss. Pen and ink, 1890.

The underlying motivation for Gladstone's campaign against charitable tax relief was his inherent distaste for inherited wealth. This led him to be particularly critical of endowed charitable organisations, many of which had been founded as the result of bequests. He thought such organisations anti-democratic (as discussed earlier in this chapter and in Chapter 5). Furthermore, it is evident that he believed in a form of the subsidy rationale as the basis for assessing the tax relief offered to charities. The combination of these two views meant Gladstone concluded that the system in its existing form was not acceptable because '... *he pictured the tax exemption as a subsidy of uncertain proportions granted by the state to institutions of question-able value'.* In his view: *'The policy was especially deplorable because the subsidy was concealed and indiscriminate, a blind contribution, for the state applied few of the checks and none of the scrutiny normally given to expenditures.'* This led him to declare: *'If we have the right to give public money, we have no right to give it in the dark. We are bound to give it with discrimination; bound to give it with supervision; bound as a constitutional Parliament, if the Hospitals are to receive a grant, to bring them within some degree of control.'*[310]

It is important to note that Gladstone had no issue with charitable organ-isations that rely on voluntary donations from the living. In fact, he thought it unfair that such organisations were at a disadvantage because they effec-tively paid tax as a result of donors' income being taxed, whereas charities set up through bequest enjoyed entirely tax-free income. While many might think the obvious solution to this problem would be to introduce tax relief for donations in order to level things up, Gladstone instead decided that the best course of action was to try to take away the existing advantages of endowed organisations.

Benjamin Disraeli, 1873.

Fortunately for the development of philanthropy in the UK, Gladstone's crusade proved somewhat quixotic, as '*his plan elicited remarkably little support either within or outside the House*'.[311] He received little support from his own Liberal Party, and his great political rival Benjamin Disraeli used the issue as an opportunity to attack him in Parliament, condemning Gladstone's proposals as '*unsound in principle and inexpedient in practice*'.[312] Disraeli even managed to win support for a version of the tax base rationale, as it is reported that he '*drew applause when he proclaimed the curious doctrine that exemption "is not a privilege – it is a right"*'.[313]

Furthermore, Gladstone's attack on charitable tax relief elicited a vehement response from the philanthropic sector at the time, and it was this, more than anything else, that put paid to his ambitions. Gladstone himself '*wryly noted [that he] was struck "by the skilful manner in which the charitable army, so to call it, has been marshalled"*'.[314] The *Times* presented a colourful account of an emergency meeting in 1863 between Gladstone and representatives of philanthropic organisations who opposed his plans, noting that it was '*one of the most influential deputations, and certainly one of the most numerous, that have ever attended at any official residence*'.[315] So numerous was it, that many members of the deputation were forced to stand or even wait outside in the corridor. Gladstone cannot have failed to be aware, as he looked up at this throng surrounding his desk, of the strength of feeling on the matter.

It is clear also from the *Times* report that the coalition of opposition to Gladstone's plans included many of the great and good of society, including the Archbishop of York, the Bishop of London, the Duke of Cambridge, the Earl of Shaftesbury, and also '*a perfect crowd of gentlemen who on this occasion attended as treasurers or secretaries of nearly all the great charities in the metropolis*'.[316] Many of these men were given the opportunity to speak about the impact the proposed changes would have on the charitable organisations they were involved with, and had marshalled a great deal of data and case studies to make a compelling case that disaster would ensue if the Chancellor proceeded in his chosen course of action.

Gladstone was left in no doubt by this deputation that the only agreeable outcome would be for him to abandon his plans. During the meeting he said '*that his only wish was to know whether the deputation wished that there should be a continuance simpliciter of the present exemption . . . To this nearly all the deputation replied "Yes, yes!".*'[317] And we can see from a report of the proceedings of Parliament in the same edition of *The Times* that the deputation's wish was swiftly granted, as Gladstone's proposals floundered before a barrage of criticism in Parliament. The newspaper noted approvingly that:

> '*With a sound though tardy judgment, the Government has resolved to withdraw the proposal for subjecting public charities to the Income Tax. Not all the rhetoric of Mr Gladstone – and never did he argue an untenable proposition with more courage and more eloquence – could have given such a scheme a chance of success. Now that all is over, and the principle of proposed impost is abandoned, it seems wonderful that it should have attracted any Chancellor of the Exchequer who was not desperate for expedients of taxation.*'[318]

Despite the abject failure of his proposals, Gladstone had certainly brought the question of the nature and justification of charitable tax breaks into the open in a way that has rarely been seen before or since. Some of the arguments he brought to light feature in the next section.

Successive governments evidently took on board the lesson of Gladstone's ill-judged assault on tax relief for charities, and attitudes towards these reliefs – at least outwardly – remained broadly supportive. For a long time, the only changes to charitable tax reliefs (barring some tightening of restrictions on charitable covenants) were positive ones, designed to improve them and to make it simpler for charities and donors to use them.

However, in 2012 the UK philanthropic sector was broadsided by a proposal in the Budget to introduce a new limit on the amount of tax relief that could be claimed by individual donors. This would have capped tax relief at the greater of £50,000 or 25% of a donor's income.[319] Clearly, this is not a measure that would have any impact on the majority of donors, whose giving would never reach the levels where the cap would apply. However, it would make a significant difference to a small number of larger donors. Given that these donors account for a large portion of the total value of charitable donations in the UK, and that their behaviour may also play an important part in setting a culture of philanthropic expectation for others (as seen in the next chapter), the detrimental effect on the voluntary sector as a whole would have been profound.[320]

As had been the case 150 years before, when the philanthropic sector found the principle of tax exemption for charities and charitable giving under attack, it very quickly mounted a coordinated and determined fight back.[321] Chancellor George Osborne learned to his cost, as Gladstone had before him, that many of the most influential people in society are staunch support-ers of charities and that in a battle between politicians and charities, the sympathies of the public are almost always with the latter. The incredulity that *The Times* expressed in 1863 at the thought that any Chancellor would think it worth getting into such an unwinnable fight seemed fitting once again. And the end result was the same as it had been for Gladstone: the proposal was eventually dropped in the face of insurmountable opposition.[322]

Implications for future philanthropy

The lesson to take from both of these attacks on charitable tax relief is that charities and philanthropists should not assume that government and public attitudes towards tax exemption for charitable activities will always remain positive. Despite Disraeli's bold assertion that such an exemption is '*not a privilege, but a right*',[323] it seems safer to accept that the principle does require some justification and that an ongoing case has to be made as to why charitable tax reliefs are appropriate and effective. This is why the theoretical justifications considered in the previous sections have real practical importance: it is only by constructing clear arguments in favour of the continuation of tax relief for charities and charitable donations that we can insure against inevitable attacks in the future.

Charitable tax relief justified in practice

Charities and philanthropists need a sound theoretical justification for char-itable tax breaks. However, there has been little clarity and consensus over the years as to what this justification should be. This is perhaps unsurprising given the organic way in which the UK system of charitable tax reliefs has evolved: rather than clear principles being established from the outset, it has been left to those in favour of the reliefs to assert *post hoc* justifications as and when required. What this means in practice is that when a challenge is presented, there is no ready-made rebuttal on which people can agree, because they all have different views on what the 'obvious' justification should be.

All three of the rationales for charitable tax relief outlined earlier in this chapter have been used at one point or another to defend charitable tax breaks against criticism. However, despite the fact that the pluralism rationale is the one that withstands the most scrutiny, it is the least used. It is far more common to see versions of the tax base or subsidy rationale being aired. Gladstone clearly believed in the subsidy rationale. And since he also believed that many charitable organisations were corrupt or incompetent, he concluded that the subsidy was not an effective one. This led him to attack the very notion of offering tax relief to charities, on the grounds that '*[he] viewed the encouragement of so-called acts of charity by what was* **in effect a gift of public money at the expense of the community** *as wrong in policy and unjust in practice'.*[324]

Disraeli, in opposing him, took great exception to Gladstone's argument and positioned himself as an eloquent advocate of the tax base rationale, clearly revelling in the opportunity to strike a blow to his great political rival:

> 'Tonight the Chancellor of the Exchequer called on us to tax the chari-
> ties of the country . . . I am quite sure, that if the principles on which he
> recommended that course had been such as would have satisfied our
> reason, no sentimental objection would have been offered to it by the
> House of Commons. But the Chancellor of the Exchequer laid down a
> principle which was the basis of the all-engrossing arguments with which
> he has treated us this evening – **that principle is, that if charities are**
> **exempted from taxation, that exemption is to be looked on as**
> **a donation from the state**. That was the foundation of the Right Hon.
> Gentleman's glittering oration of two hours and a half, to which we listened
> with so great pleasure, but with still greater surprise. Whatever his train
> of reasoning, whatever his novelty of argument, whatever his illustrations,
> they were all traceable to the original fundamental principle of his policy

– a principle which I say is utterly false in its premises, and equally fallacious in its consequences. The Chancellor of the Exchequer assumes that the exemption from taxation is the same as a contribution from the state of an equivalent amount of money to the person exempted; but is that so? I deny it. You may have exemptions that are injudicious and unjust, as, unquestionably, you may have an injudicious and unjust tax; but an exemption founded on justice – and all your exemptions should be founded on justice – is founded on the assumption that you have established your claim. On that principle you ought not to be liable to the tax, and the exemption is a just one. Exemption, then, is not a privilege – it is a right.'[325]

Arguments based on the tax base and subsidy rationales are offered at other times as well. For instance, in the US, a 1939 House of Representatives report gave a crystal-clear version of the subsidy rationale, stating: *'the exemption from taxation of money or property devoted to charitable and other purposes is based upon the **theory that the Government is compensated for the loss of revenue by its relief from financial burden which would otherwise have to be met by appropriation from public funds,** and by the benefits resulting from the promotion of the general welfare.'*[326] A 2008 Conservative Party policy paper, meanwhile, followed Disraeli in opting for a version of the tax base rationale (albeit a less fleshed-out one than he offered), arguing: *'we regard it as essential to maintain the link between rates of income tax and Gift Aid, since this embodies the principle that charitable giving should be out of untaxed income . . . Gift Aid works on the principle that **we shouldn't tax people on what they give to charity. This is a good principle'.***[327]

Implications for future philanthropy

The problem, as argued earlier in this chapter, is that there are fairly conclusive counter-arguments against both the tax base and the subsidy rationale, and the pluralism rationale is much more compelling. Concentrating on this would get us away from convoluted arguments about the theoretical basis of income tax or attempts to justify the tax treatment of charities and donations solely by reference to potential savings to the state. Instead, we could construct a positive narrative about why a generalised subsidy to support charitable giving and the financial health of civil society is a justifiable and effective use of public money.

The challenge for both charities and donors is to quantify the value of the work they do in a way that takes into account not just cost savings to the state but also less-tangible elements of value such as the importance of advocacy and campaigning, the contribution that philanthropic giving makes to individual wellbeing, the role that it plays in strengthening links between individuals and communities, and the importance of charitable giving as a symbol of the sort of society that we want to live in. This is not a simple task, but if we can spell out some of these elements of the value of philanthropy, we can offer a much stronger case for why it makes economic and political sense for the government to continue to support and encourage giving through the tax system.

CHAPTER FOUR

Philanthropy and society

We have seen that the interaction of philanthropy with the state and with democratic government has played an important role in shaping the UK. But philanthropy's role runs much deeper than this, and there are ways in which it affects our society that are entirely separate from the workings of government. The history of philanthropy can tell us a great deal about changing attitudes towards wealth and inequality; about the strength of the social contract and the notion of social responsibility; and about perceptions of property and ownership within society. Understanding these different aspects of philanthropy can give important insights into some of the challenges modern philanthropy faces as well as some clues about how we might renew its role as a positive and admired force for good.

Philanthropy and social status

Social status has been an important part of philanthropy since the idea emerged in its modern form in the Elizabethan period. As detailed in Chapter 1, this time marked the beginning of a significant shift away from traditional notions of almsgiving towards a new conception of charitable giving focused on what the gift achieved in society in the present, rather than what it would mean for the donor's immortal soul in the future. However, this does not mean that donors suddenly became entirely selfless, just that the nature of the self-interest changed. The personal pay-off from being philanthropic was no longer solely defined in terms of the judgement of the Almighty, but increasingly in the perception of one's peers and wider society. Philanthropy as a status symbol was about to come into its own.

'A Word to Grand Stand Specialists'. Cartoon by Samuel Ehrhart for the satirical magazine *Puck*, 1903. Illustration shows Puck tugging at the coat-tails of Andrew Carnegie, as he and JD Rockefeller pile money bags around the base of a statue labelled 'Fame', which they seek by endowing libraries and universities; Puck is suggesting that they could do more good for society by endowing places like a 'Home for Consumptives', saying, *'you have qualified thoroughly as modern philanthropists, now why not do some good?'*

At first, the importance of philanthropy as a mark of status was largely seen through eulogies and memorials. Society in the 16th and 17th centuries was still very fragmented, and an individual's peer groups and spheres of influence were, in most cases, limited by the simple fact that travel and communication were difficult and expensive. For most people of means, their one real opportunity to shape how society viewed them, and thereby secure their own legacy, was through the words spoken on their death and the monuments erected in their name. This meant that *'by the early and mid-decades of the 17th century, a range of memorial practices – some reshaped along lines more compatible with newer aspirations and sensibilities – employed rich visual, verbal and rhetorical resources evoking the virtue and exemplary life of the deceased, and increasingly awarding a prime place to charity and good works'*.[328] Alongside eulogies, physical memorials were *'established to provide a visual and more magnificent reflection of the grandeur, honour and virtue of charitable deeds and those engaged in them'*. These edifices were *'first and foremost a form of conspicuous consumption'* and *'[the] narrative element recording the charitable deeds of the deceased came to command centre stage'*.[329]

The phenomenon of using eulogies and memorials to record one's charitable exploits, and thereby cementing one's legacy, first emerged among the wealthy merchants and aristocrats of London. However, it was not confined to the capital: philanthropy was a major element *'not only in memorials erected in commemoration of wealthy benefactors among the gentry and urban citizens, but also in the more modest monuments and inscribed tombs that gradually filled the aisles and chancels of churches across the country'.*[330] This was largely due to an early type of peer group effect, in which individuals who wanted to secure their own good name would ape the philanthropic efforts of wealthy men. For example, sometimes a wealthy London donor left money to a charity elsewhere in the country, and thereby made themselves instantly famous in that location. These *'Londoners who left money to provincial charities became powerful figures in local memory, legends sometimes developing around them'.*[331] In other cases, though, metropolitan donors were imitated by provincial ones even if they had little or no connection with that area, simply because *'the men so praised . . . were truly famous men because of their acts of charity'.* This meant that *'in literally hundreds of wills, often of humble men and women in remote counties, bequests were left in acknowledged imitation of a famous London donor, to establish a school or an almshouse on a model prescribed by an earlier gift, or actually saying that the bequest had been inspired by an earlier and notable legacy'.* [332]

Portrait of Sir Francis Walsingham. Engraving by Jacobus Houbraken after a painting ascribed to Federico Zucchero, 1738.

The epitaph for Francis Walsingham, Elizabeth I's famed 'spymaster', is a good example of the sort of effusive praise lavished upon philanthropists. Walsingham was an enormously powerful and influential man, who played a key role in securing the execution of Mary Queen of Scots for treason, having decrypted her secret messages to co-conspirators. However, he was perhaps just as famous in his own time for his charitable exploits, and his epitaph called him variously *'the comfort of the poore', 'London's dailie friend', 'the sutor for the poore', 'the frend to fatherless and widdowes sore opprest'* and *'the knight that succourd'st those that then were like to die'.*[333]

As with many other aspects of philanthropy, its importance as a tool for gaining social status reached its zenith in the Victorian period. A wonderfully verbose editorial in *The Times* in 1850 waxed lyrical about the importance of charitable giving as the defining characteristic of English society, and one that made up for the nation's multiple failings (many of which sound eerily familiar to modern ears):

> *'... [A] trait more characteristic of the national temperament [than benevolence] could not be produced. The stranger who walks our busy streets and contemplates the moving surface of humanity scarcely dreams of the throbbing heart beneath that never ceases its activity on behalf of indigence and suffering of every kind ... It is true enough that we are a people far gone in the exclusive pursuit of money. It cannot be denied that the material preponderates largely over the spiritual in our intellectual constitution ... We are prone to good dinners, and invest the knife and fork with more dignity and authority than were ever intended for such domestic and everyday utensils. We are somewhat intolerant in our prejudices and intolerant in our bearing ... liberal as the air to the last degree but one, and in that degree, as bigoted and wrong-headed as you please. But enumerate the faults and foibles of our countrymen until there be no more to name, and there remain still to be noted the great virtues that have made our people what they are ... If Englishmen are eager of acquisition, they are spendthrifts in bounty. Their incessant anxiety to give their hard-earned money for the mitigation of pain, whether of body or soul, is more creditable to them than the greatest victory ever won over human selfishness in the tented field.'*[334]

It is clear that in Victorian society, giving to charity was no longer merely an admirable thing to do; it had become *'a social imperative, a convention observed by those who were, or wished to be, anybody'.*[335] But even among those who accepted the notion of a philanthropic obligation there was criticism of what they saw as questionable motives. Although many of the Victorian middle-class probably did accept their responsibility out of simple decency, there was a concern that others were only interested in the trappings that came with philanthropy, so that *'at its most vulgar ... this was a form of Victorian snobbism, with the comfortable off following the lead of the rich, and the rich taking their cue from the aristocratic and conforming to the tradition of paternal benevolence toward the poor and distressed'.*[336]

Not everyone is so cynical when looking back at this period. As the historian Geoffrey Finlayson argues: *'It is rather fanciful to suggest that the pursuit of often disagreeable work, seemingly quite contrary to self-interest, must have sprung from some sinister, self-interested compulsion . . . The historian of paternalism and philanthropy must allow that "good deeds" can be done for good and disinterested motives.'* Pragmatically, one has to *'be alive to the fact that "good deeds" can also be done for somewhat less than good and disinterested motives'*, and accept that in many cases *'the good and the less good can well reside within the one person or group'.*[337]

Despite this caveat, it seems clear that a desire to boost their own social status was a motivating factor in the philanthropy of many Victorians, to the extent that *'it can be argued that charity turned into a branch of fashion in the 19th century'.*[338]

Caricature of Michael Thomas Bass, by Carlo Pellegrini (aka 'Ape') for *Vanity Fair*, 1871.

And this desire for enhanced status was important to donors at all levels in society: for those at the bottom, *'contact with better-off neighbours was essential'* because it gave them an opportunity to get a foot on the ladder, and so *'acted as a spring-board for many working people who wished to integrate into the existing social and economic system'.*[339] For those of higher social status, the appeal was perhaps more frivolous and largely centred on a desire to rub shoulders with the 'celebrities' of the day because *'the first attraction that a charity could offer . . . was the presence of the "great", those leaders of the social world whose names on a charity list gave it a certain éclat'.* Charities were well aware of the lure of celebrity, and *'the value of such pillars of the worlds of fashion and power can be clearly seen when one examines the massive efforts that charities made to secure such names as vice-presidents of their institutions'.* In practical terms, *'not only was the presence of [these] names on subscription lists and their attendance at annual dinners guaranteed to attract new support, but they each had a large personal interest, that is, a retinue of dependents and hangers-on who would thus be drawn into the charitable sphere'.*[340]

'A Christmas Sermon'. Cartoon by John Pughe for the satirical magazine *Puck*, 1901. Illustration shows Puck standing on a stage for a presentation for wealthy philanthropists, including Jane Stanford, JD Rockefeller, Andrew Carnegie, Cornelius Vanderbilt, and JP Morgan. Puck is displaying a 'Plan for model tenement' and pointing to a view of current tenement housing conditions projected on a screen on the stage. In the 'Christmas sermon' Puck is asking that when they are performing their philanthropy, they consider those less fortunate and in greater need.

Many commentators at the time lampooned what they saw as gauche behaviour on the part of socially aspirant donors. Others levelled more serious accusations. *The Spectator,* for instance, suggested there was an element of mob mentality about the prevailing charitable culture, noting:

'The temptation to profess philanthropy is becoming very strong. It is the religion of the hour, in many departments of life no one can rise fast without it, it is saturating literature, and its opponents, if there are any left, are liable to obloquy of the most painful kind. They are detested alike by the good and by the mob. All men are beginning to profess love for the poor, sometimes under the most extravagant forms; half the clergy of all sects are preaching a philanthropic cult; most of the novelists devote their efforts to exciting sympathy for "the disinherited" and all politicians of all parties declare that in their hearts the one strong sympathy is for the multitude. There is not a Coriolanus left, and if there were, he would be socially lynched.'[341]

Sceptics did not limit themselves to criticising the culture of philanthropy; they were quite happy to censure individual philanthropists as well. Hence we see that many famous donors, whose names are now synonymous with the golden age of philanthropy, were the subjects of a great deal of negativity at the time. Andrew Carnegie, for instance, is often viewed as the quintessential philanthropic role model for today's billionaires,[342] yet it is still noted that *'when [he] declared in his "Gospel of Wealth" essays that he was going to give away his entire fortune and asserted that it was the duty of other rich men to give away theirs, his announcement provoked as much criticism as praise'.*[343] Many were all too willing to lambast Carnegie for giving away money that they did not think was rightfully his in the first place. The Methodist Bishop Hugh Price Hughes even accused him of being *'an anti-Christian phenomenon, a social monstrosity, and a grave political peril'.*[344]

Despite this vehement criticism from some quarters, the trend of 'aspirant philanthropy' continued throughout the 19th century. The changing nature of wealth and industry played a huge role in driving the growth of this type of giving. Many of the figures behind some of our best known brands and companies were also hugely generous philanthropists, who used their giving to cement the position in society that their wealth creation had opened up to them. In many cases this was a successful tactic, and they managed to avoid the opprobrium heaped on some of their peers. For example, of the philanthropic brewer Michael Thomas Bass, it has been said that *'if he gave because of the flattery it brought him, the Derby Public Library was a good investment. An opening day of parades, dinners and adulatory speeches reached a kind of climax when a woman with a baby in her arms ran from the crowd, crying "God bless you Mr Bass. May you live to be 100 years old".'*[345]

While philanthropy as a means of gaining social status became less significant in Britain (or at least, less overt) during the 20th century, as social and political attitudes shifted and the welfare state was created, it is interesting to note that the development of philanthropy in the US took a markedly different course. The first half of the 20th century, in particular, saw the rise of the philanthropic foundation in America as the embodiment of the philanthropic missions of wealthy individuals like Andrew Carnegie, JD Rockefeller and Olivia Sage. These institutions, and those that followed them, came to have an impact on the political and public sphere that eclipsed even the heyday of Victorian philanthropy in the UK, and cemented philanthropy as a crucial element of US society.[346]

Implications for future philanthropy

When we compare the modern philanthropic cultures of the UK and the US, this divergence in the 20th century is an important factor in understanding why the US has higher proportionate levels of giving and a more developed not-for-profit sector. However, since we cannot turn back the clock and alter the course of UK history even if we wanted to, the conclusion we actually draw from this is not obvious. As argued elsewhere,[347] if we want to raise levels of giving in the UK to match those found in the US, we need to develop a uniquely British culture of philanthropy, not simply ape that found in America. Understanding the long history of philanthropy in the UK, as detailed in this book, is a crucial part of achieving this ambition.

CASE STUDY

Philanthropy and the brands that built Britain: A good pint

We have seen that at various times in the past, there was a clear social expectation on businesspeople to do good with their money through personal philanthropy. In certain industries this took on the nature of a race, with those who competed against each other in the commercial arena also trying to outdo each other when it came to their charitable deeds.

Caricature of Sir Andrew Barclay Walker, by Liborio Prosperi (aka 'Lib') for *Vanity Fair*, 1890.

The brewing industry was one such example. In the 19th century, almost all of the figures behind the biggest beer brands of the time were significant donors. This was almost certainly in part a response to the ongoing criticism of their brewing activities by the vocal temperance movement. For instance, it is noted of the Liverpool brewer and philanthropist Andrew Barclay Walker (who gifted to the city the art gallery bearing his name)[348] that '*his business interests in the brewing trade made him a controversial political figure in a city riven by sectarian and religious differences*', and that '*many saw Walker's philanthropy as a crude attempt to establish his own cultural status in the town and to curry favour with metropolitan artistic elites*.[349] Critics saw his support for the arts (which admittedly came somewhat out of nowhere) as nothing more that an attempt to '*buy a knighthood through showy displays of philanthropy*'.[350]

Whatever the motivation behind their donations however, and notwithstanding such criticisms, it was clear that '. . . *brewers were expected to be involved with the community and to be charitable*'.[351] In fact, so ubiquitous was charitable giving among the major figures in brewing (dubbed 'the Beerage'),[352] that a failure to give was reason for raised eyebrows. Fred King, of the still-famous Greene, King and Sons, for instance, '*may be the only brewer of whom it never seems to have been claimed that he made the world a better place by some means other than his beer*'.[353]

Postcard of The Walker Art Gallery, Liverpool *circa* 1910.

Other notable examples of the Britain's philanthropic beer barons include:

- **Sir Felix Booth**, distiller of **Booth's Gin**, who financed the Ross expedition to the Antarctic which located the magnetic pole in 1831.
- John Elliot of the Stag Brewery, who was a supporter of the RHS (Royal Horticultural Society) from its foundation in 1804, and acted as Treasurer for 20 years from 1807.

Caricature of Lord Iveagh (Edward Guinness), by Leslie Matthew Ward (aka 'SPY') for *Vanity Fair*, 1891.

- William McEwan, the Scottish brewer, who gave generously to Edinburgh University, where the Graduation Hall bears his name.[354]
- Edward Guinness, whose widespread philanthropic work in Dublin and London included the establishment of many new houses for the working classes in Dublin.[355]
- Thomas Buxton, Director of the Truman Brewery in East London, who was involved in a number of major social campaigns including the abolition of the slave trade, raising the wages of Huguenot weavers, and prison reform.[356]

Inherited v created wealth

The importance of philanthropy as a means of furthering social status is inextricably linked to the changing nature of wealth. In particular, the long-term shift from inherited towards created wealth has significant implications for the expectations and perceptions society has of its wealthy individuals. This in turn has major knock-on effects on philanthropy.[357] This ongoing change is marked by occasional surges of wealth creation, such as the rise of the Tudor merchant class or the industrial revolution, which tend to be reflected in philanthropic booms.[358]

There may be a number of reasons why those who have made, rather than inherited, their wealth are more likely to be willing to give it away. One is the desire for social status mentioned above: the *nouveau riche* in a society with a rigid class system and a long tradition of hereditary wealth could still find themselves looked down upon and shut out of the upper echelons, even if they had more material wealth than almost all their peers. As a result, '*there is good reason to believe that industrial wealth was developing a quasi-aristocratic sense of obligation, that the plutocracy was doing its best to attain the status of aristocracy'.*[359] Philanthropy was an important tool for these newly-wealthy industrialists and merchants because '*munificence not only earned the gratitude of society but, more concretely, assisted in the ascent of the social ladder'.*[360] Although ostentatiously giving to charity would not necessarily overcome snobbishness on the part of the existing upper classes, it did offer a means of establishing one's position in society and in the eyes of the public that went beyond the status that comes with simply having money.

Another possible reason for the greater willingness of the self-made wealthy to give their money away is that they tend to have different attitudes to their wealth than those who have inherited it, and this shapes their general approach to philanthropy. Broadly, this difference can be characterised as that between ownership and stewardship. Those who have made their own money feel that it is theirs to do with as they like, including giving it away if they so wish. Those who have inherited their wealth, however, often feel that they are merely looking after it, and have a responsibility to ensure it is passed on to the next generation, as it was to them. This means that they can be reluctant to give the money away because they do not feel that they have the 'right' to do so.[361]

As well as having a clear sense of ownership, those who have created their own wealth have often also demonstrated a sense of gratitude and a confidence that has benefited their philanthropy: gratitude in the sense that they recognise the elements of good fortune that have made their wealth possible, or acknowledge the role that wider society has played in providing the necessary conditions, and therefore feel a responsibility to give back once they are able. And confidence in the sense that having made their fortune once, they are more willing to believe that if they lost it or gave it away they could make it again, whereas those who inherit wealth are not necessarily willing to take that risk.

CASE STUDY

Easy come, easy give: Philanthropy at the race track

One extreme example of the more relaxed attitude towards giving often displayed by those who have created their own wealth is found in the story of Baron Hirsch. Hirsch was a Jewish financier from a noted European banking family (his father was banker to the king of Bavaria), with wide-ranging charitable interests, but a core focus on Jewish causes. But it is the method he used to finance much of his philanthropy that is remarkable.

During the 1890s Hirsch, a horse-racing obsessive, decided he didn't really need the money from his winnings so he would give them all to charity. He was a racehorse owner, and an extremely well-informed gambler, so this pledge represented a significant

– if unpredictable – source of income for a handful of lucky charities:

> 'He channelled most of these sums to the London hospitals, which thus found themselves receiving handsome windfalls, as much as £30,000 in 1892 . . . This banner year was chiefly owing to the performance of the Hirsch filly La Flèche, which won the Oaks, the St Leger, the One Thousand Guineas and the Cambridgeshire . . . There was rubbing of hands in hospital offices when the Hirsch colours appeared to be having a good year, and gloom when his horses were running badly, though at such times he might supplement his winnings so that the charities would not lose too heavily.' [362]

Baron Maurice de Hirsch.

It has been estimated that Hirsh gave around £20 million in total during his lifetime – a huge sum in today's money. Whether charities nowadays would welcome a donor with his peculiar approach, when there is such a premium on predictable income, is a fair question. However, Hirsch stands as a good example of the maxim that it is far easier to give away money that you don't yet have.

The element of luck

Celebrated investor and philanthropist Warren Buffett has made it clear that he recognises the inherent element of luck that has contributed to his fortune, and the consequent gratitude that drives his philanthropy. In the letter he wrote explaining why he and Microsoft founder Bill Gates had founded the 'Giving Pledge', calling on the world's richest people to commit to give at least half of their wealth away, Buffett said:

> 'My wealth has come from a combination of living in America, some lucky genes, and compound interest. Both my children and I won what I call the ovarian lottery. (For starters, the odds against my 1930 birth taking place in the US were at least 30 to 1. My being male and white also removed huge obstacles that a majority of Americans then faced.) My luck was accentuated by my living in a market system that sometimes produces distorted results, though overall it serves our country well. I've worked in an economy that rewards someone who saves the lives of others on a battlefield with a medal, rewards a great teacher with thank-you notes from parents, but rewards those who can detect the mispricing of securities with sums reaching into the billions. In short, fate's distribution of long straws is wildly capricious.'[363]

Buffett's thoughts echo those of another famous philanthropist, Andrew Carnegie. As Carnegie's biographer explained:

> 'Warren Buffett calls himself "a member of the lucky sperm club". Carnegie made much the same point. He emphasised his good fortune in having moved to Pittsburgh with his family at precisely the moment the city was becoming a centre of iron and steel manufacturing because of its ideal location on the East-West railway network and its proximity to iron ore and coal deposits. Both men recognised that they had not earned their fortunes by themselves and thus had no right to spend them on themselves or on their families. As Carnegie put it, it was not any individual – talented and hard-working though he might be – but the community that was the true source of wealth. And it was to the community that the millionaire's dollars should be returned.'[364]

Carnegie was far from backward in putting forward his views about what others should do with their own wealth. But he was also not alone among his peers in wanting to highlight his recognition of the responsibilities that come with wealth, in order to ensure that he was seen in a positive light by wider society. Rather, he was 'part of a generation of men whose enormous wealth seemed to come to them as something of a surprise'. Although these tycoons might not have gone quite as far as openly acknowledging this fact, their *'periodic efforts to explain the logic and inevitability of their wealth to others'* suggests that they felt they had to justify their own position in some way. The memoirs of these great men (and they were almost exclusively men) usually go out of their way to *'emphasise their humble beginnings'* and *'their stories are designed to impress us with the fact that in an age filled with criticism of the way wealth had come to the wealthy, they were honest men, simple in their beliefs, and responsible to the less well off in the world around them'*.[365]

The attitudes of these self-made millionaires drove philanthropy. But just as important were the attitudes of wider society towards created wealth and the expectations placed upon those in possession of it.

CASE STUDY

Philanthropy and the brands that built Britain: Sweet charity

Perhaps the only industry that can claim to outdo brewing in terms of philanthropic heritage is chocolate-making. Although it might not have quite the quantity of notable givers found among the beer barons of former times, the confectionery trade more than makes up for this in quality, having given us some of our greatest philanthropists in members of the Cadbury, Rowntree and Fry dynasties.

The philanthropic zeal shared by these major chocolate names is not a coincidence; it is a consequence of the fact that each of them was a family-owned, Quaker company. This Quaker ideology informed each family's approach not only to philanthropy but to business, and led them to be notable for

Elizabeth Fry, by John Cochran, after Charles Robert Leslie stipple engraving, 1823.

their charitable deeds and (particularly in the case of Cadbury and Rowntree) for their forward-looking approach to employment practices and industrial relations.

The prominence of Quakers in chocolate-making was matched in a number of other areas of business in the UK: for instance, Barclays Bank, Lloyds TSB, Clarks shoes and Carr's biscuits are all companies with Quaker origins. This commercial success was partly a consequence of the Quaker's strong networks, but also of the fact that as non-conformists, they were barred from going to university or holding public office. This made the commercial arena the obvious place to direct their energies, which many of them did with great success.

Advertisement for Fry's 'Five Boys' milk chocolate.

More on the philanthropy of the Cadburys can be found in the case study of George Cadbury in Chapter 5. Of the other two, the company JS Fry is a slightly less celebrated philanthropic name, partly because the most important philanthropy was done by members of the Fry family who were not directly connected to the business, and partly because they were less sophisticated in applying their Quaker principles to the commercial operations. However, Joseph Storrs Fry II (the great-grandson of founder Joseph Fry) was a committed philanthropist, if somewhat less focused than the better-known Rowntree or Cadbury.

Perhaps JS Fry's most important contribution to philanthropy is its indirect role in the campaign for prison reform. One of the best-known figures in this field, Elizabeth Fry, was a Quaker (her mother was part of the Barclay family), who married into the Fry family via the nephew of company founder Joseph Fry.[366]

More directly, Joseph Storrs Fry II many years later left a sizeable legacy to his niece Margery Fry, who went on to continue Elizabeth Fry's pioneering working on prison reform.[367]

In the case of Rowntree's, on the other hand, philanthropy very much went hand-in-hand with business and two of the most famous Rowntree philanthropists, Joseph and his son Seebohm, were also senior figures in the company at various times. Although both men were wide-ranging in their generosity – Joseph, for instance, financed the creation of a public library and a park in their home town of York – they are best known for their focus on addressing poverty.

Perhaps more than the cause they chose to address, what is distinctive about the philanthropy of the Rowntrees is their approach. They firmly believed that it was important to look beyond the symptoms of poverty and attempt to address its root causes, which they were clear lay in structural failings of society rather than in the moral failure of the poor. To do this both men undertook detailed research, with each of them publishing a book detailing their findings.[368] They were not content merely to indulge in academic discourse: they realised that they were in a unique position, through both their philanthropy and their business, to do something about the problems they sought to understand.

Joseph Rowntree, 1906.

For the Rowntrees, the line between philanthropy, business and politics seems to have been deliberately blurred. Their endeavours in all three fields were a reflection of their Quaker beliefs and their deep commitment to addressing the problem of poverty. For instance, Joseph Rowntree was instrumental in constructing decent affordable housing for the working classes in York. He explicitly viewed this as a way to demonstrate the need for state action, rather than an end in itself. Likewise, in their own business, both Joseph and Seebohm

Rowntree introduced many innovations to improve working conditions for their employees that were informed by their beliefs and their research, such as bringing in an eight-hour day, providing a company doctor and dentist, implementing a pension scheme, and offering facilities such as a staff canteen, a library, a swimming pool and a theatre.

All of these innovations for their own employees were matched by efforts to influence wider public policy for the benefit of all workers. Seebohm, in particular, became highly influential in policymaking, and developed relationships with major figures such as Lloyd George and Beveridge.

Messrs JS Fry and Sons Manufactory, Nelson Street, Bristol.

The different aspects of the Rowntree's philanthropy are continuing today through the various charitable and non-charitable trusts that bear their name, which focus on a range of issues and activities including affordable housing, research on poverty, tackling global conflict and injustice and promoting progressive politics.[369]

Great wealth, great expectations

From the outset, a sense of duty and obligation was an important part of modern philanthropy. At first there was a strongly religious element, as Protestant teachings emphasised the idea that those with wealth are not truly its owners, but merely its stewards,[370] and that their responsibility was to ensure that the whole of society benefited from that wealth. Later on, as philanthropy became increasingly secular, similar arguments were made on the basis of concepts like the 'social contract' – emphasising the importance of society in creating freedom and prosperity for the individual and the need to play one's role within that society.[371]

Historian WK Jordan argued that this notion of social responsibility and expectation among the newly wealthy defines the character of the Tudor and Stuart eras of British history, to the extent that *'in the early 17th century the failure of a London merchant to settle some substantial and conspicuous charitable trust or gift was generally regarded as little short of shocking unless there had been a grievous wasting of the estate because of age, ill-health, or commercial misfortune'.* In Jordan's view, *'the importance of this phenomenon of habit, of the tradition of social responsibility, cannot be too strongly stated'* because it was the driving force of a philanthropic culture that defined the society of the day. He cited evidence showing that *'in many hundreds of parishes . . . one substantial foundation of, say, an almshouse would very quickly draw many other gifts either for the support of that institution or some other equally ambitious undertaking for still another need in the community'.* There was *'a kind of social osmosis from parish to parish across the face of England'* which resulted in the creation of *'an intricate network of helpful and healing social agencies which no man and no class had quite planned but which not the less expressed most perfectly the ethos of an age'.*[372]

As created wealth grew enormously during the industrial revolution and into the Victorian era, social expectation continued to be an important characteristic and a driving force behind much of the great philanthropy of the age. As we see in the case studies throughout this book, many of the great business magnates of the period, who built companies and brands that are still familiar today, were also significant philanthropists and had a strong sense of their own social responsibility. However, interpretations of the precise responsibilities that came with wealth changed over time, particularly when it came to the pronouncements of the church. While in the 17th and early 18th centuries, preachers had spared little in exhorting the rich to give their money away for the greater good, and making clear that this was a responsibility rather than a choice, their rhetoric gradually softened so that *'as the 18th century wore on, preachers began to play down the idea that the wealthy had a duty to give away their wealth – rather it was about "free and voluntary" gifts'.*[373]

This also marked a broader shift in attitudes towards the idea of wealth, particularly among Protestants: no longer was the amassing of large amounts of money seen as a burden that one should seek to overcome by giving it all away. Now, *'the getting and enjoying of wealth, rather than making it more difficult to attain salvation, was ... described as a beneficial and moral state.'* [374] So the idea that the wealthy were simply to be lauded for their riches began to take hold. In this context, not only was it no longer deemed necessary for rich people to give their money away, but *'the idea developed that it would be unreasonable, not to say dangerous, for the rich overzealously to dispossess themselves of their property, or even of their superfluities'.* This was because *'it was only in the enjoyment of such property that rank and hierarchy, as well as the true church, could be maintained'.*[375]

The question of whether the wealthy in society are entitled simply to enjoy their riches, or are under a moral obligation to give away at least some of them to help others, continues to be a source of debate today. The balance of opinion has shifted back and forth over time, and while there have been extremes like the 'greed is good' era of the 1980s (when the accumulation of personal wealth became seen as the main purpose of the individual within society), there have always been those who argued that there must be a 'social contract' in which the rich give back to the society that made their wealth creation possible. Embodiments of this idea today surface in the rise of initiatives like the 'Giving Pledge', and in the various indices that try to establish 'league tables' of philanthropy and thereby normalise the idea that giving is something that the rich should be expected to do.[376]

These attempts to develop a social norm among the wealthy rely in large part on convincing them that other 'people like them' are getting involved in philanthropy.[377] The Giving Pledge is particularly interesting in being pitched at the extremely wealthy, but yet still peer-driven: the participants are extremely wealthy people, who say they pledge to give the majority of their wealth away in the hope of encouraging other wealthy people to make a similar commitment. This helps to overcome one of the challenges inherent in discussions of the philanthropic responsibilities that come with wealth: that it is hard to talk about without straying into the politics of envy. While we all might like to lead by example in terms of giving millions of dollars away, as Bill Gates does, that is not an option open to the majority. So anything we say about the giving habits of the rich carries an unavoidable undertone of criticism, even if it is not intended.

Of course, some of those who talk about the giving – or lack of it – by wealthy individuals may be happy to be overtly critical, in the belief that this will 'shame' them into giving more. However, singling out individuals for criticism may be counterproductive in terms of encouraging them to increase their giving. There is little hard evidence to test this hypothesis, but it seems safe to at least assume that wealthy people who are already giving to charity will not respond especially well to being told that they are not doing enough. There is already a sense among many of the wealthy that they are unfairly criticised for all of society's woes, even when they are trying to give back through philanthropy. Often this is presented as a general argument about attitudes to wealth; and sometimes in rather extreme form, such as when US billionaire Tom Perkins in 2014 compared the 'persecution' of the rich in his country to the *Kristallnacht* atrocities committed against Jews in Nazi Germany, which unsurprisingly drew a barrage of criticism.[378]

Sometimes, however, wealthy people do feel that their philanthropy is not only under-appreciated, but actually used as the basis of attacks against them. Former Enron trader John Arnold, for instance, used an impassioned article in *The Chronicle of Philanthropy* to hit back at critics who had used his and his wife's philanthropic efforts as a stick to beat them with, claiming that these critics represented vested interests who felt threatened by the Arnold's philanthropy. Arnold acknowledged that '*people may not agree with every issue or policy proposal we pursue*', and claimed that he and his wife '*expect reasonable minds to disagree, and . . . welcome constructive debate on the merits of every issue in which we are involved*'. But he also made it clear that they '*will not be deterred by personal attacks, blatant lies, or self-interested campaigns to keep in place systems and policies that do not work for anyone other than the few who continue to gain from them at the expense of the rest of society*'.[379]

This just goes to demonstrate that tempers run very high around issues of wealth and responsibility. For those trying to encourage more philanthropy, there is a difficult balance to be struck between justifiably highlighting where individuals or business sectors are lagging behind their peers when it comes to giving, and simply playing to existing prejudices about the wealthy.

The challenge of maintaining a positive narrative while still questioning the philanthropic status quo has been most obvious in the technology sector in the US, which contains some of the most generous donors in the world today and also some extremely wealthy individuals whose philanthropic efforts look rather mean by comparison. Hence, for instance, Apple's eventual dominance in its long-running rivalry with Microsoft has often been contrasted with the way in which Bill Gates' philanthropy has vastly outstripped that of the late Steve Jobs.[380] Similarly, articles noting the extraordinary generosity of many successful Silicon Valley billionaires also point out that some of those you might expect to be giving a great deal are conspicuous by their absence from the lists of top donors.[381]

Giving while living, or waiting until you're gone?

Along with the general expectation that those with money should give it away to help others, there have often been views expressed about *how* they should give that money away. In particular, whether money should be given away during one's life or when one dies is a question that has often aroused strong feelings. It is sometimes suggested in discussions about the 'new philanthropy' of today's wealthy that their enthusiasm for 'giving while living' distinguishes them from their forebears.[382] However, while attitudes may have changed at various times, the question itself is far from new. The preacher John Rawlinson for instance, in a sermon in 1612, said: '*[A] blessed thing . . . it is, thus to do good, though it be but at your death. But, much more blessed should ye be in your work, not only in the sight of men, but of God himself, if in your life time ye would deale and distribute with your owne hands, that which ye cannot tell whether ye shall hold till your death; which indeed is to do good . . . to benefite others rather by your life, than by your death.*'[383] This reflects the fact that '*despite a surprisingly long life, the notion that charity was the rent on property payable to the only absolute proprietor was also fading from view*', and that in general, '*more and more clerics urged their audiences to give during their lifetimes, when they could direct and keep control over their donations, rather than give posthumously*'.[384] This was because '*charity, it was felt, could and should address itself to change, to improvement*', and unlike most charitable bequests, where the purpose was simply to provide relief, '*the charity of the living, active philanthropists could direct and promote the course of such change*'.[385]

The question of giving while living or posthumously via a bequest has aroused strong feelings among commentators for a number of reasons. One is that many have held broader critical views about inherited wealth and the effect it has on society. William Gladstone was one such critic and, as we have seen, this led him to launch an attack on charitable tax relief that met with furious opposition. Another reason people sometimes criticise legacy giving is that the creation of funds whose criteria are narrowly defined on the basis of a donor's personal wishes, which may reflect specific concerns of the donor's own time, can often end up looking anachronistic and ill-guided later on, but it is extremely difficult to do anything about it. The proliferation of such 'obsolete trusts' in Victorian England was seen as a real problem, and the efforts to combat it were largely responsible for the establishment of a permanent Board of Charity Commissioners in the middle of the 19th century (there is more on this in Chapter 5).[386]

'The Crabbed Millionaire's Puzzle'. Cartoon by John Pughe for the satirical magazine *Puck*, 1901. Illustration shows an old man labelled 'Millionaire' sitting in a chair atop a pile of moneybags, complaining that, *'If I had begun earlier I might have had some fun in giving it away. Now I must leave it either to relatives whom I hate or to churches and colleges in which I have no interest.'*

There are other, more positive, reasons why some prefer giving while living to leaving a legacy. For one thing, it can offer a stronger example to others, and for another, one can get the benefit of some of the perks that come along with philanthropy, such as increased social status. Even in the Tudor period, when legacies were a major driver of peer pressure among philanthropists, many still thought it would be better if people gave during their lifetimes instead. The Puritan preacher Thomas Gataker, while giving

the eulogy for London merchant Sir Andrew Judd in 1620, took the opportunity to contrast his generosity upon death with that of his grandson Sir
Thomas Smith, who was a generous philanthropist during his lifetime, and
said pointedly: *'. . . good done at our ende is like a lantern borne after us,
that directeth them that come after us, but afford us little light; whereas the
good done in our life time is like a light borne before us, that both benefiteth
them and us also alike'.*[387]

This debate still rages to this day. Those who believe giving while living is
the best approach use the same arguments that were heard in Tudor times,
pointing out the value of acting as a role model for others and the fact that a
live donor is in a position to get the benefits of their own philanthropy, while
a dead one is not. They have also added new angles to the argument: for
instance, making the point that the apparent increasing desire of modern
donors for 'measurable impact' is best served by taking a more engaged,
'hands-on' approach to philanthropy, and that this is something that can only
be done when one is alive.[388] However, there are still those on the other side
of the argument, who, either through their actions or their words, express
a clear view that it is better (or at least equally valid) to wait until you die to
give your wealth away. We still see stories like that of Richard Herman, a
Washington resident who died in 2013, leaving the whole of his $28 million
fortune to a handful of shocked and delighted charities, despite the fact that
he was not known to be a significant donor (or even wealthy, for that matter)
during his lifetime.[389]

For some, the decision to wait until death to make their major philanthropic gift may simply be a reflection of the practical realisation that giving
your wealth away effectively is actually much harder than it sounds, and
would take a level of time and dedication they don't feel able to commit. Or
they might not want to 'out' themselves as a wealthy donor and invite the sort
of attention this would inevitably bring (which seems to have been the most
likely motivation in Richard Herman's case). It might also be a reflection of
an individual's belief that it would be better for society if they focused on
amassing the maximum amount of wealth during their lifetime, which can
then be donated for others to do good with once they are gone. Whatever
the reason, there is still a valid choice to be made for all wannabe philanthropists about whether they want to get on with the work during their lifetimes
and be involved, or wait until they die and leave it to others to make use of
their assets for the greater good.

CASE STUDY

Ask and ye shall receive: The history of fundraising

It is often noted that building a more philanthropic society is not just about developing a culture of giving – it is also vital that there is a culture of *asking*. From the outset (and certainly since the rise of the organisational charity in the 18th century), the development of modern charitable giving has been matched by developments in the practice of fundraising, as those who have good ideas that require money try to convince those with money to give it away.

This is not the place to attempt a detailed history of fundraising. However, it is worth noting some interesting examples that highlight the fact that, as with so many other aspects of philanthropy, the approaches taken to fundraising and the challenges it faces have long histories. For instance, many charities have long recognised the importance of demonstrating the 'impact' done with donors' money and that this is often most effectively achieved through personal case studies. The Society for Promoting Christian Knowledge (SPCK), which founded many charity schools in the early 18th century, organised special 'charity services' in local churches where the children from the school would march in two-by-two, turned out in their uniforms and on their best behaviour. This demonstration of the 'impact of donations' proved very effective in encouraging people to give.[390]

Fundraisers have also long-realised that making giving into a social activity can be extremely effective at loosening people's purse-strings. The hospitals of London in the mid-18th century, for example, were masterful early exponents of the fundraising dinner:

> 'With the London Hospital, the annual festival began not long after its foundation. The sermon in one of the City churches was followed by a procession to a hall of a City Company or to a tavern for dinner ... At the first dinner, £36 14s. was collected, and at the second £82. A little more than a century later, in 1856, the diners gave up the record sum of £26,000!'[391]

The Foundling Hospital took this approach even further, realising that if offering people a way of rubbing shoulders with their peers was a powerful incentive, then offering them a chance to mix with the great and the good would be even more enticing. Thus was born the notion of celebrity charity endorsement:

> 'An astonishing number of the great of the 18th-century world were enlisted in its support... It was Hogarth who was responsible for the plan of decorating the walls of the new building with works of art and who persuaded a group of artists to contribute to the cause, with the result that the fame of the Hospital as an art gallery almost exceeded its prestige as an orphanage. The Foundling chapel was the special interest of George Frederick Handel, who donated the organ and on May 1st, 1750, gave a performance of the 'Messiah', which realised £728. His presentation of the oratorio were said to have brought in, over the years, a total of £7,000, and on his death-bed he bequeathed "a fair copy of the score and all parts" to the Hospital.'[392]

Unfortunately, in addition to introducing many ground-breaking innovations, the fundraisers of yesteryear also established some poor practices that gave their profession a bad name and which their modern counterparts are still struggling with even today. Chief among these was the aggressive targeting of donors, which became a huge problem in Victorian London, where 'collectors, paid and voluntary, were crossing and re-crossing each other's trails throughout the metropolis, frequently calling on the same individuals on behalf of identical varieties of charitable endeavour'.[393] There was even a printed 'target list' of known donors, 'The Charitable Ten Thousand', which was 'a grand index of potential contributors, almost a philanthropic "sucker-list", fitted with blank interleaves for additional names'.[394] This was a significant source of concern among the well-to-do of the day; The Times even mused gloomily: 'When a name has once been printed on a subscription list, its owner becomes a marked man. He has joined, by his own act, the unhappy class to which an appeal can be made with some chance that it will be met. From that day forward his persecution will never cease.'[395]

Not all the challenges facing fundraisers were created by bad practice within their own profession. The habits of many donors in the past also made life difficult for those trying to raise money for ongoing projects. It will come as little surprise to modern fundraisers that their forebears struggled with the challenge of a donor populace who were eminently willing to put their hands in their pockets in response to a disaster, but maddeningly hard to engage on a longer-term basis:

> 'The Indian Mutiny Relief Fund, for which about £475,000 was raised in three years, gave further evidence of the immediate and lavish response evoked by distress resulting from service to the nation. The promoters of such efforts were neither the first nor last to discover how much more readily pockets are turned inside out for a dramatic emergency or national crisis than for the year-by-year requirements of constructive philanthropy.'[396]

Clearly, those who are trying to raise money for charitable projects have faced many challenges over the years. The important thing today, as it always has been, is that the priorities and approaches of those raising funds are aligned as closely as possible with the priorities and approaches of those who have funds to give. This is far easier to say than to achieve in practice, and the ongoing challenge for fundraisers is to maximise the short-term benefits in the form of income while minimising any long-term risks in damaging public perception or donor relations.

Attitudes to poverty: enlightened self interest, morality and fear

A desire for social status and a regard for the expectations of others have been important factors in the historical growth of philanthropy. These motivations are primarily about self-interest on the part of the donor in a way that largely ignores what is actually achieved through donating. But not all factors driving philanthropy are egotistical. It is clear that many philanthropists are driven by a desire to produce outcomes with their giving; and for a long time, the vast majority of giving was focused on one broad outcome: the alleviation of poverty.

However, it is unlikely that donors making meaningful attempts to address poverty are motivated solely by altruism with no interest in the benefits of giving for themselves. There is often still an element of self-interest, but it is a more subtle 'enlightened self-interest' in which the perceived needs of beneficiaries are considered first and the benefit to the donor is a happy corollary. To understand this enlightened self-interest and the ways it has manifested itself, it is important to understand the changing attitudes to poverty and their implications for motivations for philanthropy.

It is worth noting that we should not make assumptions that poverty is definitely a problem. For a long while it was simply seen as a necessary part of the natural order, even by those who gave to help those in need. This was reinforced by the teachings of church clerics, who proclaimed that '*poverty was a providentially arranged condition, ordained by God so that men could earn salvation through the reciprocal process of kindness and gratitude*'.[397] As the direct influence of religion on giving began to wane, this idea still persisted, albeit stated more in terms of political economy or social theory than in terms of 'God's plan'. Hence '*most 19th-century philanthropists held a hierarchical view of society and assumed that distinctions between rich and poor were God-given and likely to persist. Being practical they sought to alleviate the worst abuses of society without undermining their authority. The opportunity to be charitable, after all, depended on social inequality*'.[398] Gradually this attitude receded, and more and more of the wealthy and the middle-class began to believe that poverty *was* a problem, and that philanthropy should try to solve it. They came to this conclusion for a number of reasons, which offer an insight into the changing understanding of poverty and welfare.

Awareness of need

The most positive aspect of changing attitudes towards poverty from the 16th century onwards is the simple fact that those with money were increasingly aware of the privations suffered by others. When faced with evidence of suffering there was a strong religious and social imperative to do something about it; so greater awareness of need gave rise to greater philanthropic activity. And as society changed, undergoing first an agricultural and then an industrial revolution, people became aware that the nature and scale of poverty was also changing, and the need for philanthropy to address it was greater than ever before. During the agricultural revolution, for instance, *'this awareness of acute need, no longer sustained either by the community of the land or by the ministrations of the priest, supplied an immensely powerful impulse to charity'.*[399] This philanthropic response may have played a decisive role in enabling society to overcome some of the challenges presented by the huge changes it was going through, because *'it was private charity, flowing out as it did into every nook and corner of the land, which saved England at once from disaster and from the necessity for the intervention of the state on a massive scale. The secular spirit of mankind won for itself a notable triumph in this first great trial of its strength and its sense of social responsibility'.*[400]

The industrial revolution, perhaps even more than the agricultural revolution, changed the face of British society forever. The nature of poverty also changed, becoming far more of an urban problem and giving rise to a host of new challenges such as homelessness, disease, squalor, industrial injury and child labour, and also adding to the vice and drunkenness that fired the moral indignation of many Victorian donors.

It was almost impossible for wealthy Victorians to remain ignorant of the problems in society, as they were often brought face-to-face with the poverty and deprivation all around them. For instance, it is recounted of the brewer Frederick Nicholas Charrington that:

> *'[He] experienced a religious conversion which, after a striking incident, led him to espouse the temperance cause. Outside a public house he saw a woman, with children dragging at her skirts, call her husband out of the pub into the street and ask for money to feed them. The man made no reply, but knocked her into the gutter. Charrington reported that "Just then, I looked up and saw my name, CHARRINGTON, in huge gilt letters on the top of the public house". For the rest of his life he undertook extensive philanthropic work for temperance causes, ironically all financed by brewing money.'*[401]

Similarly in an earlier period, the former sea captain and celebrated philanthropist Thomas Coram, who established the Foundling Hospital in the mid-18th century to care for the abandoned and orphaned children of London, was motivated by his personal experiences of poverty. His fundraising efforts were spurred by *'the shocking sights he had witnessed on his way to and from the City – babies, alive or dead, left by the roadside, and in one instance, so the story goes, a girl in the act of deserting her child'.*[402] Such was the charitable zeal that Coram developed as a result of these formative experiences that '*he was ruthlessly single-minded in press-ing his idea, until, as a friend remarked, "even people of rank began to be ashamed to see a man's hair become grey in the course of solicitation by which he could get nothing". In the end persistence conquered, and he was able to rally notable support in the world "of Quality and Distinction" for his project of an institution for foundlings'.*[403]

Thomas Coram, in the foreground an infant in a basket, in the background the Foundling Hospital. Line engraving by J Brooke, 1751, after B Nebot, 1741.

There is evidence that awareness of need continues to be an impor-tant factor in driving philanthropic giving even today. A 2012 study in the US found that wealthy donors who live in areas that are less economi-cally diverse are less likely to give to charity.[404] Field experiments have also shown that the reduced propensity towards giving and social action can be overcome simply by showing wealthy individuals evidence of the hardship faced by others. In one such experiment, there was a measurable difference between the levels of pro-social behaviour among a group of participants who had been shown a 46-second video about child poverty and those who had not.[405] In real-world terms, what this suggests is that wealthy people who are isolated from the wider world around them are less likely to give because they are not presented with stimuli that prompt a compassionate response. As one researcher in this field explains: '*Simply seeing someone in need at the grocery store – or looking down the street at a neighbour's modest house – can serve as basic psychological reminders of the needs of other people . . . Absent that, wealth will have these egregious effects insulating you more and more.*'[406]

John Passmore Edwards: Carnegie-lite?

John Passmore Edwards (1823–1911) is a significant figure in the history of UK philanthropy, but has not enjoyed the level of fame he might have had. He funded a large number of institutions, including 15 libraries in London and nine in Cornwall and Devon, as well as hospitals and convalescent homes. However, despite this generosity, Passmore Edwards was unfortunate to be overshadowed by his more famous philanthropic contemporary Andrew Carnegie, with whom he shared many similarities in focus and approach. In particular, Passmore Edwards' support for libraries, while admirable in its own right, somewhat pales in comparison to that of Carnegie, who was eventually responsible for financing 660 libraries around the UK, and over 2,500 worldwide.[407] To rub salt into the wound, Passmore Edwards even had a brief business collaboration with Carnegie, which did not go particularly smoothly.

Without drawing parallels with Carnegie, Passmore Edwards was in many respects an extremely admirable philanthropist. He made his fortune in publishing, but even his commercial interests pointed to his philanthropic tendencies: he was the owner of *The Echo*, a newspaper aimed at the working classes. Much like his subsequent support for libraries, his ownership of this paper was a reflection of his deep-seated belief in the importance of popular education in improving the lot of the masses. But there should be no illusions that he adhered to anything like the modern standards of editorial independence, as the paper was often used as a vehicle to push his own views on issues close to his heart such as education, peace and (that classic favourite of the moralising Victorian philanthropist), temperance.

John Passmore Edwards by George Frederic Watts. Oil on canvas, 1894.

In the latter half of his life, with his fortune secured, he increasingly focused on his charitable activities until they became pretty much a full-time pursuit. He thus demonstrated the level of commitment that is typical of a first-tier philanthropist. Allied to that, he appears to have mastered the difficult balance between action and reaction, between strategic focus and all-round benevolence, that is the hallmark of many truly great philanthropists.

His core focus was on improving the lot of the working classes through the provision of key services and access to institutions, of which he thought libraries and hospitals the most important. His strategic approach was even more considered, as he was not simply concerned with the *types* of institutions available to the working classes, but also with their *distribution:*

> *'He would try to see that [the institutions] were located at points of maximum usefulness. For, unlike some of those who pointed to the aggregate of Britain's welfare institutions, Edwards was aware how unequally and sometimes erratically these were distributed. In short, he would consciously try to improve Britain's network of hospitals and libraries, planting his benefactions in needy communities.'* [408]

This recognition of the need to try to match charitable services to the most pressing gaps in provision marks Passmore Edwards out as a particularly self-aware philanthropist. He saw that, left to its own devices and driven solely by the whims of donors, philanthropy ran the risk of adding to inequality by concentrating in certain locations, rather than being a tool to address the inequality created by inconsistencies in public and private sector provision. He tried to design his philanthropy to overcome this problem.

But Passmore Edwards did not pursue his own philanthropic projects to the exclusion of all else. He was also extremely generous in responding to fundraising requests. This led him to lend significant support to a number of high-profile projects, including the creation of the London School of Economics and the Whitechapel Gallery. This latter example throws up one anecdote that suggests that while Passmore Edwards was an admirable philanthropist in many ways, he was not devoid of human weakness: apparently he withheld his final donation to the gallery when it refused his last-minute request to name the building after him.[409]

So with hindsight, Passmore Edwards deserves recognition as one of our country's great donors. *The Times* said as much in its obituary, noting: '*In John Passmore Edwards an Englishman of great worth and value, who did more good in his time than almost any other of his contemporaries, and did it with the least possible amount of ostentation on definite and judicious lines, has been lost to the country . . . Mr Passmore Edwards gave much, and gave wisely; he was absolutely modest to the end.*'[410]

The historian David Owen certainly felt that Passmore Edwards' legacy stacked up well against those of his peers, arguing: '*Among the late Victorian philanthropists, Passmore Edwards will survive critical examination better than most. Not only were his motives above reproach . . . but his benefactions expressed deeply held and intelligent convictions about the conditions of progress in his society.*'[411]

A moral quest

For a long time – until at least the middle of the Victorian era – the prevailing view was that poverty was a failing of the individual, related to some moral weakness or sin, and the key to overcoming poverty was to address this underlying weakness. This was reflected in government policy by the introduction of harsh and punitive Poor Laws, which were designed to offer a last resort to those in need but also a strong incentive to avoid poverty at all costs. The view was also reflected in philanthropy, which in many cases became a moral quest aimed at whatever vice or ill the donor believed to be most damaging: drunkenness, idleness, godlessness, etc. Thus, *'the early Victorians were inclined to define their social problems in moral terms, and to carry over into the new urban-industrial environment answers that had been formulated in the pre-industrial age. To them the critical social evil was not mass poverty but pauperism, and this they ascribed largely to individual weakness. Unless the working classes could acquire the essential virtues of thrift, temperance, industry, and family responsibility there was little hope for British society.'*[412]

This is perhaps unsurprising when we consider that the census was only introduced in 1801, and before this (and even for some time afterwards) there was little or no understanding of social problems at a national scale. So although philanthropists were increasingly aware of the need around them, it was easy to conclude that problems were rooted with individuals, rather than stemming from failures in society.

However, it was acknowledged that some people fell into poverty as a result of genuine misfortune or circumstances not of their own making. This led to a distinction that is characteristic of the moralising approach to philanthropy of the early Victorians, and which remains contentious even today: that between the 'deserving' and 'undeserving' poor. Deciding which side of this line particular poor individuals sat on, and how to design philanthropy so that it benefited the deserving poor without providing the undeserving poor with a means to indulge their wilful indigence, was a question that greatly concerned the donors of the period because so many of them *'frowned on almsgiving, and tended to judge charitable efforts by their success in encouraging recipients to stand on their own feet'.*[413] For these donors, charity was not only a *'response to human need'*, but also *'an instrument for inculcating approved social attitudes'.*[414]

As detailed in Chapter 1, the zenith of this morally judgmental approach to philanthropy can perhaps be seen in the work of the Charity Organisation Society (COS), which not only advocated a very hard-line view on the distinction between the deserving and undeserving poor, but also argued that the failures of the Poor Laws and of philanthropists to rigorously enforce this distinction was one of the major causes of ongoing poverty. The work of the COS and its most famous leader, Charles Loch, therefore *'rested on the thesis that pauperism (and to a considerable extent, poverty) was the result of moral weakness on the part of the individual. When . . . the Charity Organisers talked, as they frequently did, of getting at 'causes' rather than mere 'symptoms', they were not thinking of what a later generation might consider causes, but simply of the individual, his family situation, his habits, and other personal factors'.*[415]

Thomas John Barnardo.
Photograph by Stepney
Causeway Studio.

The COS spent a lot of time trying to demonstrate the 'proper' way to address poverty – namely by addressing the moral failing that it was assumed must be the underlying cause – and to this end, the organisation did many things that made it increasingly unpopular. In particular, it launched a series of highly critical attacks on other philanthropists and philanthropic organisations whose methods it felt to be the 'wrong' ones. Most notable was an extraordinary attack on Dr Barnardo, who remains famous to this day (via the charity that bears his name) for his efforts to deal with homelessness and poverty among the children of London. The COS launched a highly personal assault on Barnardo through a series of allegations of impropriety, which led the trustees of his charity to conduct a full investigation. Barnardo was cleared of all serious charges, although his case was not helped by the fact that *'his . . . medical degree was shown to be of the mail-order variety'.*[416]

Despite the undermining of his credentials, Barnardo survived the assault. The reputation of the COS took a buffeting, however. Its extreme moralising approach *'helped to fasten . . . its reputation as a charity kill-joy more interested in checking inefficient philanthropy than in promoting positive efforts'.*[417]

The COS's views, and in particular the controversial distinction between the 'deserving' and 'undeserving' poor, is not merely a historical curiosity. It is a recurrent theme in discussions of government attitudes to welfare spending: in 2011, for instance, the then Archbishop of Canterbury, Dr Rowan Williams, warned against what he saw as the *'quiet resurgence of the seductive language of "deserving" and "undeserving" poor'*[418] in government pronouncements on welfare. The example of the COS provides a clear lesson in the dangers of applying such a moralistic view of poverty to philanthropy.

Philanthropy and the brands that built Britain: good journeys

Thomas Cook, 1892.

Popular tourism in the UK has clear philanthropic origins, thanks to the involvement of one man: Thomas Cook, of the eponymous travel agency that is still one of the most famous in the world. Cook was a cabinet-maker and ardent temperance supporter, who strongly believed that almost all the problems besetting the working classes were down to the demon drink. One day he was walking from Market Harborough, where he lived, to a temperance meeting in nearby Leicester, and was struck by a thought about *'the practicability of employing the great powers of railways and locomotion for the furtherance of this social reform'*.[419]

Acting on this inspiration, Cook organised his first publicly advertised excursion: taking 540 temperance campaigners from Leicester to a rally in Loughborough (12 miles away) for the price of one shilling per head. Emboldened by the success of this experiment, Cook went on to organise a range of excursions around the Midlands over the following years, primarily for temperance groups and Sunday schools. This was a purely philanthropic endeavour, as he made no money from any of the trips.

In 1845, Cook embarked on his first commercial venture: a train trip to Liverpool. For this he charged 15 shillings for first class passengers and 10 shillings for second, and he also produced a pamphlet detailing his research about the route and the destination – the world's first holiday brochure. From this beginning, the commercial travel business grew and grew, and

Cook's profile rose even further when in 1851 Joseph Paxton, architect of the Crystal Palace, persuaded him to devote himself to bringing workers from Yorkshire and the Midlands to London for the Great Exhibition.

Composite image of the four friezes on the front of the Thomas Cook Building in Leicester, England. The panels depict excursions offered by the travel company.

Cook eventually expanded to tours around the whole of the UK and Ireland and in 1855 he took his first group of tourists to the continent. Although by now this was very much a commercial operation, Cook continued to see the company as a vehicle for his own philanthropic activities and a way to push the message of temperance. However, his son, John Mason Cook, who also worked for the business, did not share his views on these matters, and this was a source of great disagreement between the two men. Both Thomas Cook and his son died in the 1890s, and the company passed to John Mason Cook's sons. At this point the link with the firm's philanthropic origins was severed, although the company itself continued to play a key role in the social history of Britain throughout the 20th century.

Guilt

Gradually, as the scale of social problems became clear, the view that poverty was a moral failing of the individual began to recede. A growing number of affluent people saw poverty as a failing of society, and philanthropy as part of a strong obligation to address this failing. This obligation might have been religious or secular in nature, but it was fundamentally linked to a realisation that society is unavoidably interconnected and one therefore has responsibilities to those less fortunate than oneself. This sense of responsibility was often accompanied by a sort of guilt or existential angst that made the philanthropy into a deeply personal mission.

For instance, the founder of the temperance movement in Scotland, John Dunlop, was so consumed by his concern about drunkenness that he suffered physical symptoms. He recalled that he '*got no sleep except dozing all night, and dreamed of drunken women and boys, till I overheard myself groaning, so that I was afraid I might disturb those that slept in the next room'*.[420] The historian and social reformer Arnold Toynbee captured this palpable sense of guilt felt by many of the affluent in the later Victorian period – and their desire to distance themselves from what they saw as the negative approaches to philanthropy taken by their forebears – when he said in a speech to a working-class audience:

> '*We – the middle classes, I mean, not merely the very rich – we neglected you; instead of justice we have offered you charity, and instead of sympathy we have offered you hard and unreal advice, but I think we are changing . . . You have to forgive us, for we have wronged you; we have sinned against you grievously – not knowingly always, but still we have sinned, and let us confess it; but if you will forgive us . . . we will devote our lives to your service.'*[421]

Fear of unrest

As well as enlightened self-interest in trying to sculpt society according to one's own moral views, or assuaging one's own guilt about the inherent unfairness of the world, there is another form of self-interest that has driven philanthropy and is based on a far simpler motivation: fear. At various times in our history, the wealthy and those in power have had a tangible fear that the scale of poverty and social unrest in the country would give rise to rebellion among the poor and so threaten their own position and livelihood. Philanthropy was seen as an important tool for quelling unrest and thereby ensuring one's own safety and security and that of the realm.

The enthusiasm for charitable giving among Tudor monarchs, for instance, was arguably underpinned by such concerns of political expediency, which meant that '*their steady concern with the eroding poverty of their age proceeded not from any sentimental concern for the poor but rather from an astute understanding that unrelieved, uncontrolled want constituted a grave threat to the stability of the realm. It is not too much to say that the Tudors viewed charity as a necessary aspect of public policy rather than as a requirement of Christian morality'.*[422] For those in government and for individual wealthy citizens, therefore, *'paternalism and philanthropy . . . might be a way of upholding law and order, and protecting property from attack. They might also be a means of defending the established social order, to which most philanthropists belonged, against radical criticism'.*[423]

This calculating approach to philanthropy, driven by fear of the poor and a desire to appease unrest, is seen even more strongly in the 18th century. The political unrest in France that eventually gave rise to the French Revolution was a source of grave concern for the upper classes in England, and many of them sensed that there were likely to be *'imminent and important changes in the political and social structure of the nation'.*[424] Some even *'feared an impending war between the haves and have nots'.*[425] In this context, philanthropy took on a new importance. For some, this reflected a positive sense that philanthropy was a force for good in difficult times. The *Charity Record & Philanthropic News* commented that benevolence helped *'crush out that class feeling which at times threatens to turn this England of ours into two hostile camps',*[426] while the philanthropist Jonas Hanway thought *'the role of charity was central [because] only charity could mediate between rich and poor and act as a counterbalance to 'all the evil passions of envy, covetousness, revenge, so frequent, so pernicious'.*[427] Charity thus offered the *'only . . . possible remedy for "the hunger of the poor crying aloud"'.*[428]

For others, however, while philanthropy was an important tool to quell unrest, it was more about suppressing the poor than supporting them. Hence their giving was *'to a degree, insurance against revolution, a means of keeping the populace, if not contented, at least reasonably submissive'* and as a result *'even in the hands of those whose intentions were above reproach, seemed to take on a cautious and calculating, almost harsh, tone'.*[429] While it had long been the case that *'the ruling classes largely took it for granted that deference would flow from their philanthropy',*[430] it was only when social tensions were brought to boiling point by events like the French Revolution or the Napoleonic Wars that '*they openly expressed a desire to subordinate the lower classes through charitable agencies*'.[431]

Fear of unrest as a motivating force for philanthropy ebbed and flowed with the prevailing social mood, but it never really went away. In the Victorian era, there was often concern about aspects of poverty that reflected the specific fears of the middle and upper classes. For instance, '*concern was often expressed about the rough living and working conditions of the railway navvies*' and while this was '*partly influenced by a genuine religious or humanitarian solicitude that men should have to live in such circumstances*', it was also driven by '*the widespread fear that bands of navvies – whose style of life was, to say the least, robust – might constitute a threat to public order and to property as they move around the countryside*'.[432]

Although the element of fear motivating philanthropy was often unspoken, many were well aware of it and some of the biggest names in the philanthropy world of the 19th century had little or no compunction about exploiting these fears. Thomas Barnardo, for example, '*was well aware of the role of philanthropy in staving off social unrest . . . and he used this argument to add to others in his appeals for funds*'.[433] He made the case for the importance of his own work by arguing that '*every boy rescued from the gutter . . . is one dangerous man the less*', and that he feared there would come a time '*when this seething mass of human misery will shake the social fabric, unless we grapple more earnestly with it than we have yet done*'.[434]

We have already seen that by the end of the Victorian era, most had abandoned the idea that philanthropy could provide an effective solution to the problems of poverty. But it did not seem to be particularly effective as a means of quelling unrest in the long term either, as the underlying tensions between rich and poor only intensified as time wore on. At the start of the 20th century, future Prime Minister Winston Churchill argued:

> '*The greatest danger to the British Empire and to the British people is not to be found among the enormous fleets and armies of the European Continent, nor in the solemn problems of Hindustan . . . nor any danger in the wide circuit of colonial and foreign affairs. No, it is here in our midst, close at home, close at hand in the vast growing cities of England and Scotland, and in the dwindling and cramped villages of our denuded countryside. It is there you will find the seeds of Imperial ruin and national*

decay – the unnatural gap between rich and poor . . . the awful jumbles of an obsolete Poor Law, the constant insecurity in the means of subsistence and employment which breaks the heart of many a sober, hard-working man, the absence of any established minimum standard of life and comfort among the workers, and, at the other end, the swift increase of vulgar, joyless luxury – here are the enemies of Britain. Beware lest they shatter the foundations of her power.'[435]

Implications for future philanthropy

The relationship between inequality and philanthropy is a complex one, and continues to present a challenge to philanthropists today. On the one hand philanthropy is seen as a tool to address inequality, because it offers a means for redistribution from the wealthy in society to those who have far less. On the other, however, inequality is a necessary condition for philanthropy to exist in the first place, as it requires that there be haves and have-nots. While the rich might not be entirely to blame for society's failure to distribute wealth more evenly, the very fact that they are rich while others are poor is the root of the problem. Furthermore, the ways in which those at the top of society have amassed their wealth (and indeed, the ways they choose to spend it) may well exacerbate the situation by perpetuating structures that create further inequality.

This does not mean that philanthropy aimed at addressing poverty and inequality cannot be successful. But we cannot assume that it will be so automatically, without careful consideration of the right approach to take. In pragmatic terms, our only real option is to work with the world as we find it, rather than railing against the system that allows inequality to exist while denouncing the efforts of those who are trying to do something to mitigate it.[436] This means finding ways of doing philanthropy that minimise its contribution to the problem of inequality, while maximising its impact on the underlying causes. This is clearly a huge challenge, but the recent prominence of inequality as an issue on the global political agenda shows that it is one we must face up to.

CHAPTER FIVE

Criticisms of philanthropy

Philanthropy has often been a powerful force for good in our country, and has played a major role in shaping the society we live in today. The contention of this book is that it should continue to play an important role in modern Britain, and that by looking at some of the key issues facing philanthropy through a historical lens we will get a much better understanding of what that role should be. But philanthropy has also come in for its fair share of criticism over the years. *The Atlantic* magazine noted in an article about the history of criticisms of philanthropy in the US: *'The debate about the legitimacy of large benefactions became so heated that in 1909 one New Orleans newspaper quipped that philanthropy had become "the recognisable mark of a wicked man".'*[437] While we may not have reached this point in the UK, criticism of philanthropy has still been widespread and has taken various forms, many of which have already been discussed in this book. However, we can also distinguish some broader recurring themes. It is only by understanding these criticisms and seeing how they might be overcome that we can successfully craft a positive narrative about the role of philanthropy as a force for good in society.

'Philanthropy is ineffective'

Perhaps the criticism most often levelled at philanthropy is that it is simply not effective as a way of dealing with social problems. This seems fairly stark and straightforward, but in fact this censure is more complex than

it first appears. It can take many forms – some merely attack the way philanthropy is done in practice, while others challenge the very notion of
philanthropy as an enterprise.

Macro-level criticism of effectiveness

As detailed in Chapter 2, the failure of philanthropy to meet the welfare
needs of society adequately at the end of the 19th century was a large part
of the impetus for the creation of the welfare state. Some saw this failure as
evidence of a fundamental flaw in philanthropy. They concluded that philanthropy could never be an effective way of meeting need because even if
individual charitable interventions were effective, overall it was just not up
to the scale of the challenge. For instance, *The Guardian* in 1891 carried
the following withering attack on the notion of philanthropy as a remedy for
social ills:

> 'It cannot be too strongly asserted that there is no heroic solution of the
> social problem in any degree possible. Indeed, the very expression "social
> problem", where it is not merely rhetorical, is to be deprecated, for it encour-
> ages in the public mind that radical misconception of the subject-matter
> of religion and philanthropy, which thinks of it, speaks of it, and proposes
> to deal with it, as something simple, measurable, and defined, a rotten
> limb which may be amputated, not a subtle poison diffused through the
> whole body. There is no "social problem", but there is an infinitely complex
> network of social relationships existing under abnormal and perplexing
> conditions, and deriving from them elements of special danger and dif-
> ficulty. Heroic remedies ignore the character of the disease which they
> pretend to cure. They are naturally confined to social quacks, whose igno-
> rance may be honest, but is always profound, and whose confidence is
> invariably absolute. Any scheme or project which proposes a solution of
> the entire "social problem" is self-condemned.'[438]

Others have drawn similarly critical conclusions from a historical perspective about the Victorian notion of philanthropy as a panacea. Benjamin
Kirkman Gray, in his posthumously published 1908 book *Philanthropy
and the State* (which he had apparently toyed with calling *The Failures of
Philanthropy*) echoed *The Guardian*'s conclusions, pointing out: 'A century
ago philanthropy was regarded as having what would now be called a
socio-political function . . . [and that] conception was a possible one, so

long as the extent of the problem was not recognised.' However, he argued: 'As knowledge of social facts became more complete and precise, so it began to appear that private corporations could not adequately deal with difficulties which result not from personal but from public causes, and which are as extensive as society itself.'[439]

He went on to accuse Victorian philanthropists of hubris for believing that 'it was theirs to heal the hurts of the people'. He notes: 'They were ready at any moment and without training to run the longest race ... Private individuals were confident of their power to discharge a public function, and the government was willing to have it so.' Eventually, however, 'it was left to experience to determine that the work was ill done and was by no means equal to the need'.[440]

Historian David Owen, writing in 1961, came to a similar conclusion, albeit less harshly-phrased, about the overall success of the grand edifice of Victorian philanthropy. He argued: 'As measured against the problem, voluntary effort was performing no miracle. It had not succeeded in bridging the gap between rich and poor, if, indeed, this had been a serious aim, nor had it taken more than a tentative step or two toward civilising the brutish masses or improving their material environment ... Taken all in all, however hesitant and muddled their work may have been, public authorities did more to improve city life than did private charity.'[441]

The question of the macro-level effectiveness of philanthropy as a means of meeting the welfare needs of society is considered primarily in the context of the Victorian era because that was the only time – in our country at least – that there was a real attempt to test this approach. Most would agree that the experiment was a failure; perhaps a glorious failure, but a failure nonetheless. And the lesson we take from this failure is largely up to us. There are those who have seen it as conclusive proof of an inherent flaw in philanthropy. Kirkman Gray, for instance, drew the conclusion that philanthropy was doomed to failure because it could never keep pace with need. He argued: 'On the one side is charity, full of generous impulses, though shrinking from the appropriate hard means; on the other the interminable ranks of the ragged army of sorrow; individuals come and go, pass across our field of vision and vanish from sight, while others always continually supply their place ... The want, which charity, not always unavailingly, has endeavoured to assuage, does nevertheless renew itself with perpetual iteration.'[442] And he wondered why, given this ongoing imbalance, people persisted with philanthropy, asking: *'Whence then this strange entangle-ment around the action of pity, so that the thing desired is never the thing done? What explanation may be given of the contradiction, growing ever more sharp, between the needs of the needy and the spirit of humanity?'*[443]

This is essentially the same argument put forward by the Mexican bil-lionaire Carlos Slim Helú, currently the world's richest man, who has been criticised widely for his lacklustre approach to philanthropy. Part of his reasoning for not having made greater efforts when it comes to charitable giving, despite the high-profile achievements of his peers such as Bill Gates and Warren Buffett, is that he is sceptical about the macro-level effective-ness of philanthropy. He argues: *'We have seen donations for 100 years . . . We have seen thousands of people working in non-profits, and the problems and poverty are bigger. They have not solved anything.'*[444] This led Slim Helú to maintain for many years that he could *'do more good by building solid companies than by "going around like Santa Claus" donating money'*.[445] This echoes very clearly the view of American oil tycoon J Paul Getty, who said: *'If I were convinced that by giving away my fortune I could make a real contribution towards solving the problems of world poverty, I'd give away 99.5% immediately. But a hard-eyed appraisal of the situation convinces me that this is not the case. The best form of charity I know is the art of meeting a payroll.'*[446]

Implications for future philanthropy

It is not necessary to draw quite such gloomy conclusions about philan-thropy, however. The lesson from its failure to deliver effective universal welfare or solve all of the world's problems need not be that it is a flawed concept. Rather, these expectations are unfounded: philanthropy is not an appropriate tool to deliver such a national system of welfare services and neither can it solve all of society's problems by itself. As argued in Chapter 2, philanthropy is unable to meet requirements like guaranteeing universality and equity, and voluntary giving is not of the right degree of magnitude to be properly comparable to public spending in any case. But since neither the state nor the private sector has been successful in eradicating need despite hundreds of years of trying, it is hard to see why we should expect the philanthropic sector to have fared any better. Philanthropy has had some notable successes, but it cannot work miracles.

None of the intractable problems in society today are likely to be solved by any one sector acting on its own. It will only be when we find a way of effectively combining the best of the public, private and philanthropic sectors to address some of these issues, which have multiple, complex causes, that we stand a chance of overcoming them. The role of philanthropy is not, therefore, to provide an alternative to taxation-funded public services, or to the market, but to supplement both and bring its own unique strengths to efforts to address the problems facing society. How we make this collaboration and cooperation happen in practice is a challenge that policymakers and practitioners need to address.

Micro-level criticism of effectiveness

The macro-level criticism outlined above still allows that the majority of (or indeed all) individual philanthropic efforts may be effective; it just argues that they do not add up to a sufficient whole. However, many have also criticised individual philanthropic efforts themselves, on the basis that they are perpetuating interventions or remedies for which there is little or no evidence of success, and which are argued to be totally ineffective in delivering the desired outcomes (or, in some cases, even actively harmful).

This is clearly not an argument against philanthropy as a whole; merely against certain approaches to it. As discussed earlier, this was part of the rationale behind the 'scientific' philanthropy movement epitomised by the Charity Organisation Society, which held nothing back in criticising what it viewed as the ill-guided and ineffective charity of others, and saw itself very much as an antidote to such wrong-headedness. This sort of normative approach, which distinguishes between 'good' and 'bad' philanthropy on the grounds of effectiveness, is very much in evidence today. In fact, it may have found its purest expression in the 'effective altruism' movement that has evolved from the work of philosopher Peter Singer.[447] Plenty of people are sold on the idea that we should use data and evidence to determine how best to address particular social issues, but effective altruism goes one step further and argues that the cause to which you give should be determined by the numerical evidence of where the most social good can be produced.[448] In effect, it postulates that some causes are better than others.

Effective altruism is interesting because it has provoked great controversy, even among those who firmly believe in the importance of effectiveness in philanthropy,[449] in much the same way that the Charity

Organisation Society made waves in Victorian philanthropic circles. This just goes to show that a positive motivation – in this case to ensure maximum impact by applying rigour to charitable giving – can have unintended negative consequences if applied in the wrong way (for instance, if organisations are deemed to be dogmatic or overly-judgmental of the philanthropic efforts of others). As argued in Chapter 1, the desire to make philanthropy rigorous could damage it by stifling the motivations that lie at its core, or introduce sectarian divisions between organisations and individuals who might otherwise be working towards a common cause.

Moral criticism of effectiveness

Some have taken the normative approach to philanthropy further by incorporating a moral argument. For such critics, ineffective philanthropy is not just bad because it fails to achieve results; it is reprehensible because it embodies a moral failing. This 'moral failing' is usually tied to a belief in the distinction between the deserving and undeserving poor. The argument is that philanthropy which fails to acknowledge this distinction rewards those who have 'chosen' to live off handouts (the 'undeserving poor') just as much as those who find themselves in poverty through no fault of their own (the 'deserving poor'), and thereby removes the incentive for the poor to 'better themselves'.

Alexis de Tocqueville is most often cited for his enthusiastic comments about voluntary association in the US in *Democracy in America*. But he presented a much less appealing side of himself in putting a vehement case against the moral evil of indiscriminate charity in his *Memoir on Pauperism*:

> 'Man, like all socially organised beings, has a natural passion for idleness. There are, however, two incentives to work: the need to live and the desire to improve the conditions of life. Experience has proven that the majority of men can be sufficiently motivated to work only by the first of these incentives. The second is only effective with a small minority. Well, a charitable institution indiscriminately open to all those in need, or a law which gives all the poor a right to public aid, whatever the origin of their poverty, weakens or destroys the first stimulant and leaves only the second intact. The English peasant, like the Spanish peasant, if he does not feel the deep desire to better the position into which he has been born, and to raise himself out of his misery (a feeble desire which is easily crushed in the

majority of men) – the peasant of both countries, I maintain, has no interest in working, or, if he works, has no interest in saving. He therefore remains idle or thoughtlessly squanders the fruits of his labours.'[450]

Alexis de Tocqueville.

As we have seen, this moral point of view was put into practice by the Charity Organisation Society, which *'pushed its crusade against mendacity, indiscriminate almsgiving, and laxity in Poor Law administration with enormous zeal . . . secure in the fashionable thesis that ill-considered and unsystematic philanthropy was the chief source of pauperism'.*[451] Even though many disagreed with the COS's approach, and with the underlying notion that there are 'deserving' and 'undeserving' poor people, most would agree that indiscriminate charity is not ideal because it necessarily implies a certain amount of wastefulness, and we should be seeking to eradicate such waste. There have been those, however, who are willing to defend indiscriminate charity, on the grounds that it is preferable to the alternative of overly-discriminating charity. The 19th century cleric Cardinal Manning, for instance, declared that he *'welcomed indiscriminate charity as the lightening conductor which saves us'*, and that *'as to waste and wisdom [of donations]'*, he was *'content that many unworthy should share rather than one worthy case be without help'.*[452]

The moral criticism was taken even further by those such as the economist JA Hobson, who no longer characterised the failing as one of 'bad' philanthropy, but as an inherent failing of philanthropy of any kind. Hobson argued: *'It is more socially injurious for the millionaire to spend his surplus wealth in charity than in luxury . . . for by spending it on luxury, he chiefly injures himself and his immediate circle, but by spending it in charity he inflicts a graver injury upon society.'* His central thesis was that charity undermines the drive for self-advancement and improvement that is necessary for a true solution to the problem of poverty. Charity, he argued, *'weaken[s] the personal springs of social reform, alike by the "miraculous" relief it brings to the individual "case" that is relieved, and by the softening influence it exercises on the hearts and heads of those who witness it . . . It [thus] substitutes the idea and the desire of individual reform for those of social reform, and so weakens the capacity for collective self-help in society'.*[453]

Some may find this moral criticism of charity compelling, depending on their views about poverty and individual responsibility. To many people, the more extreme forms of this moral position almost certainly seem unpalatable. However, in more restrained forms it is an argument that we still see today, when people accuse charity of creating and perpetuating dependency.[454]

The Malthusian criticism of effectiveness

Thomas Robert Malthus,
by John Linnell, 1833.

Even the extreme form of the moral criticism outlined above is topped by the nihilistic argument occasionally put forward by those who subscribe to the teachings of the population theorist Thomas Robert Malthus.[455] These critics also contend that philanthropy is morally questionable, but not because it is ineffective – rather, precisely because it *is* effective. By saving the lives of people who might otherwise die due to poverty or disease, it is argued, philanthropists are adding to the problem of unsustainable population growth, which Malthus identified as the greatest threat to society. As a consequence, they are not really helping those who are the recipients of their efforts – merely condemning them to prolonged misery. The 19th century Liberal and economic journalist Walter Bagehot took such a misanthropic point of view, arguing: *'Great good, no doubt, philanthropy does, but then it also does great evil. It augments so much vice, it multiplies so much suffering, it brings to life such great populations to suffer and be vicious, that it is open to argument whether it be or be not an evil to the world.'*[456]

Although many have rejected Malthus' original analysis, the arguments at the core of his work have continued to generate much debate over the last 200 years. There is even a broad school of 'neo-Malthusian' thought, which takes as its starting point the hypothesis that unchecked population growth is unsustainable, and attempts to develop arguments that go beyond those available to Malthus in the early 18th century.[457] However, while population growth is still very much a current issue, it is unusual for charity or philanthropy nowadays to be criticised on these grounds. The idea of deliberately withholding assistance from those in need would be extremely unpalatable to most modern audiences.

'Philanthropy is inefficient'

Slightly different to the idea that philanthropy is ineffective, but still occupying similar territory, is the criticism that it is *inefficient*. Proponents of this view allow that philanthropy may well be able to achieve social goals, but argue that the way philanthropy works in practice means that it takes greater resources to do so than is necessary. Once again there are both macro- and micro-level interpretations of this criticism: the former contends that the philanthropy marketplace as a whole is inefficient, while the latter focuses on the perceived inefficiencies of specific philanthropic initiatives.

Market-level inefficiency

The accusation that there are 'too many charities' and that they are guilty of duplicating each other's efforts and thereby reducing the efficiency of the philanthropic sector as a whole has been levelled by critics many times over the years. We still hear it aired today with reliable regularity,[458] but there have been times in history when the issue was felt far more keenly.

Inefficiency was a source of great concern to many in the Victorian era. They worried that although significant amounts of money were being given to charitable causes, the range of organisations making up the philanthropic sector was so great in number and divergent in quality that a lot of this money was wasted. Hence, *'the charity [world], they insisted, [was] full of small, inefficient, redundant agencies, which had yielded no benefits proportional to their number and to the pounds, shillings and pence collected for them'.*[459]

A particularly pressing problem for the Victorians was the growing number of obsolete charitable trusts. These were legal structures set up on the bequest of a donor to provide funds for some specified charitable purpose, but where that purpose had subsequently become redundant. There was a mechanism for overcoming this problem: the so-called 'cy-près' rule, which allowed trustees to use funds to address charitable purposes that were sufficiently close in spirit to the original donor's wishes where possible. However, many of these 'zombie' trusts had purposes that were so specific and obscure that it was impossible in practice to apply a cy-près approach. So there were a growing number of charities in Victorian England that no longer had a purpose, but whose incomes continued to rise through the interest they earned.

There are many weird and wonderful examples of these sorts of trusts, which give some sense of why people were struggling so much with the tension between respecting the wishes of donors in the past and meeting the needs of the present. Examples include:

- Funds to support sermons celebrating the defeat of the Spanish Armada and the failure of the Gunpowder Plot.[460]
- Various funds for the ransoming of Christian captives from the Turks or Barbary pirates.[461]
- A charitable trust solely dedicated to providing funds for killing ladybirds on Cornhill, in the City of London.[462]
- A trust whose purpose was to maintain an oil lamp at the corner of Billingsgate 'for ever'.[463]
- A (possibly apocryphal) fund to buy faggots of wood for burning heretics.[464]

The problem was particularly acute in London, which was awash with such oddball bequests and funds. And this was a source of great annoyance to those in the capital who were expending a great deal of energy trying to fundraise, as all the time they could see this growing pot of money set aside for charitable causes, yet tantalisingly beyond their reach. Eventually, the problem got so bad that a Parliamentary Inquiry was established to look into it. This led to the introduction of new legislation, which imbued the Charity Commissioners with enhanced powers in the case of City parochial charities (of which there were over 1300). The Commissioners were now, for the first time, permitted to ignore founders' wishes and proceed on a utilitarian basis in freeing up the money in these trusts for good causes. The process of doing this turned out to be exceedingly complex, and took nearly a decade. The end result was the consolidation of the existing dormant charities into a single fund (the City Parochial Foundation, which survives to this day as Trust for London[465]), which immediately made a series of significant grants. Although this was designed to deflect any criticism by releasing funds as quickly as possible, it was only partly successful. There were still many who had concerns that the City Parochial Foundation represented a dangerous precedent in its ability to override the wishes of donors after the event.

The problem of obsolete or awkwardly-defined charities did not disappear with the formation of the City Parochial Foundation, and continued to be a source of frustration well into the 20th century. In Beveridge's 1948 book *Voluntary Action,* for instance, an appendix is dedicated to the issue of obsolete charitable trusts, which even contains a 'Charities' Chamber of Horrors' detailing particularly egregious examples of the genre.[466] As an example, take The Brown Animal Sanatory Institution, highlighted in the case study below.

CASE STUDY

The Brown Animal Sanatory Institution[467]

Thomas Brown died in 1852 and left property worth more than £20,000 to the University of London to found an institution for studying and treating (for free) diseases in animals or birds 'useful to man'. This in itself would have been fine, but unfortunately he added additional stipulations that it had to be 'within a mile of Westminster, Southwark or Dublin', and that if the University of London did not use the money within 19 years (or used it improperly), it should instead go the University of Dublin for the exclusive purpose of establishing professorships in *'at least three of the following languages: Welsh, Slavonic, Russian, Persian, Chinese, Coptic and Sanskrit'.*[468]

The University of London quickly realised that Brown's first condition was going to be almost impossible to meet (particularly because the terms of the bequest explicitly forbade the use of any part of the fund to purchase either a leasehold or freehold interest in land in England, so they would have to find a way of purchasing suitable land separately). At that point an unedifying three-way legal battle ensued: between Brown's heirs, who claimed that the whole bequest was invalid, the University of London, who proposed that it should be allowed to keep the money but use it in a more effective manner, and the University of Dublin, who argued that as the first criterion in the bequest could not legally be met, it should receive the money immediately instead.

The Brown Institution, Vauxhall, for the study and treating of diseases in animals or birds 'useful to man'.

The University of London won the case, and then sat on the money for the maximum term of 19 years. It did eventually build an institution in line with Brown's wishes, but it was clear that the original stated purpose of the bequest was out-dated (for one thing, the number of animals in central London had fallen significantly by this point).

The animal hospital was closed at the outbreak of the Second World War and subsequently destroyed in an air raid. There then followed a further 25 years of legal wrangling about what to do with the remaining charitable funds (as the University of

London had not spent the full amount on the original hospital). It was eventually decided that they should be shared between the University of London and Trinity College Dublin, which finally happened in 1971 – 120 years after Thomas Brown's bequest was made.

Implications for future philanthropy

Although systematic regulation of charities has done a lot to overcome the problems caused by obsolete or ill-considered charities, market-level inefficiency remains a challenge for the voluntary sector in the UK, as it does for philanthropic sectors around the world. There is a difficult balance to strike between preventing undesirable proliferation and duplication, and respecting the right of individuals to come together and set up an organisation to address a cause in which they have a shared belief. At the end of the day, philanthropy is an unavoidably voluntary activity, based on the free choices of individuals and communities. If this means that there is some inefficiency in the overall marketplace of philanthropic organisations, then maybe we just have to accept that. Perhaps the lesson is simply that we must adjust our expectations of what an optimal philanthropic sector looks like.

Organisational inefficiency

The claim that philanthropy is inefficient, because individual charitable organisations waste money on things like fundraising or administration, is still heard with depressing regularity.[469] But, like so many things about philanthropy, it is far from new. There were many in the heyday of Victorian philanthropy who suggested that a significant amount of money was spent by charities on things that benefited themselves or their donors, rather than their supposed beneficiaries:

'The numerous charity balls, philanthropic dinners and conversaziones, the pretentious central offices, the pages of print devoted to lists of subscriptions, the elegant membership cards – the very organisation of the philanthropic world itself (not to speak of the causes on which its resources were spent) all ensured that such redistribution of the national income as did take place in the 19th century gave pleasure to and even financially profited many of the not-so-poor before it finally filtered down to those in

real need. Any modern visitor to the London headquarters of the British and Foreign Bible Society, for instance, finds himself amid an architectural splendour worthy of the Medici in their most palmy days.'[470]

Implications for future philanthropy

It is impossible to offer a knock-down argument against this criticism, because there is undoubtedly an element of truth in it: some charities, past or present, do spend their money wastefully. But then this is not a problem unique to charities – the same is true of any sector, as there will always be organisations that either deliberately or unintentionally mismanage their financial affairs. The important thing is that critics do not extrapolate from isolated incidents to a general argument that all charitable endeavours are wasteful. And charities must continue to demonstrate that this is not the case by providing evidence that they are using the donations they receive in an appropriate way.

As argued in Chapter 1, if charities fail to face up to this challenge, then donors will simply decide for themselves how to determine which organisations are effective. This may mean that they rely on unhelpful metrics such as administration costs or salary levels to make their decisions, which will benefit neither donors nor charities. Not only are these poor measures of the actual effectiveness of an organisation (see Chapter 1 for further detail), but often people are basing their decisions on perception rather than actual data anyway. For instance, over half of the UK public believe that charities spend too much on salaries and administration,[471] but it is also clear that people tend to overestimate quite badly the proportion of charitable money that is actually spent on such things.[472]

'Philanthropy is conventional or lacking in ambition'

Philanthropy has occasionally come under fire for becoming trapped in convention or stifled by lack of ambition. Given that one of the things most often cited as the *raison d'être* of philanthropy is its ability to fund unfashionable causes or take on issues that have not yet made it onto the mainstream political agenda, this is a particularly damaging accusation.

Despite the plaudits we often bestow on the Victorians for their philanthropic culture, some have argued that the quantity of their giving was not matched by their level of imagination when it came to picking causes or organisations. Rather, it is claimed, '*the chief impression left by late-century bequests is not that of eccentricity but of conventionality*'. If we examine wills from the Victorian period, '*few . . . contained anything particularly venturesome or imaginative. Money went, on the whole, to maintain established institutions or to create new ones of the same sort. Hospitals, orphanages, almshouses, church organisations, such eminently respectable national charities as the RSPCA and the RNLI – these were the philanthropies that commonly figured in wills, together with an occasional public park, gift to a library or art gallery, or scholarship or university chair*'.[473]

Some contemporary critics, frustrated by this perceived lack of imagination and ambition, fell back on the 'if in doubt, compare the UK unfavourably with the US' approach. Owen notes: '*There was dissatisfaction in some quarters over the behaviour of British philanthropists*' and that '*a critic might complain of the "great lack of originality on the part of rich men in the disposition of their wealth".*' *The Times* newspaper took a stance on this issue, and '*was inclined to credit American testators with greater liberality and more interesting ideas than their British counterparts. The bulk of British bequests, the editor insisted, came from childless persons, with no family responsibilities, and went for pretty conventional objects*'.[474]

The accusation of lacking ambition remains one of the most damning that can be levelled at philanthropy. It strikes at the very heart of one of philanthropy's main claims to importance and value – its ability to address causes that others will not take on, or address them in ways that others are unwilling to. If philanthropy is unwilling to break the bounds of convention or afraid to think beyond the *status quo*, then what is the point of it?

In the case of the Victorians, the criticism seems to be that most people were simply lacking imagination, so they went for obvious causes or organisations because that offered the path of least resistance. In more modern cases where we see people or organisations accused of lacking ambition, the criticism is often less about a lack of imagination than an unwillingness to take necessary risks. For instance, a 2012 report on philanthropy and risk in an international development context argued: '*Philanthropy offers genuine potential to actively seek opportunity (with its associated risk) and seek out creative solutions to the most intractable development and social problems . . . [but] in order to innovate, philanthropists need to be much more accepting of failure and recognise that to achieve large-scale change many of their resources may be wasted along the way. Occasional failure should be seen as the acceptable cost of innovation.'* Unfortunately, however, the same report concluded: *'There is evidence that philanthropists are not willing to take the risks they could with their philanthropy.'*[475] And this conclusion was backed up by research from the Bank of America, who found in a survey of wealthy US donor households that only 2.3% were willing to 'take substantial financial risk' in their philanthropy.[476]

Some have suggested that this risk aversion is an unintended consequence of the demands for a more rigorous, strategic approach to philanthropy. Their argument is that because such a strong emphasis is placed on measurable evidence of 'impact', donors are driven to support established, lower-risk programmes rather than untested innovations where the risk of failure may be very high. For instance, an article in the *Stanford Social Innovation Review* in 2014 suggested: *'Over the last decade, many funders have lost their appetite for experimentation and risk, even as they trumpet their desire to make big bets. The strategic philanthropy movement has swept across the field and helped funders align their programmes and grantmaking with carefully designed theories of change to produce clear and quantifiable results. But the pendulum may now be swinging too far, to a place where foundations are willing to support only safe, established programmes.'*[477]

Implications for future philanthropy

This highlights one of the ongoing challenges for philanthropy: it is subject to myriad variables – economic, political, psychological or emotional. And many of them we do not even understand properly. This means that, as with any complex system, making changes in one area (even if those changes themselves seem positive) can have significant and unexpected impacts in other areas. This is something to continually guard against. If it is true that efforts to make philanthropy more rigorous are reducing the capacity of donors to take risks, this is a real source of concern. Risk taking, imagination and innovation are central to what makes philanthropy a valuable and positive force in our society, so we must do whatever we can to make sure that they are not stifled.

Samuel Morley: All the gear, but no ideas?

Samuel Morley, by Manesse.

Samuel Morley (1809–1886) was, in many ways, an unremarkable philanthropist. As heir to an established business and a man of strong religious convictions, he had the financial assets and moral framework common to many philanthropists of the Victorian era. The interest in Morley's case comes from two things: firstly, the criticism he attracted for his somewhat pedestrian approach, and secondly, the one time he deviated from his usual pattern, which gave rise to his most notable philanthropic legacy.

There is no doubt of Morley's generosity of spirit. He was clearly committed to philanthropy throughout his life, and it was said of him: *'Charity was no afterthought in the evening of a life given over . . . to building his fortune. His outlook on philanthropy, as on other matters, reflected his devout Nonconformist faith . . . To Morley with his convictions on Christian stewardship and his own simple, even austere, habits of life, charitable giving was a continuous obligation, not a single magnificent gesture.'* [478]

However, he gave little strategic thought to how his fortune could best be put to good use, choosing instead to be almost entirely responsive in his charitable giving. So, while he was known for his diligence and generosity in responding to fundraising requests, he was criticised after his death as an example of the lack of purpose displayed by many philanthropists at the time. *The Spectator* magazine, for instance, damned him with faint praise in concluding: *'Mr Samuel Morley was in no way a great man, belonging as he did essentially to the British middle class, sound in feeling, hard of head, and narrow in thought; but the general appreciation of him after his death is nevertheless well founded . . . If he took up a cause heartily, he spent on it not only money, but time, thought, energy, and that capacity for organisation which is the great money-makers' gift, and which seems often to relieve them from the necessity of possessing any high intellectual quality whatever.'*[479] *The Spectator's* ire seems not to have been particularly directed at Morley himself, but rather at a certain sort of unsophisticated approach to philanthropy that the magazine disapproved of, and which he was taken to exemplify. Hence it goes on to complain about *'the kind of catholicity which distinguishes English middle-class philanthropists. They seem to give to everything good, rather than to any cause; to find more pleasure in helping on everything they approve, than in carrying on any one work all by themselves'.*[480] This, *The Spectator* concludes, is the difference between the ideal of philanthropy and the reality, because *'the dreamer who dreams what he would do with money takes up "a cause" in his visions, and thinks it would, were he once rich, prove all-absorbing; but the actually rich philanthropist divides his benefactions, and finds so many objects deserving of help that he completes no single work at all'.*[481] And the article expresses the wish that *'we should like some day to see a Mr Morley concentrate his wealth and his powers on some immortal deed'.*[482]

The major irony is that the one philanthropic project Samuel Morley was involved with which has had the greatest lasting impact was also his biggest deviation from his normal patterns of giving: his support for the Old Vic theatre. This was an odd fit for Morley, the pious Christian, given that he had little interest in frivolity and that the Old Vic at this time enjoyed a less than salubrious reputation. Even the theatre's own official history admitted that it was *'fair to assume that it discharged its*

Caricature of Samuel Morley, by Adriano Cecioni for *Vanity Fair*, 1872.

functions of bar and brothel with something like the maximum of grossness'.[483] Morley's enthusiasm for supporting the Old Vic was initially prompted by a plan to reinvent it as a temperance music hall, but he ended up saving it from financial ruin in 1884 with a sizeable donation that secured its future.

This strange mismatched marriage of donor and cause means that the Old Vic survives to this day, and the name of Samuel Morley is still remembered, even though *'no doubt it would astonish the pious businessman to find himself remembered today as a kind of patron saint of the Old Vic, the single instance in which he deviated markedly from his established pattern of giving'.*[484]

'Philanthropy is patronising or dehumanising'

It has sometimes been said of philanthropy that it is not a desirable way to address social issues, because it is patronising or dehumanising from the point of view of beneficiaries. This can be framed as an overall criticism of philanthropy as an idea, if you accept that the relationship between donor and recipient is inherently and unavoidably one of patronage. Or it can be framed as a criticism of particular, 'bad' ways of doing philanthropy that embody unhealthy donor-beneficiary relationships, while allowing that there are 'good' ways that avoid these problems.

These sorts of criticisms are often levelled by those for whom class is a crucial issue (in particular, socialists and political radicals, because they believe that philanthropy helps to perpetuate broader attitudes and structures they would like to do away with). And perhaps they have a point: there have certainly been proponents of philanthropy who were quite open about the fact that they see its ability to reinforce existing social hierarchies as part of its appeal. The 18th century churchman Richard Grey, for example, argued: *'Charitable foundations . . . give the poor in general grateful and honourable sentiments of and inspire them with a proper Love and Reverence toward their Superiors, to see them thus Active and Solicitous for Their Good; and by consequence promote the Harmony and Subordination, in which the Peace and Happiness of Society consists.'*[485]

One of the most famous critics of charity on the grounds that it is degrading to the recipient was Oscar Wilde. He used his 1891 essay *The Soul of*

Man Under Socialism to argue that charity is a negative force because it allows people to turn their attentions towards addressing the symptoms of society's problems, rather than their root causes. For Wilde, the only real answer to these problems was the adoption of socialism:

> 'With admirable, though misdirected intentions, [philanthropists] very seri-ously and very sentimentally set themselves to the task of remedying the evils that they see. But their remedies do not cure the disease: they merely prolong it. Indeed, their remedies are part of the disease . . . They try to solve the problem of poverty, for instance, by keeping the poor alive; or, in the case of a very advanced school, by amusing the poor. But this is not a solution: it is an aggravation of the difficulty. The proper aim is to try and reconstruct society on such a basis that poverty will be impossible. And the altruistic virtues have really prevented the carrying out of this aim . . . Men who have really studied the problem and know the life – educated men who live in the East End – [are] coming forward and imploring the community to restrain its altruistic impulses of charity, benevolence, and the like. They do so on the ground that such charity degrades and demoralises. They are perfectly right. Charity creates a multitude of sins.'[486]

This socialist critique of philanthropy has been adopted in recent times by, among others, the Marxist philosopher and cultural critic Slavoj Žižek, who gave a lecture on the ethical implications of charity in which he quoted Wilde approvingly.[487]

For such socialist critics, although the objects of their ire are the capital-ist system and the wealthy individuals who (in their view) embody its failings, the poor are also to blame for some of the problems with philanthropy. By buying into the notion of charity, rather than taking a principled stand and refusing to engage with a system that is flawed, many of the poor, it is argued, are complicit in perpetuating society's problems. This was a core part of the doctrine of many Victorian political radicals, who *'incorporated this hatred of charity into their political creed – the dole was the poor man's equivalent of the hated upper-class pension'.*[488] The radical writer and jour-nalist William Godwin (the father of Mary Shelley, of *Frankenstein* fame) for instance, drew attention to *'the pauper fawning with abject vileness upon his rich benefactor, and speechless with sensations of gratitude for hav-ing received that, which he ought to have claimed with an erect mien, and with a consciousness that his claim was irresistible'.*[489] And Wilde made a similar point, distinguishing between what he saw as the 'right' and 'wrong' attitudes of the poor towards charity:

> 'We are often told that the poor are grateful for charity. Some of them are, no doubt, but the best amongst the poor are never grateful. They are ungrateful, discontented, disobedient, and rebellious. They are quite right to be so. Charity they feel to be a ridiculously inadequate mode of partial restitution, or a sentimental dole, usually accompanied by some impertinent attempt on the part of the sentimentalist to tyrannise over their private lives. Why should they be grateful for the crumbs that fall from the rich man's table? They should be seated at the board, and are beginning to know it.'[490]

Even if one does not accept the strong Marxist critique of philanthropy, many of the arguments used to justify it do tell us something important about philanthropy in practice. Approaches that embody ideas of subservience and gratitude from beneficiaries, and create an undesirable power imbalance between donors and recipients, paint philanthropy in a poor light and undermine its legitimacy as a means of addressing social ills. For instance, the socialist historian Benjamin Kirkman Gray, who was not opposed to the idea of philanthropy in principle, still criticised the approaches of many Victorian donors, because he saw them as typifying unwelcome attitudes of patronage. He argued: 'Another motive that influenced alike the managers of the charities and the subscribers was the love of power . . . [the suspicion] that a love of patronage is at the root of much so-called charity, is confirmed by a remark of Alcock's some half-century earlier. "It's greatly for the interests of charity," he writes, "that the objects of it should be respectful and grateful. We think our kindness in a manner repaid, when it is thankfully received. It's a pleasure then to have done it, and an incitement to do more" . . . The need to foster this sense of adventitious superiority may account for the letters of thanks which patients were instructed to write to their patrons.'[491]

Those who believe philanthropy can be a positive force for change would do well not to ignore the arguments of socialist critics. They pose serious challenges, and philanthropic activities need to be done in such a way that they are not open to the same criticisms. As a salutary lesson in how *not* to do things, it is worth noting the example of the Victorian 'voting charity'. This was a fashion in some philanthropic organisations of the time, where donors would be given the opportunity to select for themselves the beneficiaries of their charitable largesse. Although it started out as a way of ensuring accountability, this system quickly became corrupted and led to some of the least edifying scenes of 'philanthropy' one could imagine, in which the needy recipients of charity became little more than trading cards or betting chips in a game of competitive altruism among the wealthy. It is reported that *'elections resembled the casino or the race track as rival subscribers backed favoured candidates'*,[492] and the tactics employed would not have been out of place in either of those locations, as *'one hears that the walls of the London Tavern were placarded with the names of candidates, sponsors offering to exchange two "Idiots" for a "Governess", or three "Governesses" for one "Female Orphan"... About it all there was a certain excitement and an appeal to the sporting instincts of the sponsors'.*[493]

This tactic of playing to the competitive instincts of donors, while evidently distasteful, does seem to have been successful, as it was widely felt that *'seeing an applicant home in a highly competitive field was no small achievement'*[494] and that *'to pick a winner, to bring one's candidate through at the head of the poll was akin, in a morbid fashion, to any triumph on the track, the playing field, or the stock market'.*[495] In this context, success was deemed important, as it *'highlighted the influence of the sponsor and the indebtedness of the nominee'.*[496]

'Philanthropy is self-indulgent or ideologically-driven'

Philanthropy is ultimately reliant on the choices and actions of individuals. This is one of its strengths, because it means that it is able to harness people's personal motivations by offering them a way of expressing their social preferences. It can, however, quickly become a weakness and a focus for criticism if those choices and actions are seen as self-indulgent or overly ideological.

The self-indulgent living

Chapter 1 highlighted that one of the defining moments in the development of modern philanthropy was the shift from a Catholic to a Protestant conception of charity, with the accompanying change of focus from what the act of giving meant for one's soul in the afterlife to what it achieved in the world as a result of the gift. However, not all Protestant philanthropy was impeccably strategic and selfless. Although the focus was now ostensibly

'A Christmas Reminder'. Cartoon by Udo Keppler for the satirical magazine *Puck*, 1901. Illustration shows Puck addressing Andrew Carnegie who is poring over the 'Plan for the Carnegie Library'; Puck gestures toward an elderly couple standing at the door in the cold winter wind and snow and says, *'books are already so cheap and libraries so abundant that even the poorest man has all the literature he wants. Now, why not provide respectable homes for the people who are too old to work and who were never able to save anything from their scanty wages; – and so keep them from beggary, starvation or suicide?'*

on what giving achieved in terms of improving the world, many still paid more attention to how it made them feel personally, and used philanthropy as a way of shoring up their own beliefs. So, in the 18th century, we increasingly see the idea of charity as *'a sentimental escape from the troubles of this world'*. Now, *'rather than face the reality of public distress or private misfortune, the 18th-century man or woman delighted to take refuge in a comfortable and unreal haven of sentimentality.'* And for these donors, *'giving was a pleasure that made them forget worry and fear; the agreeable sensations which attend the charitable drove away harsh thoughts of injustice and pain'.*[497]

The criticism of self-indulgence is one we also see directed at the Victorians. Although the scale of their charitable endeavours and the pervasiveness of philanthropy in their society are clear, there was a suspicion that a large body of this philanthropy was primarily an agreeable pastime for the middle classes. For many donors and volunteers *'the daily or weekly round among the poor was a source of immense pleasure [because] . . . despite encounters with hardship and disease, it could be the one bright spot in an otherwise dreary landscape . . . To be needed, to be counted* upon, to be called "dear" and "friend" by those more obviously in distress was a great reward'.[498] It might well have been the case that 'reclaiming the intemperate was . . . as effective a remedy for boredom and invalidism as alcohol itself', and 'many well-to-do housewives certainly came to look on "slumming" as a pleasure'.[499]

Of course, if the philanthropy of the Victorian 'do-gooders' was achieving effective results, then it would not necessarily matter if the motivations for doing it were not exactly as we might wish. However, it has been argued that the desire to undertake philanthropy as a pleasant hobby led too many Victorian donors to shy away from the really pressing problems facing their society – many of which were uncomfortable and difficult to address – and instead focus on marginal or even frivolous issues that better met their need to feel good about themselves. Contemporary critics bemoaned the arbitrariness and shallowness of much 19th-century charity; the religious and political orator William Johnson Fox wrote: 'The worst of the moral sensibility of the English public . . . is that it is so irregularly and partially excited, that it penetrates so little below the surface and that it so very often diverts attention and exertion from the root and trunk of national immorality to some petty branch or quivering twig.'[500]

Even when the accusation of arbitrariness cannot be made, and the issues being tackled are clearly valid charitable causes, philanthropists can still come in for criticism from those who have a different view of where priorities lie. Standard Oil founder and celebrated philanthropist JD Rockefeller, for instance, came under fire during an investigation by the US Congress Commission on Industrial Relations for the focus of his donations:

'Frank Walsh, the chairman of the commission, recalled the complaint of a Colorado coal miner about $250,000 of Rockefeller Foundation money that had been allocated for a retreat for migratory birds. That money, the miner insisted, had come from the labor of men like him who should have had a say in how it was spent. "He protested against this apportionment of the wealth to the migratory birds," Walsh remembered. "He said he wanted first to see established a safe retreat for his babies and his wife".'[501]

This is a criticism that we still see today, when the causes a donor chooses to support are called into question for being self-indulgent. Google founder Larry Page's plans to use his wealth to support the establishment of a colony on Mars, for instance, met with scepticism from some quarters. The

US website *Inside Philanthropy* made the point: '*The real problem here is that philanthropic dollars are a finite resource, so how they are spent is exceedingly important.*' It suggested that Page's approach was problematic because, '*imagine if every philanthropist thought like Page: we'd have a lot of grandiose plans for solving problems that don't really exist while the more pressing issues get ignored. So through this lens, it starts to look less like philanthropy, and more like some rich kid's fantasy*'.[502]

This sort of censure raises once again questions about the role of philanthropy, the responsibilities of those with wealth, and what the rest of society is entitled to expect of them. It also throws into sharp focus the fact that the element of donor choice that lies at the heart of philanthropy can lead to criticism if the issues a donor chooses to focus on are perceived to be frivolous or self-indulgent, and if others believe that the donor has an obligation to address more pressing needs.

Implications for future philanthropy

This tension between personal freedom and responsibility to society is one that all philanthropists must grapple with when choosing where to focus their efforts. It is not for other people to tell an individual what to do when it comes to giving their money away, but that individual should also recognise that others may disagree with their choices, and if they want to counter such criticism, they should be prepared to defend those choices.

CASE STUDY

Thomas Holloway: The good, the bad and the ugly of philanthropy?

Thomas Holloway (1800–1883) was a wealthy Victorian businessman who made his fortune selling patent medicine, and put a large portion of it towards philanthropic works. He is probably best known today for founding Royal Holloway College, now part of the University of London.

Engraving of Thomas Holloway, from a photograph by Elliott & Fry, 1884.

Holloway is interesting because his charitable works encapsulate both some of the best, and what many might consider some of the worst, aspects of philanthropy. On the plus side, Holloway did not choose easy or popular causes: Royal Holloway College was conceived as a college of higher education for women, with a view to it becoming a standalone women's university, at a time when there were very few higher education opportunities available for women. Likewise, Holloway's other main project, The Holloway Sanatorium, was designed as a curative institution for the mentally ill, based on research into approaches on the continent and in the US, and was a long way from the normal mode of the Victorian insane asylum.

Also counting in his favour was the considered and strategic approach that Holloway took to choosing his philanthropic projects. It was this that led him to focus on a small number of major projects rather than spread his generosity more widely. It is noted: *'There was nothing impulsive about his choice of philanthropies. On the contrary, he studied the possibilities with exemplary deliberation, took counsel from a variety of advisers, and reached his decision only after years of reflection. Apparently he saw in the benefactions of George Peabody, the American, a challenge and even a rebuke to wealthy Englishmen. From the beginning he made it clear that he would concentrate on one or two important projects of national utility rather than scatter his resources on a variety of minor schemes.'* [503]

The flipside of this is that Holloway was clearly driven by a desire to boost his own status and rather enamoured of the image of himself that he obtained through his good works. By choosing to found physical institutions, he was able to attach his own name to them and ensure that everyone was aware of his role in their construction. This suited Holloway because *'he obviously enjoyed the twin satisfactions of contributing to social progress and wielding power, albeit in the interests of benevolence ... Unlike many of his well-to-do contemporaries, [he] was little tempted to scatter his wealth semi-anonymously over the charity terrain.*

Instead, he elected to put the bulk of it into bricks and mortar (and endowment) for the two institutions that he founded'.[504]

Royal Holloway College, the upper quadrangle.

Apart from the slight question mark over the purity of Holloway's motivations, it was his dogmatism and micro-management when it came to the construction of the institutions he was funding that brought the most criticism. He refused, for instance, to listen to those who suggested that his choice of location for Royal Holloway College (Egham in Surrey) would make it isolated from all the other existing academic centres. He drew further disapproval for the design of the college, which many felt to be ridiculously opulent. One can see his critics' point: rather than adopting a practical, low-cost approach, Royal Holloway was built as a foot-by-foot replica of Château Chambord in the Loire Valley (albeit in brick, rather than stone). The blame for this rested solely with Holloway, as he obsessively micro-managed the project from beginning to end. As a case in point, one (possibly apocryphal) story has it that when the architect submitted the final plans to him for approval, Holloway travelled to Chambord to check that nothing had been missed. Apparently all was perfect, except for a small and inaccessible dormer window on the east front that was lacking in the architect's plans. Holloway immediately demanded that the architect draw up new plans to rectify the omission.

Holloway is an intriguing and confusing figure, and is in many ways an anomaly among donors of his time. But whatever questions there might be about his motivations or methods, in purely financial terms he was one of the most significant donors of his age:

> 'If a portrait [of a "typical" Victorian philanthropist] could be drawn,
> it would bear little resemblance to Thomas Holloway. He seems, per-
> haps to have less in common with his English contemporaries than
> with certain American multimillionaires, who during most of their
> careers were concerned only with business success and whose sense
> of social responsibility flowered late. For Holloway lacked the inter-
> est in a profusion of good works that marked the characteristically
> charitable Victorian, and religious motivation, if it existed at all,
> was not conspicuous in his activities. Yet measured by the total of
> his benefactions, which totalled well over a million pounds . . .[he]
> was certainly one of the two or three preeminent philanthropists of
> this time.'[505]

Telescopic philanthropy

A specific condemnation made in some quarters in the past was that too
many donors chose to focus on giving overseas (often for missionary work),
rather than addressing the multiple pressing needs at home. Charles
Dickens coined the term 'telescopic philanthropy' to describe this phenomenon, and mocked it in his novel *Bleak House*. In this book, Mrs Jellyby
is set up as a figure of ridicule for giving all of her attention to overseas
philanthropic projects (including the wonderfully-named 'Borrioboola-Gha
venture'), while ignoring the plight of the poor on her doorstep. Even her
own family are left to fall into poverty and destitution while she continues to
pour her energies into projects in Africa.

The Times took a particularly scathingly position on telescopic philanthropy, accusing such donors of taking the soft option:

'Philanthropy in former days was not an agreeable pastime. A man who
devoted himself to raise the fallen, to succour the indigent, to cleanse the
gaol or transport-hulk, or slave ship, had need of a vigorous will, a burning
and yet constant enthusiasm, a strong frame and not over-delicate nerves;
for in those days men did things themselves, and not through the agency
of societies, with an office, a secretary and an organisation for colossal
begging . . . But modern philanthropy does not run such dangers . . . The
parliamentary lover of his kind leads a by no means unpleasant life. He
converts the heathen, succours the afflicted and civilises the barbarian,

without ever seeing a ragged garment or a tawny skin. He is the chairman of meetings and the lion of soirees, on account of his interest in populations which he has never visited and his knowledge of the moral state of islands which he could not point out on a map.'[506]

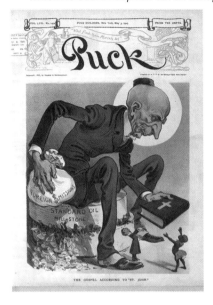

'The Gospel according to "Saint John"'. Cartoon by Udo Keppler for the satirical magazine *Puck*, 1905. It shows John D Rockefeller holding a bag labelled 'Foreign $ Missions' close to his side, sitting on millstones labelled 'Standard Oil Millstone', grinding or squeezing money from people caught between the two stones; with his left hand he offers a copy of the Bible to a native man.

The newspaper even reprinted a poem from the satirical magazine *John Bull*, entitled 'Ode to Modern Philanthropy', which mocked telescopic philanthropists in verse:

'To common optics objects will appear
Dim or distinct, as they're remote or near;
Distance invariably decreasing clearness:
While objects, to the philanthropic-eyed,
At distance more distinctly are descried,
But rendered petty and obscure by nearness.

Your thorough-bred philanthropists can glance
Their pitying eyes over the earth's expanse,
Till sorrow all their bosoms discomposes
For their black brethren sold to whips and chains;
And not a single sympathy remain
For starving whites who die beneath their noses.'[507]

Although we do not see quite the same language used nowadays, similar sentiments are sometimes expressed by those who take exception to the work of international development charities. There are clearly a host of wider issues to do with the effectiveness and efficiency of aid spending, but the old adage that 'charity begins at home' is still used and abused to suggest that those who give to international development causes (including governments) should think about the needs in their own country first.[508]

The road to hell: paved with good intentions and asphalted with ideology?

Even in those cases where Victorian philanthropists did choose to face up to the big issues of the day, they sometimes brought ideological baggage with them that undermined the good they were trying to do. The Charity Schools movement of the late 17th and 18th centuries is a case in point. Charity schools were free schools for children of the poor, designed to offer them a basic education. On the face of it, this seems a sensible solution to an obvious need. However, it became apparent that the schools were less about providing an education for the working classes than a way to serve an ideological desire to prevent the spread of Catholicism in order to protect the middle classes.

The curriculum in these Charity Schools was deliberately limited and joyless; designed to inculcate the poor with the necessary knowledge and habits of hard work and sobriety to meet the country's future needs for factory workers and labourers. The conflict between the desire to give the poor a little education and the concern not to give them too much led to heavy criticism. According to many of these critics, it failed to meet either its own aims or the needs of its supposed beneficiaries. Lord Kames, a central figure of the Scottish enlightenment,[509] accused Charity Schools of being *'more hurtful than beneficial . . . [because] young persons who continue there so long as to read and write fluently become too delicate for hard labour and too proud for ordinary labour'.*[510]

The necessity to look beyond ideology in picking philanthropic approaches remains just as relevant for today's donors. Even when people display a high level of commitment to addressing a real social issue, if they choose to do this in the wrong way on the basis of their preconceptions and beliefs about the nature of the problem, they can do more harm than good. The best-known example of this phenomenon is the 'scared straight'

'An Object Lesson'. Cartoon by John Pughe for the satirical magazine *Puck*, 1901. Illustration shows Charles M Schwab holding a moneybag labelled 'Schwab', standing next to Andrew Carnegie who is sitting on the ground, holding a moneybag labelled 'Carnegie' and with a basket labelled '$10,000,000 for Scotch Universities' overflowing with money next to him. Schwab gestures toward factories on the left as he addresses Carnegie; in the background, on the right, is a line of old men wearing caps and gowns and carrying 'Diplomas' under their arms, emerging from a building labelled 'University'. Schwab says to Carnegie, *'this is the school most people must go to, and the one that has always turned out the biggest men. That other school is for the few and is already turning out too many doctors, ministers, lawyers and clerks. Don't you think we ought to improve conditions in our school rather than in that other one?'*

approach that originated in the US in the 1970s and continues to be used in various guises. Scared straight programmes are based on the idea that young people can be dissuaded from a life of crime (often gang membership or drug dealing) by educating them about the realities of those things through contact with former offenders and law enforcement officers. In many ways this sounds eminently plausible. Unfortunately, repeated evaluations have shown that scared straight programmes not only don't work, they actually *increase* the likelihood of participants subsequently getting involved in crime.[511] Despite this clear evidence, some people continue to advocate for the scared straight approach because it fits with their ideological view of how criminal justice should work.[512] For philanthropists, this offers a cautionary tale about the dangers of placing ideology first when choosing their approach, as they risk not only undermining their own efforts, but furthering the very problems they are trying to solve.

The frivolous dead

Concerns about self-indulgence extend beyond the philanthropy of the living: if anything, those who choose to give after their death in the form of a bequest have come in for even more severe criticism on these grounds. As we saw in the section on inefficiency earlier in this chapter, the tension between respecting the wishes of donors in the past and meeting the needs of today's society has presented a challenge for many years. The previous discussion assumed that even if a donor's choice of cause or their stipulations about how the money was to be spent were problematic, their original motivations were broadly good. However, there are plenty of instances in which it is hard to take such a generous interpretation.

Numerous individuals have attempted to leave legacies that seem frivolous, bizarre or even deliberately designed to offend. For instance:

- Cornelius Christmas, who, taking his own name as a basis, left a bequest from which the income was to be distributed in the form of bread, coals and money '*to the poor of Great Yarmouth, in the week before Christmas Day, every year hereafter and at no other time, for ever*'.[513]
- A man named Greene left a bequest that aimed to supply women with green waistcoats trimmed with green lace, while a man named Gray provided for garbing the poor in grey.[514]
- A woman who left her money to an Oxford University College to '*pay the gate fines of those young men who loved life so well that they returned over-late in the evening*'.[515]
- Thomas Nash, who attempted to leave a bequest in order to insult his wife. Nash left money to the bell-ringers of Bath Abbey on condition that every year on the anniversary of his wedding they should '*[ring] the whole peal of bells with clappers muffled various solemn and doleful changes allowing proper intervals for rest and refreshment from eight o clock in the morning until eight o clock in the evening*' and that conversely, on the anniversary of his death, they should '*ring a grand bob major, and merry mirthful peals unmuffled, during the same space of time, and allowing the same intervals as above-mentioned, in joyful commemoration of my happy release from domestic tyranny and wretchedness*'.[516]
- A story recounted in *The Times* of '*[a] Toronto lawyer, [who] with that quiet irony which lawyers sometimes use to season their dreary*

tasks, has recently bequeathed a fortune of two million dollars to persons of a carefully chosen inappropriateness. Valuable brewery shares go to strongly Prohibitionist Methodist ministers on condition that they play their full part as directors. Shares in racing courses are allotted to well-known opponents of the Turf, on the same terms of active participation. If the bequests are refused they go after nine years to whichever woman in Ontario has had the largest family in the meantime. That lawyer indulged to the full the natural human impulse to make an impressive exit and to leave a stir behind'.[517]

Some of these examples were successfully challenged on the grounds that they did not demonstrate sufficiently charitable purposes. However, some – and worse examples besides – were found to be valid and survived. They became grist to the mill for those charity reformers who argued that such trusts exemplified why the 'dead hand of the donor' needed to be challenged. The fight to achieve this aim contributed greatly to the establishment of a permanent Board of Charity Commissioners, which put the regulation of charities on a more official footing (and led, eventually, to the formation of the modern Charity Commission for England & Wales). Added to that, the clarification of what constitutes an acceptable charitable purpose in law via a succession of legal cases (the most important being the *Pemsel Case* of 1891, in which the judge's ruling outlined the 'four heads of charity)[518] went some way towards removing the grey area that had allowed frivolous and bizarre trusts of this kind to exist.

Implications for future philanthropy

As argued earlier in this book, donor choice is vital. The right for people to choose where to give money of their own free will is a defining principle of philanthropy. It is not for government or society to tell a donor what to give to, but crucially they can set limits by defining the boundaries of what constitutes an acceptable charitable purpose. This may also set the eligibility criteria for tax relief on charitable donations by specifying that only organisations that fall within these boundaries (or perhaps a subset of them) are valid recipients of tax-effective gifts. Once these limits are set, however, the principle of free choice must be respected. In some cases we may not particularly like the causes a donor chooses to give to, but we either have to accept it as the price we pay for having a culture of philanthropy, or challenge the definition of charitable purposes that includes that cause.

The serious lesson from the slightly oddball examples given above, therefore, is that what constitutes an acceptable charitable purpose is an ongoing source of debate. Modern philanthropists should be aware that even if they are operating within the bounds of existing laws, they may come in for criticism on the grounds that they have chosen to focus on causes or organisations that others view as contentious. If this is the case, they may have to be prepared to make a renewed case for why their activities should be viewed as charitable.

'You can't do good with bad money'

Some have argued that any positive impact that philanthropy might have is undermined by the negative impact of the methods used to accumulate the underlying wealth in the first place. Again, this can be phrased as a general criticism of philanthropy as an idea, or as a specific censure of individual philanthropists and their approaches.

Those who object to philanthropy as an idea tend to argue that the capitalist system itself produces social ills such as inequality, so anyone accumulating wealth within that system is contributing to the perpetuation of these problems, regardless of any subsequent good they try to do with their money. This is somewhat similar to the Marxist criticism of philanthropy outlined earlier in this chapter, where it is really capitalism that is being judged at fault, rather than philanthropy itself. An argument of this kind was at the heart of the case made by Peter Buffett, son of billionaire philanthropist Warren Buffett and a major donor in his own right, when he wrote an article in the *New York Times* criticising philanthropy and what he termed the 'charitable industrial complex':

'As more lives and communities are destroyed by the system that creates vast amounts of wealth for the few, the more heroic it sounds to "give back". It's what I would call "conscience laundering" – feeling better about accumulating more than any one person could possibly need to live on by sprinkling a little around as an act of charity . . . But this just keeps the existing structure of inequality in place. The rich sleep better at night, while others get just enough to keep the pot from boiling over. Nearly every time someone feels better by doing good, on the other side of the world (or

street), someone else is further locked into a system that will not allow the true flourishing of his or her nature or the opportunity to live a joyful and fulfilled life.'[519]

'A phase of our tax system - the greater the service, the heavier the tax'. Cartoon by Udo Keppler for the satirical magazine *Puck*, 1911. Illustration shows two men labelled 'Charity Worker' addressing an oversized man sitting on a throne, taking money from a box labelled 'Rents'. The men are saying, *'We thank you for your generous contributions for the relief of the suffering poor, but why don't you replace those rookeries with model tenements and relieve their miseries in that way?',* to which the enthroned tenement-house owner replies, *'Why? Why because, if I did, the city would fine me with increased valuations and heavier taxes!'*

The response to this is broadly the same as to the Marxist argument. Although it raises important questions in a theoretical sense, from a pragmatic viewpoint there is no option but to work within the current capitalist system to minimise the negative impact of the way money is created, while at the same time maximising the positive impact of philanthropy. The relationship between philanthropy and inequality is complex and multi-faceted, and it is not easy to use philanthropy as a tool to address inequality. However, it is possible to continue to harness the best of philanthropy in its current form to address the problems of society right now. This still leaves it open to challenge the broader framework of capitalism at the same time, although admittedly this can be a difficult balance to strike.

Those who criticise individual philanthropists and their approaches are willing to allow that capitalism can be a positive force, and that wealth accrued within this system can be used for social good, but argue that in some cases the line of work or business practices of an individual donor undermine their philanthropic efforts. No less a figure that George Bernard Shaw found himself embroiled in a controversy over this question of whether it was possible to 'do good with bad money' through philanthropy. His play *Major Barbara* is about a young female Salvation Army officer, Barbara Undershaft, who becomes disillusioned when the organisation accepts donations from an arms manufacturer (who happens to be her father) and a whisky distiller. Many critics thought this represented a blistering attack by Bernard Shaw on the hypocrisy of charities that accept donations from questionable sources. However, in a preface to later versions of the play, he made it clear that he thought it was eminently sensible for charities to take money from any source, because at least that way some good would be done with it.

> 'Even the handful of mentally competent critics got into difficulties over my demonstration of the economic deadlock in which the Salvation Army finds itself. Some of them thought that the Army would not have taken money from a distiller and a cannon founder: others thought it should not have taken it: all assumed more or less definitely that it reduced itself to absurdity or hypocrisy by taking it. On the first point the reply of the Army itself was prompt and conclusive. As one of its officers said, they would take money from the devil himself and be only too glad to get it out of his hands and into God's. They gratefully acknowledged that publicans not only give them money but allow them to collect it in the bar – sometimes even when there is a Salvation meeting outside preaching teetotalism . . . On the point that the Army ought not to take such money, its justification is obvious. It must take the money because it cannot exist without money, and there is no other money to be had. Practically all the spare money in the country consists of a mass of rent, interest, and profit, every penny of which is bound up with crime, drink, prostitution, disease, and all the evil fruits of poverty, as inextricably as with enterprise, wealth, commercial probity, and national prosperity. The notion that you can earmark certain coins as tainted is an unpractical individualist superstition.'[520]

Bernard Shaw exhibits an intriguing mixture of pragmatism and cynicism in his defence of philanthropy against this criticism, but many charities today would not be quite so phlegmatic about taking money from sources that overtly conflicted with their mission. The Red Cross, for instance, found itself in such a situation in 1997, when it was approached by Andrew Morton, author of a controversial biography of Princess Diana, who wanted to donate proceeds from an updated version of his book to charity (the new version had attracted particular disapproval because it was seemingly rushed out in the wake of Diana's death). The Guardian, in an editorial on the story, asked: 'Should the Red Cross take the bent Morton penny?' and referred to Bernard Shaw's earlier views, noting: *'Shaw . . . was robust about such moral dilemmas: donations from contaminated sources should always be accepted so long as the recipients were confident that they would not be contaminated. He would have wanted the Red Cross to accept the cash – and condemn the giver. No donation – however large – alters the moral position of an immoral act.'* [521] However, the paper disagreed with Bernard Shaw's conclusion, arguing: *'Moral organisations can be demeaned by their donors, particularly if the donors are seeking to make themselves look more moral. That's why the major cancer research charity is right to reject all grants from the tobacco industry – and why the Red Cross is right to be wary of Mr Morton.'*[522]

George Bernard Shaw by Elliott & Fry, 1900.

Even if an individual's line of work does not raise ethical issues when it comes to their philanthropy, the way in which they run their business can still present problems. The great industrial philanthropists of the early 20th century such as Rockefeller and Carnegie faced strong censure on these grounds. Rockefeller, in particular, brought this issue to the frontline of public discourse in 1905, when his gift of $100,000 to the American Board of Foreign Missions met with strong criticism.[523] Many felt that Rockefeller's money was 'tainted' by his unethical business practices, and that the American Board should not accept his donation because that would mean an implicit pardoning of these practices.[524] This led to a furious debate in which all the ethical, legal and practical considerations were considered at length. Although the American Board ended up keeping the money, there was no clear conclusion on the bigger question of what to do with such 'tainted donations'.

Carnegie faced similar criticisms and addressed them head-on, although his argument is not one that paints philanthropy in a particularly favourable light. It amounted basically to the claim that it was justifiable for him to maximise his profits through questionable work practices, rather than improve pay and conditions for his employees, because that way he would have more money to spend on philanthropy. This was in the workers' interests, he argued, because he could be better-trusted to address their needs through his philanthropy than they could be to look after themselves if the money was in their own pockets:

'Workingmen on both sides of the Atlantic questioned whether the Pittsburgh steelmaker's huge charitable donations would have been better spent on higher wages, improved working conditions, and an eight- rather than 12-hour workday. Carnegie responded in a speech in Pittsburgh that he kept wages low to remain competitive, and that even had it been possible for him to share some of his profits with his workers, it would have been neither "justifiable or wise" to do so. "Trifling sums given to each every week or month . . . would be frittered away, nine times out of ten, in things which pertain to the body and not to the spirit; upon richer food and drink, better clothing, more extravagant living, which are beneficial neither to rich nor poor." The lower the costs of labour, the higher the profits. Far better, in his view, to squeeze money from workers' paycheques, aggregate it, and give back to the community in the form of public libraries and concert halls.'[525]

One would hope that this sort of paternalistic justification would not be used by many of today's philanthropists, and that they would instead acknowledge the need to implement fair working practices and pay structures at the same time as undertaking philanthropic activities. However, this fight has not yet been won, by any means. Some, for example, have criticised the philanthropy of Mexican billionaire Carlos Slim Helú on the grounds that the damage done by his approach to business outweighs any good he might be doing through his donations. A *New York Times* article reported: '*Sceptics argue that the value of Mr Slim's philanthropy has to be measured against the damage his telephone monopoly did to the economy*,' and carried a quote from a professor at a Mexican university who said: '*At some level I can applaud his philanthropy, but it would be better for Mexico if he stopped blocking competition first.*'[526]

It seems increasingly unfeasible, however, to maintain a 'left hand/ right hand' distinction between business and philanthropy in which the purposes to which money is put are seen as totally separate from the way in which it was made. Increasingly, there is an emphasis on companies and their leaders taking a 'responsible business' approach, in which social and environmental concerns are woven into day-to-day business practices.[527] For individual philanthropists who buy into this ideal, it is clear that seeing philanthropy as totally distinct from one's wealth creation does not really wash, as the same underlying motivations and considerations apply to both.

CASE STUDY

George Cadbury: Sweet charity with a hard centre

George Cadbury, 1909

Along with the other famous Quaker confectionery families, the Rowntrees and the Frys, the Cadbury family had a huge impact on the history of philanthropy in the UK (more on the history of philanthropy in the chocolate industry can be found in the case study in Chapter 4). George Cadbury (1839–1922) was perhaps the most notable of the Cadbury donors. Like many of those whose philanthropic legacy has lived on to the present day, he made real efforts to address the underlying causes of social issues rather than just addressing their symptoms because '*in spite of his deep compassion, Cadbury was not much interested in relieving temporary distress, nor in applying what he thought of as palliatives. He could deplore the way in which philanthropists seemed satisfied to deal only with "superficial evils", and . . . [made efforts] to assist "those who are seeking to remove their underlying causes"*.[528]

What really distinguishes George Cadbury is his holistic approach. Many others also applied philanthropic principles to their business activities, or combined campaigning philanthropy with politics, but Cadbury was notable for the sheer extent to which he saw no distinctions between philanthropy, business and politics. For him, they were all merely an extension of his Quaker beliefs, and he saw no contradiction in combining them: *'To an extent that his business contemporaries found more than a little mysterious, almost traitorous, Cadbury's whole career was, in the broad sense, a venture in philanthropy. He was contemptuous of the rich men who devoted the morning and noon of their lives to making money and the evening to giving it away, and of those who kept the money-making and their benevolent activities in well-insulated compartments.'*[529]

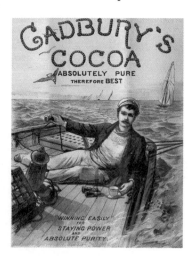

Cadbury's Cocoa advert, 1874.

On the question of whether it is possible to 'do good with bad money' considered above, Cadbury was very firmly of the mind that it is not, because he believed that philanthropy cannot be considered in isolation from how the underlying wealth was created in the first place. As far as he was concerned *'making money and giving it away formed . . . a single pattern, and making it could be as constructive socially as giving it away. No amount of philanthropic giving could take the curse off a fortune that had been accumulated carelessly or without regard for the welfare of the workpeople who had laboured for it'*.[530]

Probably the most famous way in which Cadbury put his views into practice was in the construction of the model workers' village of Bournville, built to provide affordable housing for the working classes (including his employees) when the Cadbury factory expanded and moved to the countryside outside Birmingham.

A suggestion box for workers at the Cadbury factory in Bournville – just one of the many innovative employment practices introduced by Cadbury. In the first seven months after the system was introduced more than 1,000 suggestions were received; a high percentage of them were found to be sufficiently useful to be adopted.

Cadbury's views on responsible business sound forward-thinking even to modern ears, so one can only imagine what his contemporaries must have made of them. However, the commercial success of the Cadbury business, despite the application of such unconventional approaches, provided a compelling argument for Cadbury's vision. And this was important to him, because *'he saw [his approach] as a pilot experiment in social welfare which, if successful, might provide a model for industry as a whole. And . . . he demonstrated that such unconventional views were by no means incompatible with a wildly profitable business'.*[531] Unfortunately, none of his peers seemed willing to follow Cadbury's example. This is perhaps unsurprising when we consider that it is only now, nearly 100 years after his death, that the commercial world as a whole is starting to catch up with Cadbury's vision and accept that principles of social and environmental responsibility can be incorporated into successful mainstream businesses.

Cadbury was also unafraid to take on issues with a clear political element, and once again to use all the tools at his disposal to do so. In the same way as his contemporary John Passmore

Edwards (see case study in Chapter 3), Cadbury used his ownership of a newspaper as a means to exert political pressure and further his social aims. This included promoting the introduction of old-age pensions and highlighting the exploitation of workers in sweatshops. His opposition to the Boer War also acted as a catalyst for him developing a high-profile role as an anti-imperialist and pacifist.

Cadbury stands as a towering figure in UK philanthropy: a man for whom philanthropy was not a limited activity to be tacked on to commercial and political endeavours, but an ethos that pervaded every aspect of his life and work. His blurring of the boundaries between business and philanthropy, in particular, sets an example that even now we are still trying to understand how to follow.

CHAPTER SIX

Where next for philanthropy?

This book has focused on the long and proud history of philanthropy in Britain. Philanthropy predates the idea of government welfare and has subsequently developed alongside it; shaping state provision through its own successes and failures. It has enabled the safeguarding of the cultural and natural heritage of the country for future generations, as the charitable trust structure offers a means of long-term stewardship of assets that is not subject to short-term political considerations. Philanthropy has also acted as a vital safeguard in the development of modern democracy, allowing people to escape the political strictures of their time in order to drive social progress and challenge the status quo. But is philanthropy now facing something of an identity crisis?

We live in a country where the state guarantees most of our basic needs and rights, and the market offers us the opportunity to buy additional goods and services to enhance our lives, so is there a need for anything else? Furthermore, many of the needs that were once only likely to be met by charitable organisations are now being provided for by other kinds of organisations: some have become part of the commercial realm, while others remain broadly within the scope of 'social goods'. The range of options for people to fund these social goods has grown to incorporate new, non-charitable models such as social enterprise, impact investing, crowd-funding and digital activism. In this brave new world, is there still a place for people voluntarily giving their money away for the benefit of others, with no expectation of any financial return, or is this an anachronism that will slowly die out?

The purpose of this book is to argue that there is still a crucial role in our society for philanthropy and charitable giving. There are many ongoing problems in society that have proved resistant to our efforts to combat them; in some cases for hundreds of years. Although charities are as much at fault as the state and the market for our failure to solve these problems, they have often done more than any other kind of agency to limit their impact. Given that none of these problems are going to disappear overnight, we can assume that it will remain important to nullify their effects as far as possible, even while we look for solutions to their underlying causes.

Furthermore, it seems fanciful to suppose that we can always find new ways of addressing these problems that can ensure the same social benefits that charities have been bringing for hundreds of years, yet also deliver financial returns. This may be feasible in some cases – and the potential of social enterprise and social investment in these areas is huge – but in many instances it will not be possible. In these cases, the only real option is to continue to rely on the work of charitable organisations, funded by philanthropic donations.

Philanthropy, then, has a role to play in overcoming the failings of the state and the market in meeting social needs. It does this by addressing gaps in provision and by offering an alternative model where existing public or private sector provision is not meeting the requirements of those it is supposed to be helping. But it is important not to extrapolate from this and assume that philanthropy is a viable substitute for state funding or fair markets. The lesson from the problems that beset Victorian philanthropy, which led to state intervention in many areas and eventually to the creation of the welfare state, is that if the demands we make of philanthropy are too great and our expectations unrealistic, it is almost certainly doomed to fail.

In crude arithmetical terms, philanthropic giving is simply not of the same magnitude as public spending. As noted before, the total value of voluntary donations in any one year in the UK tends to be around £10–11 billion, whereas Total Managed Expenditure by government in 2012/13 was an order of magnitude higher, at £675 billion. Furthermore, philanthropy has features that make it ill-designed for meeting the requirements of welfare provision at a systemic, national level. For one thing it is capricious: philanthropic giving is fundamentally a voluntary act – an expression of choice and preference on the part of the donor. While this can be a strength, because it means philanthropy is able to harness people's personal motivations in a unique way, it does not provide a sound basis for delivering a consistent, fair system for meeting the needs of society. Apart from anything else, if we compare the current profile of charitable giving and that of public spending, it is obvious that there would have to be a massive change in the nation's philanthropic preferences for the two to even come close to matching. A society that tried to rely on philanthropy to replace public spending would find itself very short of money and with most of that money concentrated in a few areas.

Even if philanthropy should not be expected to replace public spending, it can play a vital role in any system of public services by providing a means to challenge existing provision. It can do this by demonstrating better ways of doing things, in the hope that the state takes its ideas on board (or – more likely nowadays – offers the charity a contract to deliver the given service on its behalf). It can also challenge provision through campaigning and advocacy designed to get the state to change the way it delivers services. This is a role that philanthropy has played to great effect many times.

But while its function in supporting and challenging service provision is important, it is not all that philanthropy is about. This is a narrow frame of mind that politicians too often seem to have adopted: assuming that the only reason charities funded by voluntary donations might be important is either because they could be viable candidates to deliver public services under contract in the future, or because the work they do fills gaps in state provision or augments it, and so reduces the onus on the state to address its own failings. The danger is that this ignores the true value of charities and charitable giving, which is about much more than service delivery.

As we saw in Chapter 3, a central feature of philanthropy has been its role in challenging the status quo – and sometimes even the democratic system itself – through campaigning and advocating for social change. Often this has been on issues that would otherwise have been marginalised, and in the face of a lack of political will from the leaders of the time, such as the campaigns for the abolition of slavery or for gay rights. Philanthropy has been vital in providing a means of dragging these issues into the main-stream, and in building up an evidence base and a sufficient mass of public support to force those in power to take them seriously. From a short-term perspective, this is probably the feature of charities that politicians like the least, as they are often on the receiving end of this campaigning. However, from the point of view of the overall health of our democracy and society, the challenge that philanthropically-funded organisations are able to pose through their advocacy and campaigning is absolutely vital. It sits alongside a free press as one of the most important elements of the system of checks and balances in our democracy.

This is why the actions and pronouncements of politicians who suggest that campaigning is 'not a suitable activity' for charities, and the support for legislation like the Lobbying Act in the UK, which sends out such a negative message about the government's view of charity campaigning, are so pernicious. The wilful failure to distinguish between 'political' and 'party political' allows politicians to accuse charities of straying outside the bounds of what is allowed, when usually what they mean is simply that the charity has had the temerity to criticise one of their policies or pronouncements.

It is often implied that this sort of criticism is a new phenomenon, which represents charities somehow 'straying' from their traditional remit. Of course, as this book has shown, nothing could be further from the truth: charities have been acting as a critical voice to those in power in our society for more than 300 years. Obviously no-one likes being criticised, and it takes a significant amount of equanimity to fight for the rights of those who are likely to criticise you, but it is important that politicians look beyond the short term and recognise that the right of charities to campaign and challenge is vital to ensuring that our society continues to be free and fair to all its citizens.

Understanding that campaigning is just as important as delivering services has important ramifications for any policy approach to philanthropy. For instance, it forces us to be clearer about the justification for offering tax relief on donations. More often than not, this is justified after the event with reference to some argument about savings to the public purse, but this once again falls into the trap of thinking about charities only in the context of public service delivery. If, however, we take into account the campaigning role of charities, it is hard to see how this can be justified by any version of the 'subsidy rationale' outlined in Chapter 3, as it does not represent something that the state would otherwise have to pay for itself. This reinforces the argument that the 'pluralism rationale' for charitable tax relief is the only defensible one – that it should be seen as a generalised subsidy for the sustenance of a healthy civil society, rather than a subvention for any particular service or outcome. This explains why it is justifiable for the government to subsidise the campaigning work of charities through Gift Aid and other reliefs: because this is a vital element of the sort of healthy civil society that it wants to support.

Recommendations

It is clear, then, that philanthropy still has a vital role to play in our society. It can support the delivery of services that address needs outside the responsibility of the state, or of services that bridge the gaps in state provision or bring added value to existing public services. It can also offer challenge: challenge to public service provision, challenge to government policy and legislation and even challenge to our democratic system.

To make the most of the value that philanthropy can bring to society, it is vital that policymakers, charities and donors have a shared understanding of what it is, how it works and what its strengths and limitations are. This book considers some of these issues: the wider social factors that affect philanthropy, the way in which the practice of philanthropy has changed over the years, and some of the criticisms that have been levelled at it. Hopefully, this provides food for thought for philanthropists, policymakers and anyone else interested in these issues, and some clues as to how we can arrive at the sort of shared understanding suggested.

It is not possible to prescribe such a shared understanding here. As noted many times throughout this book, philanthropy's reliance on personal choice and voluntary action make it a powerful tool but an extremely difficult thing to fit into neat compartments. Instead, this book proposes a set of key principles to guide our understanding of philanthropy. These distil many of the lessons suggested by the historical examples detailed, and will hopefully provide a starting point for others to use in shaping their own approaches to philanthropy policy and practice.

Key principles of philanthropy
Philanthropy is about people and their choices
The freedom for individuals to choose where they direct their gifts lies at the heart of philanthropy and gives it much of its strength. But this also means that it is not good at providing consistency or equality at a systemic level. Rather than trying to overcome this by forcing philanthropy to be something

it isn't, we should respect and cherish the importance of donor choice and tailor our expectations accordingly.

Philanthropic choices are about both head and heart

Not only is philanthropy about individual choice, but those choices are informed by a wide range of considerations, both rational and emotional. On the rational side there is a demand for evidence – of where need lies and how best to address it. On the emotional side is a complex mixture of factors – some are personal or cultural (which lie outside the remit of this book), and some are societal, such as prevailing attitudes towards wealth and need (as considered in Chapter 4). Philanthropy is therefore a product of both head and heart, and the balance between the two varies between donors.

Philanthropy is not the same as public spending and cannot replace it

Philanthropic giving is nowhere near the same order of magnitude as public spending, and the profile of giving does not match the profile of need at a societal level. The element of voluntary choice and the influence of emotional factors also make philanthropy ill-suited to meeting needs at a systemic level. Hence it is not a feasible or appropriate replacement for public spending.

Philanthropy is often 'political' (and that is a good thing)

A key distinguishing feature of philanthropy is that it has a purpose or goal. In most cases this can be framed as a problem that needs to be overcome or a change that needs to be made in society. By giving to a particular cause, a philanthropist is expressing a view about a way in which our society, our laws or government policies need to be different. This is an inherently political act. It is only if we incorrectly conflate 'political' and 'party political' that there is a problem. If we instead reclaim the proper understanding of what the sphere of politics includes, then it is clear that philanthropy is, and always has been, a valuable tool for people to express their beliefs within that sphere.

Philanthropy should be progressive

Philanthropy, properly understood, is about trying to improve society by tackling the root causes of problems, rather than just addressing their symptoms. Philanthropy should therefore be progressive, not regressive or conservative. Philanthropy is not about maintaining the status quo or turning back the clock, but about moving society forward by overcoming failings in existing government, welfare provision or legislation.

Philanthropy should be prepared to take risks

Philanthropy is often aimed at intractable problems that have proved resistant to the efforts of government and the market to solve them. To succeed where these other actors have failed, philanthropy needs to try new and different approaches, and this means taking risks. The voluntary nature of philanthropy and its basis in the social motivations of individuals mean that philanthropy is able to take risks that would not be possible either for public sector organisations, which are accountable to taxpayers, or for private sector organisations, which are accountable to shareholders. This tolerance for risk is one of philanthropy's greatest assets.

Philanthropy can enable a long-term view

Philanthropy is not beholden to the political cycle or to the short-term demands of the market. That means that it should be able to take a longer-term approach to dealing with social problems than either businesses or government. This is a great strength of philanthropy, as there are many issues that clearly require long-term solutions and philanthropic organisations may be the only bodies capable of identifying and delivering them.

Tax relief on philanthropic donations is not a subsidy for services the state would otherwise have to provide

Offering tax relief for individuals on their charitable donations is a valuable tool for governments to support a philanthropic culture. It is not a given that donations should not be taxed, so the relief does count as a subsidy by government. But it should not be seen as a subsidy for the provision of particular services that the state would otherwise have to provide. The tax relief only makes sense when seen as a generalised subsidy reflecting a government view that a healthy civil society is important (including its role in advocacy and campaigning), and that supporting individuals to make voluntary donations is an effective way of ensuring this health.

Bibliography

Books and book chapters

Abrahamson, E. (2013). *Beyond Charity: A Century of Philanthropy Innovation.* [Online]. New York: Rockefeller Foundation. Available from: https://assets.rockefellerfoundation.org/app/uploads/20131001184008/Beyond-Charity.pdf.pdf

Abrahamson, E., Hurst, S. and Shubinski, B. (2013) *Democracy & Philanthropy: The Rockefeller Foundation and the American Experiment.* [Online] New York: Rockefeller Foundation. Available from: http://centennial.rockefellerfoundation.org/page/-/USA_PDF_eBook_11.21.13.pdf

Abramitzky, R. and Braggion, F. (2003) Malthusian and Neo-Malthusian Theories. In *Oxford Encyclopaedia of Economic History.* Vol 3. Oxford: Oxford University Press. 423–427.

Alcock, T. (1752) *Observations on the Defects of the Poor Laws.* London: R Baldwin. Reproduced by Hathi Trust (2011). Available at: http://hdl.handle.net/2027/hvd.hxjnf9

Andrew, D. (1989) *Philanthropy and Police: London Charity in the Eighteenth Century.* Oxford: Princeton University Press.

Ben-Amos, I. (2008) *The Culture of Giving: Informal Support and Gift-Exchange in Early Modern England.* Cambridge: Cambridge University Press.

Bernard Shaw, G. (1907) 'Preface to Major Barbara: First Aid to Critics' in *Major Barbara.* New York: Brentano's. Reproduced by Project Gutenberg, 2009. Available at: www.gutenberg.org/files/3789/3789-h/3789-h.htm

Beveridge, W. (1948) *Voluntary Action: A Report on Methods of Social Advance.* London: George, Allen & Unwin.

Bishop, M. and Green M. (2010) *Philanthrocapitalism: How Giving Can Save the World.* London: Bloomsbury.

Bremner, R. (1996) *Giving: Charity and Philanthropy in History.* New Brunswick: Transaction Publishers.

Brendon, P. (1991) *Thomas Cook: 150 Years of Popular Tourism.* London: Secker & Warburg.

Brenton, M. (1985) *The Voluntary Sector in British Social Services.* London: Longman.

Burlinghame, D. (ed.) (1992) *The Responsibilities of Wealth.* Indianapolis: Indiana University Press.

Carnegie, A. (1901) *The Gospel of Wealth, and Other Timely Essays.* New York: The Century Co. Reproduced by the Internet Archive, 2008. Available at: https://archive.org/stream/gospelwealthand00carngoog#page/n4/mode/2up

Churchill, W. (1909) *Liberalism and the Social Problem*. London: Hodder and Stoughton. Reproduced by Project Gutenberg, 2006. Available at: www. gutenberg.org/files/18419/18419-h/18419-h.htm

Cunningham, H. (2015) Philanthropy and its Critics. In: Morvaridi B (ed.) (2015) *New Philanthropy and Social Justice*. Bristol: Policy Press.

Cunningham, H. and Innes, J. (eds.) (1998) *Charity, Philanthropy & Reform from the 1690s to 1850*. London: Palgrave.

Davis Smith, J., Rochester, C. and Hedley, R. (eds.) (1995) *An Introduction to the Voluntary Sector*. London: Routledge.

Davis Smith J., (1995) The Voluntary Tradition: Philanthropy and Self-Help in Britain 1500–1945. In: Davis Smith, J., Rochester C. and Hedley, R. (eds). *An Introduction to the Voluntary Sector*, London: Routledge. 9–40.

de Tocqueville, A. (1835) *Memoir on Pauperism*. Translated by Seymour Drescher, 1968. Reproduced by Civitas, 1997. Available at: www.civitas.org.uk/pdf/Tocqueville_rr2.pdf

Deakin, N. The perils of partnership: The voluntary sector and the state, 1945–1992. In: Davis Smith, J., Rochester C. and Hedley, R. (eds.) (1995) *An Introduction to the Voluntary Sector*. London: Routledge. 40–66.

Dobkin Hall, P. (2006) A Historical Overview of Philanthropy, Voluntary Associations, and Nonprofit Organizations in the United States, 1600–2000. In: Powell, W. and Steniberg, R. (eds). (2006) *The Nonprofit Sector: A Research Handbook, (2nd ed)*. New Haven: Yale University Press. 32–65.

Drassinower, A. (2001) The Doctrine of Political Purposes in the Law of Charities: A Conceptual Analysis. In: Phillips, J., Chapman, B. and Stevens, D. (2001) *Between State and Market: Essays on Charities Law and Policy in Canada*. Montreal: McGill-Queen's University Press. 288–316.

Finlayson, G. (1994) *Citizen, State and Social Welfare in Britain, 1830–1990*. Oxford: Oxford University Press.

Friedman, L. and McGarvie, M. (2002) *Charity, Philanthropy, and Civility in American History*, Cambridge: Cambridge University Press.

Gladstone, D. (ed.) (1999) *Before Beveridge: Welfare Before the Welfare State*. London: Civitas.

Godwin, W. (1797) *An Enquiry Concerning Political Justice, Vol 2*. Book VIII 'Of Property'. London: G.G.J. and J. Robinson. Reproduced by the Online Library of Liberty, 2006. Available at: http://lf-oll.s3.amazonaws.com/titles/236/0164-02_Bk.pdf

Habermas, J. (1962) *The Structural Transformation of the Public Sphere: An Inquiry into a Category of Bourgeois Society*. Translated by Thomas Burger, 1989. Cambridge, MA: MIT Press.

Harding, M. (2014) *Charity Law and the Liberal State*. Cambridge: Cambridge University Press.

Harris, J. (1990) Society and the state in twentieth century Britain. In Thompson, F. (ed.) (1990) *The Cambridge Social History of Britain 1750–1950, Volume 3: Social agencies and institutions*. Cambridge: Cambridge University Press. 63–119.

Healey, E. (1984) *Lady Unknown: The Life of Angela Burdett-Coutts*. London: Sidgwick and Jackson.

Himmelfarb, G. (1992) *Poverty and Compassion: The Moral Imagination of the Late Victorians*. London: Vintage.

Hobson, J. (1914) *Work and Wealth: A Human Valuation*. New York: MacMillan. Reproduced by the Internet Archive, 2008. Available at: https://archive.org/details/workwealthhumanv00hobsrich

Illingworth, P., Pogge, T. and Wenar, L. (eds.) (2011) *Giving Well: The Ethics of Philanthropy*. Oxford: Oxford University Press.

Innes, J. (1998) State, Church and Voluntarism in European Welfare, 1690–1850. In Cunningham, H. and Innes, J. (eds.) (1998) *Charity, Philanthropy & Reform from the 1690s to 1850*. London: Palgrave. 15–66.

Jordan, W. K. (1959) *Philanthropy in England 1480–1660*. London: George Allen & Unwin.

Jones, G. (1969) *History of the Law of Charity 1532–1827*. Cambridge: Cambridge University Press.

Joseph Rowntree Memorial Trust and Carnegie United Kingdom Trust. (1978) *The Future of Voluntary Organisations: Report of the Wolfenden Committee*. London: Croom Helm.

Karl, B. (1992) Andrew Carnegie and his Gospel of Philanthropy: A Study in the Ethics of Responsibility. In Burlinghame, D. (ed.) *The Responsibilities of Wealth*, Indianapolis: Indiana University Press. 32–51.

Kirkman Gray, B. (1905) *A History of English Philanthropy: From the Dissolution of the Monasteries to the Taking of the First Census*. London: P.S. King & Son. Reproduced by the Internet Archive, 2008. Available at: https://archive.org/stream/ahistoryenglish00graygoog#page/n6/mode/2up

Kirkman Gray, B. (1908) *Philanthropy and the State; or Social Politics*. London: P.S. King & Son. Reproduced by the Internet Archive. Available at: https://archive.org/details/philanthropyand00graygoog

Lloyd, T. and Breeze, B. (2013) *Richer Lives: Why Rich People Give*. London: Directory of Social Change.

Low, S. (1850) *The Charities of London: Comprehending the benevolent, educational, and religious institutions; their origin and design, progress, and present position*. London: Sampson Low. Reproduced by the Internet Archive, 2007. Available at: https://archive.org/details/charitiesoflondo00lowsrich

Lupton, R. (2011) *Toxic Charity: How Churches and Charities Hurt Those They Help (and How to Reverse It)*, New York: Harper Collins.

Macadam, E. (1934) *The New Philanthropy: A Study of the Relations Between the Statutory and Voluntary Social Services*. London: George Allen & Unwin.

Malthus, T. (1798) *An Essay on the Principle of Population*. London: J Johnson. Reproduced by Electronic Scholarly Publishing Project, 1998. Available at: www.esp.org/books/malthus/population/malthus.pdf

Mayr, U., Harbaugh, W. and Tankersley, D. (2008) Neuroeconomics of Charitable Giving and Philanthropy. In: Glimcher, P., Fehr, E., Camerer, C. and Poldrack, R. (eds.) (2008) *Neuroeconomics: Decision Making and the Brain*. Waltham, MA: Academic Press. 303–319.

McCarthy, T. (1989) Introduction. In: Habermas, J. (1962) *The Structural Transformation of the Public Sphere: An Inquiry into a Category of Bourgeois Society*. Translated by Thomas Burger, 1989. Cambridge, MA: MIT Press.

Miller, R. (2012) *The House of Getty*. London: Bloomsbury Reader.

Morvaridi, B. (ed.) (2015) *New Philanthropy and Social Justice*. Bristol: Policy Press.

Owen, D. (1964) *English Philanthropy, 1660–1960*, Cambridge, MA: Harvard University Press.

Partridge, E. (1973), *The Routledge Dictionary of Historical Slang*. London: Routledge.

Phillips, J., Chapman, B. and Stevens, D. (2001) *Between State and Market: Essays on Charities Law and Policy in Canada*. Montreal: McGill-Queen's University Press.

Powell, W. and Steinberg, R. (eds.) (2006) *The Nonprofit Sector: A Research Handbook, (2nd ed)*. New Haven: Yale University Press. 32–65.

Price, R. (1999) *British Society, 1680–1880*. Cambridge: Cambridge University Press.

Prochaska, F. (1980) *Women and Philanthropy in 19th Century England*. Oxford: Oxford University Press.

Prochaska, F. (1988) *The Voluntary Impulse: Philanthropy in Modern Britain*. London: Faber & Faber.

Prochaska, F. (1990) Philanthropy. In: Thompson, F. (ed.) (1990) *The Cambridge Social History of Britain 1750–1950, Volume 3: Social agencies and institutions*. Cambridge: Cambridge University Press. 357–395.

Reich, R. (2006) Philanthropy and its Uneasy Relation to Equality. In: Damon, W. and Verducci, S. (eds.) (2006) *Taking Philanthropy Seriously: Beyond Noble Intentions to Responsible Giving*. Indianapolis: Indiana University Press.

Reich, R. (2011) Towards a Political Theory of Philanthropy. In: Illingworth, P., Pogge, T. and Wenar, L. (eds.) (2011) *Giving Well: The Ethics of Philanthropy*. Oxford: Oxford University Press. 177–196.

Roberts, M. (1998) Head versus Heart? Voluntary Associations and Charity Organisation in England c. 1700–1850. In: Cunningham & Innes (eds.) (1998) *Charity, Philanthropy and Reform From the 1690s to 1850*. London: Palgrave.

Rodgers, B. (1949) *Cloak of Charity: Studies in Eighteenth Century Philanthropy.* London: Methuen & Co.

Ross, C. and Chapman, C. (2013) *Philanthropy: The City Story*. London: Sutton's Hospital.

Rowntree, B.S. (1908) *Poverty: A Study of Town Life*. London: Macmillan & Co. Reproduced by the Internet Archive, 2009. Available at: https://archive.org/details/povertyastudyto00rowngoog

Sievers, B. (2010) *Civil Society, Philanthropy and the Fate of the Commons.* Hanover, N.H.: University Press of New England.

Singer, P. (2011) What Should a Billionaire Give – and What Should You? In: Illingworth, P., Pogge, T. and Wenar, L. (eds.) (2011) *Giving Well: The Ethics of Philanthropy.* Oxford: Oxford University Press. 13–26.

Slack, P. (1995) *The English Poor Law 1531–1782*. Cambridge: Cambridge University Press.

Thomas Dolby Publisher (1825). *The Spirit of the Times V1-2: Concentrating Every Week, All That Is Worthy of Being Preserved from the Whole of Our Periodical Literature (1825)*. Reprint Montana: Kessinger, 2010.

Thompson, F. (ed.) (1990) *The Cambridge Social History of Britain 1750–1950, Volume 3: Social agencies and institutions.* Cambridge: Cambridge University Press.

Waddington, K. (2000) *Charity and the London Hospitals, 1850–1898*, Suffolk: Boydell and Brewer Ltd.

Wilde, O. (1909) *The Soul of Man Under Socialism*. London: Arthur L. Humphreys. Reproduced by Project Gutenberg, 1997. Available at: www.gutenberg.org/files/1017/1017-h/1017-h.htm

Zunz, O. (2012) *Philanthropy in America: A History*. New Jersey: Princeton University Press.

Journal papers

Andreoni, J. (1990) Impure Altruism and Donations to Public Goods: A Theory of Warm-Glow Giving. *The Economic Journal*, 100 (401), 464–477.

Anik, L., Aknin, L., Norton, M. and Dunn, E. (2009) Feeling Good about Giving: The Benefits (and Costs) of Self-Interested Charitable Behavior, *Harvard Business School Working Paper*, 10-012.

Archer, I. (2002) The Charity of Early Modern Londoners. *Transactions of the Royal Historical Society*, Sixth Series, 12, 223–244.

Bekkers, R. and Wiepking, P. (2011) Who Gives? A Literature Review of Predictors of Charitable Giving I – Religion, Education, Age and Socialization. *Voluntary Sector Review*, 2 (3), 337–365.

Bekkers, R. and Wiepking, P. (2012) Who Gives? A Literature Review of Predictors of Charitable Giving II – Gender, Family Composition and Income. *Voluntary Sector Review*, 3 (2), 217–245.

Bielenberg, A. (2002) Late Victorian Elite Formation and Philanthropy: The Making of Edward Guinness. *Studia Hibernica*, 32, 133–154.

Bittker, B. and Rahdert, G. (1976) The Exemption of Nonprofit Organizations from Federal Income Taxation. *The Yale Law Journal*, 85 (3), 299–358.

Bittle, W. and Todd Lane, R. (1976) Inflation and Philanthropy in England: A Re-Assessment of WK Jordan's Data. *The Economic History Review*, New Series, 29 (2), 203–210.

Bosworth, D. (2011) The Cultural Contradictions of Philanthrocapitalism. *Society* 48 (5), 382–388.

Bremner, R. (1956) 'Scientific Philanthropy', 1873–93. *Social Service Review*, 30 (2), 168–173.

Bremner, R. (1959) Modern Attitudes toward Charity and Relief. *Comparative Studies in Society and History*, 1 (4), 377–382.

Brooks, A. (2007) Income Tax Policy and Charitable Giving. *Journal of Policy Analysis and Management*, 26 (3), 599–612.

Carnegie, A. (1889) The Best Fields for Philanthropy. *The North American Review*, 149 (397), 682–698.

Clough, S. (1960) Philanthropy and the welfare state in Europe. *Political Science Quarterly*, 75 (1), 87–93.

Curti, M. (1958) American Philanthropy and the National Character. *American Quarterly*, 10 (4), 420–437.

Curti, M. (1961) Tradition and Innovation in American Philanthropy. *Proceedings of the American Philosophical Society*, 105 (2), 146–156.

Davis Smith, J. and Oppenheimer, M. (2005) The Labour Movement and Voluntary Action in the UK and Australia: A Comparative Perspective. *Labour History,* 88, 105–120.

Dinello, N. (1998) Elites and Philanthropy in Russia. *International Journal of Politics, Culture, and Society*, 12 (1), 109–133.

Dobkin Hall, P (2013) Philanthropy, the Nonprofit Sector & the Democratic Dilemma. *Dædalus, the Journal of the American Academy of Arts & Sciences*, 142 (2), 139–158.

Eikenberry, A. (2007) Philanthropy, Voluntary Association, and Governance Beyond the State. *Administration & Society*, 39 (7), 857–882.

Fabricant, S. (1961) An Economist's View of Philanthropy. *Proceedings of the American Philosophical Society*, 105 (2), 162–166.

Fack, G. and Landais, C. (2010) Are Tax Incentives for Charitable Giving Efficient? Evidence from France. *American Economic Journal: Economic Policy*, 2 (2), 117–141.

Feingold, M. (1987) Philanthropy, Pomp, and Patronage: Historical Reflections upon the Endowment of Culture. *Daedalus*, 116 (1), 155–178.

Goose, N. (2006) The rise and decline of philanthropy in early modern Colchester: the unacceptable face of mercantilism? *Social History*, 31 (4), 469–487.

Habermas, J., Lennox, S. and Lennox, F. (1974) The Public Sphere: An Encyclopedia Article (1964), *New German Critique,* 3, 49–55.

Harrison, B. (1966) Philanthropy and the Victorians. *Victorian Studies*, 9 (4), 353–374.

Huntington, J. (1892) Philanthropy and Morality. *International Journal of Ethics*, 3 (1), 39–64.

Jordan, W. K. (1961) The English Background of Modern Philanthropy. *The American Historical Review*, 66 (2), 401–408.

Jones, G. (1967) Frances Moore's Reading on The Statute of Charitable Uses. *The Cambridge Law Journal*, 25 (2), 224–238.

Karl, B. and Katz, S. (1981) The American Private Philanthropic Foundation and the Public Sphere 1890–1930. *MINERVA,* XIX (2), 236–270.

Karl, B. and Katz, S. (1987) Foundations and Ruling Class Elites. *Daedalus*, 116 (1), 1–40.

Kidd, A. (1996) Philanthropy and the 'Social History Paradigm'. *Social History*, 21 (2), 180–192.

Moore, J. (2004) The Art of Philanthropy? The formation and development of the Walker Art Gallery in Liverpool. *Museum and Society*, 2 (2), 68–83.

Moore, M. (1971) Social Service and Social Legislation in Edwardian England: The Beginning of a New Role for Philanthropy. *Albion: A Quarterly Journal Concerned with British Studies*, 3 (1), 33–43.

Obler, J. (1981) Private Giving in the welfare state. *British Journal of Political Science,* 11 (1), 17–48.

Page, B., Bartels, B. and Seawright, J. (2013) Democracy and the Policy Preferences of Wealthy Americans. *Perspectives on Politics*, American Political Science Association, 11 (01), 51–73.

Pelling, H. (1966) Review of 'English Philanthropy 1660–1960' by David Owen. *The Historical Journal*, 9 (2), 244–246.

Pifer, A. (1987) Philanthropy, Voluntarism, and Changing Times. *Daedalus*, 116 (1), 119–131.

Piff, P., Kraus, M., Keltner, D., Côté, S. and Hayden Cheng, B. (2010) Having Less, Giving More: The Influence of Social Class on Prosocial Behaviour. *Journal of Personality and Social Psychology*, 99 (5), 771–784.

Pullan, B. (2005) Catholics, Protestants, and the Poor in Early Modern Europe. *The Journal of Interdisciplinary History*, 35 (3), 441–456.

Ramdas, K. (2011) Philanthrocapitalism: Reflections on Politics and Policy Making. *Society,* 48 (5), 393–396.

Rogers, R. (2011) Why Philanthro-Policymaking Matters. *Society,* 48 (5), 376–381.

Sievers, B. (2010) Philanthropy's Role in a Liberal Democracy [Online]. *The Journal of Speculative Philosophy*, 24 (4), 380–398. Available from: http://pacscenter.stanford.edu/sites/all/files/Philanthropy's%20Role%20in%20a%20Liberal%20Democracy.pdf

Singer, P. (1972) Famine, Affluence and Morality, *Philosophy and Public Affairs*, 1 (1), 229–243.

Sturges, P. (1996) Beer and Books: Michael Thomas Bass, Derby Public Library and the Philanthropy of the Beerage. *Libraries & Culture*, 31 (2), 247–71.

Tananbaum, S. (1997) Philanthropy and Identity: Gender and Ethnicity in London. *Journal of Social History*, 30 (4), 937–961.

Vallier, K. and D'Agostino, F. (2013) Public Justification [Online]. In: Zalta, E. (ed). *The Stanford Encyclopedia of Philosophy (Spring 2014 Edition)*. Stanford. Available at: http://plato.stanford.edu/archives/spr2014/entries/justification-public

Van Leeuwen, M. (2012) Giving in early modern history: philanthropy in Amsterdam in the Golden Age. *Continuity and Change*, 27 (02), 301–343.

Wilson, G. (1979) The Brown Animal Sanatory Institution. *The Journal of Hygiene*, 82 (1), 155–176.

Wines, F. (1898) Sociology and Philanthropy. *Annals of the American Academy of Political and Social Science*, 12, 49–57.

Discussion and conference papers

Breeze, B. (2010) *How Donors Choose: Findings of a study of donor perceptions of the nature and distribution of charitable benefit*. Occasional Paper 1, Centre for Charitable Giving and Philanthropy/University of Kent.

Cunningham, H. (2013) *A History of Western Philanthropy*. Occasional Paper, Centre for Charitable Giving/Cass Business School.

Dobkin Hall, P. (2000) *Philanthropy, The welfare state and the Transformation of American Public and Private Institutions, 1945–2000*. Working Paper 5, The Hauser Center for Nonprofit Organizations, John F Kennedy School of Government, Harvard University.

Fack, G. and Landais, C. (eds.) (2010) *Charitable Giving and Tax Policy: a Historical and Comparative Perspective*. Paris School of Economics, France.

Fishman, J. (2008) *The Political Use of Private Benevolence: The Statute of Charitable Uses*. [Online]. Pace Law Faculty Publications, Paper 487. Available from: http://digitalcommons.pace.edu/lawfaculty/487

Harlock, J. (2013) *Impact measurement practice in the UK third sector: a review of emerging evidence*. Working Paper 106, Third Sector Research Centre, Birmingham.

Sadeh, J., Tonin, M. and Vlassopoulos, M. (2014) Why Give Away your Wealth? An Analysis of the Billionaires' View. Discussion paper 1417, University of Southampton.

Smith, S. (2012) Increasing charitable giving – what can we learn from economics? Working Paper 12/29, Centre for Markets and Public Organisation, University of Bristol.

Smith, S. and Scharf, K. (2010) The price elasticity of charitable giving: does the form of tax relief matter? Working Paper 10/247, Centre for Markets and Public Organisation, University of Bristol.

Wright, K. (2001) Generosity versus altruism: Philanthropy and charity in the US and UK, Civil Society Working Paper 17, The Centre for Civil Society, London School of Economics and Political Science.

Newspaper and magazine articles

Arnold, J. (2014) Attacks and Vitriol Will Not Deter Me From Supporting Fixes to Public Policy [Online]. *Chronicle of Philanthropy*, 31 March. Available from: philanthropy.com/article/AttacksVitriol-Will-Not/153337

BBC News. (2012) Budget 2012: Charities could lose big donors [Online]. 21 March. Available from: www.bbc.co.uk/news/business-17458362

Bloomberg Businessweek. (2014) A Tangled Web of Charity [Online]. 8 May. Available from: images.bwbx.io/cms/2014-05-14/feat_billionaires_970.png

Buffett, P. (2013) The Charitable-Industrial Complex [Online]. *New York Times,* 26 July. Available from: www.nytimes.com/2013/07/27/opinion/the-charitable-industrial-complex.html

Chapman, C. (2012) Giving While Living [Online]. *Philanthropy Impact*, 29 November. Available from: www.philanthropy-impact.org/trend/giving-while-living

Chorley, M. (2014) 'Charity begins at home': Ukip's Nigel Farage calls for foreign aid budget to be used to help flood-hit communities [Online]. *Daily Mail*, 6 February. Available from: www.dailymail.co.uk/news/article-2552969/Ukips-Nigel-Farage-calls-foreign-aid-budget-used-help-flood-hit-communities.html

Eaton, G. (2011) Archbishop of Canterbury: 'no one voted' for the coalition's policies [Online]. *New Statesman,* 8 June. Available from: www.newstatesman.com/blogs/the-staggers/2011/06/rowan-williams-government

Eisenberg, P. (2013) 'Strategic Philanthropy' Shifts Too Much Power to Donors [Online]. *Chronicle of Philanthropy*, 20 August. Available from: philanthropy.com/article/Strategic-Philanthropy-/154451

Fiennes, C. and Reed, E. (2014) Moneyball Philanthropy? Not Always [Online]. *Forbes*, 30 June. Available from: www.forbes.com/sites/skollworldforum/2014/06/30/moneyball-philanthropy-not-always

Gentilucci, M. (2014a) Meet the 12 Most Generous Tech Leaders. . . And 6 of the Least [Online]. *Inside Philanthropy*, 18 March. Available from: www.insidephilanthropy.com/tech-philanthropy/2014/3/18/meet-the-12-most-generous-tech-leaders-and-6-of-the-least.html

Gentilucci, M. (2014b) Larry Page's Philanthropic Vision Could Save Humanity. If It Doesn't Doom Us First [Online]. *Inside Philanthropy*, 26 March. Available from: www.insidephilanthropy.com/tech-philanthropy/2014/3/26/larry-pages-philanthropic-vision-could-save-humanity-if-it-d.html

Gose, B. and Gipple, E. (2012) Rich Enclaves Are Not as Generous as the Wealthy Living Elsewhere [Online]. *Chronicle of Philanthropy*, 19 August. Available from: https://philanthropy.com/article/Rich-Enclaves-Are-Not-as/156255

Gowen, A. (2013) Philanthropist Richard A. Herman leaves fortune to local charity, symphony, opera. *Washington Post*, 5 February. Available from: www.washingtonpost.com/local/philanthropist-richard-a-herman-leaves-fortune-to-local-charity-symphony-opera/2013/02/05/88c49b4c-6fb3-11e2-aa58-243de81040ba_story.html

Green, C. (2014) There are too many charities doing the same work, claims Charity Commission chief executive [Online]. *The Independent*, 25 June. Available from: www.independent.co.uk/news/uk/home-news/there-are-too-many-charities-doing-the-same-work-claims-charity-commission-chief-executive-9562997.html

Henley, J. (2012) The New Philanthropists [Online]. *The Guardian*, 7 March. Available from www.theguardian.com/society/2012/mar/07/new-philanthropists-wealthy-people

Hillier, A. and Cook, S. (2014) Gagging Clauses in Public Sector Contracts [Online]. *Third Sector,* 1 April. Available from: www.thirdsector.co.uk/gagging-clauses-public-service-contracts/policy-and-politics/article/1287885

Hu, E. (2014) Billionaire Compares Outrage Over Rich In SF To Kristallnacht [Online]. *NPR*, 26 January. Available from: www.npr.org/blogs/alltechconsidered/2014/01/26/266685819/billionaire-compares-outrage-over-rich-in-s-f-to-kristallnacht

Hudson, S. (2010) Mission drift on the rise as charities go where the money is [Online]. *Third Sector*, 20 December. Available from: www.thirdsector.co.uk/mission-drift-rise-charities-go-money-is/finance/article/1047274 (subscription only)

Jack A, (2013) A Different Kind of Philanthropy [Online]. *Financial Times*, 30 April. Available from: www.ft.com/cms/s/0/2e40a226-ae68-11e2-8316-00144feabdc0.html#axzz3Ez4M5MpZ

Jenkins, S. (2006) The welfare state is waning. Bring on the philanthropists [Online]. *The Guardian*, 28 June. Available from: www.theguardian.com/commentisfree/2006/jun/28/comment.policy

Jewish Chronicle. (1885) Improved Dwellings for the Poor, 13 March.

Kasper, G. and Marcoux, J. (2014) The Re-Emerging Art of Funding Innovation [Online]. *Stanford Social Innovation Review*, Spring. Available from: ssir.org/articles/entry/the_re_emerging_art_of_funding_innovation

Kenny, C. (2014) Why Private Donations Aren't Helping America's Poor [Online]. *Bloomberg Businessweek,* 13 October. Available from: www.bloomberg.com/bw/articles/2014-10-13/why-private-donations-arent-helping-americas-poor

Lieu, D. (2010) George Soros Fights Back After an Attack by Glenn Beck [Online]. *Chronicle of Philanthropy*, 11 November. Available from: philanthropy.com/article/George-Soros-Fights-Back-After/194099

Malkin, E. (2007) New Commitment to Charity by Mexican Phone Tycoon [Online]. *New York Times*, 28 June. Available from: www.nytimes.com/2007/06/28/business/worldbusiness/28slim.html

Mider, Z. (2014) The $13 Billion Mystery Angels [Online]. *Bloomberg Businessweek,* 8 May. Available from: www.bloomberg.com/bw/articles/2014-05-08/three-mysterious-philanthropists-fund-fourth-largest-u-dot-s-dot-charity#p1

Nasaw, D. (2006) *Looking the Carnegie Gift Horse in the Mouth: The 19th-century critique of big philanthropy* [Online]. *Slate.com*, 10 November. Available from: www.slate.com/articles/news_and_politics/history_lesson/2006/11/looking_the_carnegie_gift_horse_in_the_mouth.html

Parker, R. (1975) As the financial crisis gets tougher, it is the smaller charities that are feeling the pinch [Online]. *The Times,* 24 December. Available from: www.thetimes.co.uk/tto/archive (subscription required)

Porter, M. and Kramer, M. (2011) Creating Shared Value [Online]. *Harvard Business Review,* January/February. Available from: hbr.org/2011/01/the-big-idea-creating-shared-value

Preston, C. (2012) World's Richest Man Steps Up Giving Despite Wariness About Charity [Online]. *Chronicle of Philanthropy*, 30th September. Available from: www.carlosslim.com/preg_resp_philanthropy_art01_ing.html

Preston, C. (2013) Philanthropy Must Do More to Influence Policy, Say Government Officials [Online]. *Chronicle of Philanthropy,* 13 February. Available from: https://philanthropy.com/article/Philanthropy-Must-Do-More-to/155373

Pudelek, J. (2013) Too many 'careerists' in the voluntary sector, says philanthropist [Online]. *Third Sector*, 6 March. Available from: www.thirdsector.co.uk/careerists-voluntary-sector-says-philanthropist/finance/article/1173686

Reuben, A. (2013) Sunday Times Rich List: The changing face of wealth [Online]. *BBC Business News*, 18 April. Available from: www.bbc.co.uk/news/business-22188762

Sellers, P. (2010) Billionaire Peer Pressure: behind the Buffett-Gates challenge. *Fortune*, 16 June. Available from: www.fortune.com/2010/06/16/billionaire-peer-pressure-behind-the-buffett-gates-challenge

Serrano, A (2007) Billionaire Pokes Fun At Philanthropy [Online]. *CBS Moneywatch*, 13 March. Available from: www.cbsnews.com/news/billionaire-pokes-fun-at-philanthropy

Sorkin, A. (2011) The Mystery of Steve Jobs's Public Giving [Online]. *New York Times*, 29 August. Available from: http://dealbook.nytimes.com/2011/08/29/the-mystery-of-steve-jobss-public-giving

Soskis, B. (2014a) Dirty Money: From Rockefeller to Koch [Online]. *The Atlantic*, 7 March. Available from: www.theatlantic.com/business/archive/2014/03/dirty-money-from-rockefeller-to-koch/284244

Soskis, B. (2014b) The Importance of Criticizing Philanthropy [Online]. *The Atlantic*, 12 May. Available from: www.theatlantic.com/business/archive/2014/05/the-case-for-philanthropy-criticism/361951

Strom, S. (2010) Pledge to Give Away Fortunes Stirs Debate [Online]. *New York Times*, 10 November. Available from: www.nytimes.com/2010/11/11/giving/11PLEDGE.html?pagewanted=all&_r=0

Sullivan, P. (2014) Private Citizen Bloomberg on Philanthropy [Online]. *New York Times,* 25 April. Available from: www.nytimes.com/2014/04/26/your-money/private-citizen-bloombergs-philosophy-on-philanthropy.html?_r=0

The Gentleman Magazine (1790) Character of Mr Howard Cleared from Misrepresentation. 67 (4), part I, 287–289.

The Guardian (1885) Employers and Employed. [Online]. 21 October, 581. Available from http://newspaperarchive.com

The Guardian (1891) The Selection of Social Agencies. 22 April, 629. Available from http://newspaperarchive.com

The Guardian (1997) When donations demean. The Red Cross is right to question Mr Morton's money. 7 October. Available from http://newspaperarchive.com

The Spectator (1886) Diffuse Benevolence [Online]. 11 September, 9–10. Available from: archive.spectator.co.uk/article/11th-september-1886/9/diffuse-benevolence

The Spectator (1893) The Hypocrisy of Philanthropy [Online]. 25 November, 11. Available from: archive.spectator.co.uk/article/25th-november-1893/11/the-hypocrisy-of-philanthropy

The Times (1840) Ode to Modern Philanthropy. 28 December, 3. Available from: www.thetimes.co.uk/tto/archive (subscription required)

The Times (1843) Philanthropy. 27 January, 3. Available from: www.thetimes.co.uk/tto/archive (subscription required)

The Times (1850) Charitable London. 7 September, 6. Available from: www.thetimes.co.uk/tto/archive (subscription required)

The Times (1856) Among the many considerations which make an Englishman proud of his country . . . 8 August, 6. Available from: www.thetimes.co.uk/tto/archive (subscription required)

The Times (1857) Philanthropy in former days. 11 March, 8. Available from: www.thetimes.co.uk/tto/archive (subscription required)

The Times (1863a) Proposed Taxation on Charities. 5 May, 10. Available from: www.thetimes.co.uk/tto/archive (subscription required)

The Times (1863b) In the House of Lords last night . . . 5 May, 11. Available from: www.thetimes.co.uk/tto/archive (subscription required)

The Times (1869) Miss Coutts New Market at Bethnal Green. 29th April 1869. Available from: www.thetimes.co.uk/tto/archive (subscription required)

The Times (1880) We publish this morning a list of charitable appeals . . . 1 July, 11. Available from: www.thetimes.co.uk/tto/archive (subscription required)

The Times (1899) The Custom of Charitable Bequest. 25 September, 5. Available from: www.thetimes.co.uk/tto/archive (subscription required)

The Times (1911) Death of Mr Passmore Edwards. 24 April, 11. Available from: www.thetimes.co.uk/tto/archive (subscription required)

The Times (1926) Bequests, 26 December, 15. Available from: www.thetimes.co.uk/tto/archive (subscription required)

The Times (1949) Voluntary Effort – Recognition by the State. 23 June, 2. Available from: www.thetimes.co.uk/tto/archive (subscription required)

Wessel, M (2011) Idolize Bill Gates, Not Steve Jobs [Online]. *Harvard Business Review*, 1 November. Available from: www.bloomberg.com/bw/management/idolize-bill-gates-not-steve-jobs-11012011.html

West, M. (2014) Charitable Gifts from Wealthy Koch Brothers Often Prompt Partisan Reactions [Online]. *Wall Street Journal*, 3 August. Available from: online.wsj.com/articles/charitable-gifts-from-wealthy-koch-brothers-often-prompt-partisan-reactions-1407117054

Yu, E. (2014) At 'Wit's End': Scared Straight Programs Remain Popular Among Parents Despite Warnings. [Online]. *Juvenile Justice Information Exchange,* 9 May. Available from: http://jjie.org/at-wits-end-scared-straight-programs-remain-popular-among-parents-despite-warnings

Additional materials

Non-government policy & research materials

CAF publications

Charities Aid Foundation (1974) *1924–1974: Half Way to a Centenary.* Kent: Charities Aid Foundation.

Charities Aid Foundation (2011) *Charities spend a lot less on fundraising than we think.* Press release, 11 July.

Charities Aid Foundation (2015) *UK Giving 2014: An overview of charitable giving in the UK during 2014.* [Online]. London: Charities Aid Foundation. Available from: www.cafonline.org/docs/default-source/cafcdodocuments/CAF-UKGiving2014

Charities Aid Foundation and NCVO (2012) *UK Giving 2012* [Online]. London: Charities Aid Foundation and NCVO. Available from: www.cafonline.org/docs/default-source/cafcdodocuments/UKGiving2012Full.pdf

Davies, R. (2011) The Wages of Sin? Doing good with 'bad' money. *CAF Giving Thought blog.* [Online]. Posted 6 December. Available from: http://givingthought.org/2011/12/06/the-wages-of-sin-doing-good-with-bad-money

Davies, R. (2012) Getting good service: Is the Social Value Act just the beginning? *CAF Giving Thought blog* [Online]. Posted 29 March. Available from: http://givingthought.org/2012/03/29/getting-good-service-is-the-social-value-act-just-the

Davies, R. (2013) Are some causes better than others? The 'effective altruism' debate. *CAF Giving Thought blog* [Online]. Posted 27 November. Available from: http://givingthought.org/2013/11/27/are-some-causes-better-than-others-the-effective-philanthropy-debate

Davies, R. (2014a) *Give Me a Break: Why the UK should not aspire to a 'US-Style' culture of charitable giving* [Online]. London: Charities Aid Foundation. Available from: www.cafonline.org/docs/default-source/about-us-publications/give-me-a-break--giving-thought-discussion-paper-no-1.pdf

Davies, R. (2014b) Inequality and Philanthropy: part of the solution or part of the problem? *CAF Giving Thought blog* [Online]. Posted 19 March. Available from: http://givingthought.org/2014/03/19/inequality-and-philanthropy-part-of-the-solution-or-part-of-the-problem

Davies, R. (2014c) Not a Measured Approach? Does the Hewlett Foundation's decision indicate the failure of impact-measuring approaches to philanthropy? *CAF Giving Thought blog* [Online]. Posted 10 April. Available from: http://givingthought.org/2014/04/10/not-a-measured-approach-does-the-hewlett-foundations-decision-indicate-the-failure-of-impact-measuring-approaches-to-philanthropy

Livingston Booth, D. and Brophy M. (1999) *CAF 25th Anniversary.* Kent: Charities Aid Foundation.

Pickering, A. (2014) *Future World Giving: Enabling an Independent Not-for-profit Sector.* [Online]. London: Charities Aid Foundation. Available from: https://www.cafonline.org/docs/default-source/about-us-publications/caf-independence-report-finalv2.pdf

Other publications

Arnsberger, P., Ludlum, M., Riley, M. and Stanton, M. (2008) A History of the Tax-Exempt Sector: An SOI Perspective. Washington, DC: Internal Revenue Service.

Atlantic Philanthropies (2010) *Turning Passion into Action: Giving While Living.* [Online] New York: Atlantic Philanthropies. Available from: www.atlanticphilanthropies.org/sites/default/files/uploads/GWL_050510_1723%20%282%29.pdf

Bagwell, S., de Las Casas, L., van Poortvliet, M. and Abercrombie, R. (2013) *Money for Good UK: Understanding donor motivation and behaviour.* [Online]. London: NPC. Available from: www.thinknpc.org/publications/money-for-good-uk/money-for-good-uk-2/?post-parent=7442

Bank of America and Center on Philanthropy at Indiana University (2012) *2012 Bank of America Study of High Net Worth Philanthropy.* [Online]. New York/Indianapolis: Bank of America/ Indiana University. Available from: http://newsroom.bankofamerica.com/files/press_kit/additional/2012_BAC_Study_of_High_Net_Worth_Philanthropy_0.pdf

Bernholz, L. (2013) *Philanthropy and the Social Economy: Blueprint 2014, The Annual Industry Forecast.* [Online]. New York: Foundation Center. Available from: www.grantcraft.org/assets/content/resources/blueprint_2014.pdf

Bowie, B. and Lioz, A. (2012) *Auctioning Democracy: The Rise of Super PACs and the 2012 Election.* [Online]. New York/Washington DC: Demos/US PIRG. Available from: www.demos.org/sites/default/files/publications/AuctioningDemocracy-withAppendix.pdf

Bowman v Secular Society (1917), A.C. 406.

Breeze, B. (2006) UK Philanthropy's Greatest Achievements. London: Institute of Philanthropy.

Brophy, M. (2014) Witness: A personal account of the changes in the charity sector, 1980 – 2010, with reflections on what next. [Online]. Presentation given to Voluntary Action History Society seminar at the Institute of Historical Research, 17 February. Audio available from: http://podcast.ulcc.ac.uk/accounts/SAScasts/VoluntaryActionHistory/IHR_17_02_14_Voluntary_Action_History.mp3

Buffett, W. (2010) My Philanthropic Pledge. [Online]. Available from: http://givingpledge.org/Content/media/My%20Philanthropic%20Pledge.pdf

Charity Tax Group and Nuffield Foundation (2012) Charity Tax Map. 2nd Edition. [Online]. London: Charity Tax Group and Nuffield Foundation. Available from: www.ctrg.org.uk/files/tax_map/CTG_Charity_Tax_Map_Second_Edition_03-12-12.pdf

Congressional Budget Office (2011) Options for Changing the Tax Treatment of Charitable Giving. [Online]. Washington, DC: Congressional Budget Office. Available from: www.cbo.gov/sites/default/files/112th-congress-2011-2012/reports/charitablecontributions.pdf

Conservative Party (2008) A Stronger Society – Voluntary Action in the Twenty First Century [Online]. Green paper, London: Conservative Party. Available from: www.conservatives.com/~/media/Files/Green%20Papers/Voluntary_Green_Paper.ashx?dl=true

Coutts (2014) Million Pound Donors Report 2014. Available from: http://philanthropy.coutts.com

Davies, R. (2009) Value in Public Services. [Online]. London: Policy Exchange. Available from: www.policyexchange.org.uk/images/publications/value%20in%20public%20services%20-%20july%2009.pdf

Fiennes, C. (2013) Good charities spend more on administration than less good charities spend. Giving Evidence blog. [Online]. Posted 2 May. Available from: http://giving-evidence.com/2013/05/02/admin-data

Gash, T. and Roos, T. (2012) Choice and competition in public services: learning from history. [Online]. London: Institute for Government. Available from: www.instituteforgovernment.org.uk/sites/default/files/publications/Choice%20and%20competion%20in%20public%20services_0.pdf

Giving USA Foundation (2008) Giving During Recessions and Economic Slowdowns. Giving USA Spotlight 3. Glenview: Giving USA Foundation.

Gousmett, M. J. (2009) The Charitable Purposes Exemption from Income Tax: Pitt to Pemsel 1798 – 1891. [Online]. PhD, University of Canterbury. Available from: http://ir.canterbury.ac.nz/bitstream/10092/3448/2/thesis_fulltext.pdf

Grant, Peter Russell (2012) Mobilizing Charity: non-uniformed voluntary action during the First World War. [Online]. PhD, City University London. Available from: http://openaccess.city.ac.uk/2075/1/Mobilizing_Charity.pdf

Harrison, B. (2014) Volunteering and Democracy in Britain Since the 1790s. [Online]. Presentation given to Voluntary Action History Society seminar at the Institute of Historical Research, 17 February. Audio available from: http://podcast.ulcc.ac.uk/accounts/SAScasts/VoluntaryActionHistory/IHR_03_02_14_Voluntary_Action_Historu.mp3

Higher Education Funding Council For England (2014) Recurrent Grants for 2012–13: Final Allocations. [Online]. London: Higher Education Funding Council For England. Available from: www.hefce.ac.uk/media/hefce/content/pubs/2014/201427/HEFCE2014_27.pdf

Hobhouse, A. (1868) A lecture on the characteristics of charitable foundations in England. London: Longman Green & Co. Reproduced as part of Bristol Selected Pamphlets collection [Online]. Available from: www.jstor.org/stable/60248376

Howell, P. (1979) Buxton, Sir Thomas Fowell (1837–1915). In Nairn, B. and Serle, G. (eds.) (1979) Australian Dictionary of Biography. Melbourne: Melbourne University Press. Reproduced online, available from: http://adb.anu.edu.au/biography/buxton-sir-thomas-fowell-5455/text9265

International Association for Scottish Philosophy (n.d.) *Henry Home, Lord Kames (1696–1782)*. [Online]. Available from: www.scottishphilosophy.org/lord-kames.html

Ipsos MORI (2014) *Public trust and confidence in charities*. [Online]. London: Ipsos Mori. Available from: www.ipsos-mori.com/Assets/Docs/Publications/sri-charities-public-trust-and-confidence-in-charities-2014.pdf

Jacobellis v Ohio (1964) 378 US Supreme Court 84.

Jenkins, S. J. (2001) *The Intellectual Framework of Voluntary Social Service c. 1940–1960*. [Online]. PhD, University College London. Available from: http://discovery.ucl.ac.uk/1317670/1/268449.pdf

Kindell, J. and Reilly, J. (1997) Lobbying Issues. [Online]. In: Internal Revenue Service. (1997) *Internal Revenue Service Continuing Professional Education Manual*. Washington DC: Internal Revenue Service. Available from: www.irs.gov/pub/irs-tege/eotopicp97.pdf

London School of Economics and Political Science [n.d.] *Poverty Maps of London*. [Online]. Charles Booth Online Archive. Available from: http://booth.lse.ac.uk/static/a/4.html

Macdonald, L. (2011) *Public Libraries: Briefing Paper*. [Online]. Dunfermline: Carnegie UK Trust. Available from: http://carnegieuktrust.org.uk/CMSPages/GetFile.aspx?guid=f57df5fb-a063-4690-9351-511483ad44a2

Morice v Bishop of Durham (1805) EWHC Ch J80.

Morris, S. (2006) *The greatest philanthropic tradition on earth? Measuring the extent of voluntary activity in London, 1874–1914*. [Online]. Presentation given to Voluntary Action History Society seminar at the Institute of Historical Research, 9 February. Available from: www.vahs.org.uk/wp-content/uploads/2006/03/The_Greatest_Voluntary_Tradition_on_Earth%5B1%5D.pdf

National Council for Voluntary Organisations (2014) *UK Civil Society Almanac*. London: NCVO.

New Philanthropy Capital, The Smith Institute and The Peabody Trust (2013) *Rebuilding the Relationship Between Affordable Housing and Philanthropy*. [Online]. London: New Philanthropy Capital, The Smith Institute and The Peabody Trust. Available from: www.thinknpc.org/publications/rebuilding-the-relationship-between-affordable-housing-and-philanthropy/rebuilding-the-relationship-between-affordable-housing-and-philanthropy-2/?post-parent=8541

nfpSynergy (2014) *Public thinks charity spending on admin is more than double their acceptable level*. [Online]. Available from: http://nfpsynergy.net/press-release/public-thinks-charity-spending-admin-more-double-their-acceptable-level

NHS England (2013) *NHS Allocations for 2013/14*. [Online]. Available from: www.england.nhs.uk/allocations-2013-14

Pallotta, D. (2013) *The way we think about charity is dead wrong*. [Online]. Video of a talk given at the TED2013 conference. Available from: www.ted.com/talks/dan_pallotta_the_way_we_think_about_charity_is_dead_wrong?language=en

Petrosino, A., Turpin-Petrosino, C., Hollis-Peel, M. and Lavenberg, J. (2002) *Scared Straight and Other Juvenile Awareness Programs for Preventing Juvenile Delinquency: A Systematic Review*. [Online]. Updated (2012) Campbell Systematic Reviews 2013:5. Oslo: The Campbell Collaboration. Available from: www.campbellcollaboration.org/lib/download/2818/Petrosino_Scared_Straight_Update.pdf

Prochaska, F. (2006) Working Class Philanthropy in Britain. *Social Affairs Unit blog*. [Online]. Available from: www.socialaffairsunit.org.uk/blog/archives/000616.php

Prochaska, F. (2014) *The State of Charity*. [Online]. Transcript of lecture given at Charity Commission annual public meeting, 17 September. Available from: https://www.gov.uk/government/uploads/system/uploads/attachment_data/file/356191/Lecture_-_Dr_Frank_Prochaska.pdf

Quakers in the World (n.d.) *Profile of Elizabeth Fry*. [Online]. Available from: www.quakersintheworld.org/quakers-in-action/13

Quakers in the World (n.d.) *Profile of Margery Fry*. [Online]. Available from: www.quakersintheworld.org/quakers-in-action/84

Resource Alliance and Rockefeller Foundation (2012) *Risk and Philanthropy: Systematisation, Education and Professionalisation*. London/New York: Resource Alliance/Rockefeller Foundation.

Social Finance (2014) *Introduction to Social Impact Bonds*. [Online]. London: Social Finance. Available from: www.socialfinance.org.uk/wp-content/uploads/2014/07/Introduction-to-Social-Impact-Bonds.pdf

Thane, P. (2011) There Has Always Been a 'Big Society'. *History Workshop blog.* [Online]. Available from: www.historyworkshop.org.uk/there-has-always-been-a-big-society

The Victorianist (2011) *'The Most Remarkable Woman in the Kingdom.' Or, The Philanthropy of Angela Burdett-Coutts.* [Online]. Available from: http://thevictorianist.blogspot.co.uk/2011/04/most-remarkable-woman-in-kingdom-or.html

Thomas Cook (n.d.) *Thomas Cook History.* [Online]. Available from: www.thomascook.com/thomas-cook-history

Unwin, J. (2012) *Philanthropy Then, Philanthropy Now.* [Online]. Transcript of lecture given at Gresham College, 29 March. Available from: www.gresham.ac.uk/sites/default/files/29mar12juliaunwin_philanthropythenphilanthropynow.doc

Wixley, S. and Noble, J. (2014) *Mind the Gap: What the public thinks about charities.* [Online]. London: New Philanthropy Capital. Available from: www.thinknpc.org/publications/mind-the-gap/mind-the-gap-what-the-public-thinks-about-charities-2/?post-parent=9831

Žižek, S. (2009) First as Tragedy, Then as Farce. [Online]. Lecture for the RSA. Available from: www.thersa.org/discover/videos/event-videos/2009/11/first-as-tragedy-then-as-farce

Parliamentary and governmental materials

Reports and statistics

Great Britain, Charitable Trusts Committee (Nathan Committee) (1952) *Report of the Committee on the Law and Practice relating to Charitable Trusts.* London: The Stationery Office (Cm. 8710).

Great Britain, HM Treasury (2013) *Public Expenditure Statistical Analyses.* [Online]. London: The Stationery Office (Cm. 8663). Available from: www.gov.uk/government/uploads/system/uploads/attachment_data/file/223600/public_expenditure_statistical_analyses_2013.pdf

Great Britain, HM Treasury and HMRC (2012) *Delivering a cap on income tax relief: a technical consultation.* [Online]. London: HM Treasury and HMRC. Available from: www.gov.uk/government/uploads/system/uploads/attachment_data/file/81450/consult_income_tax_relief_cap_130712.pdf

Great Britain, House of Commons Culture, Media and Sport Committee (2011) *Funding of the Arts and Heritage: third report of session 2010–11.* [Online]. London: The Stationery Office (HC464-I). Available from: www.publications.parliament.uk/pa/cm201011/cmselect/cmcumeds/464/464i.pdf

Great Britain, Parliament, House of Commons (2012) *Public Services (Social Value) Act.* London: The Stationery Office. 2012 c.1.

Great Britain, Parliament, House of Commons (2014) *Transparency of Lobbying, Non-party Campaigning and Trade Union Administration Act.* London: The Stationery Office. 2014, c.4.

Phillips, P. (2012) *Philanthropy Beyond London: A report commissioned by the Secretary of State for Culture, Media & Sport.* [Online]. London: Department of Culture, Media & Sport. Available from: www.gov.uk/government/uploads/system/uploads/attachment_data/file/78577/philanthropy_in_the_regions.pdf

Seely, A. (2013) *Income tax – cap on unlimited reliefs.* [Online]. House of Commons Library Standard Note SN603. London: House of Commons Library. Available from: www.parliament.uk/briefing-papers/sn06303.pdf

United States, Congressional Budget Office (2011) Options for Changing the Tax Treatment of Charitable Giving. [Online]. Washington, DC: Congressional Budget Office. Available from: www.cbo.gov/sites/default/files/112th-congress-2011-2012/reports/charitablecontributions.pdf

United States, Senate Committee on Finance (2013) Tax-Exempt Organizations and Charitable Giving: Senate Finance Committee Staff Tax Reform Options for Discussion. [Online]. Washington, DC: United States Senate Committee on Finance. Available from: www.finance.senate.gov/imo/media/doc/06132013%20Tax-Exempt%20Organizations%20and%20Charitable%20Giving.pdf

United States, US Senate (1917) *War Revenue Act*.

Woodhouse, J. (2015) *The Voluntary Sector and the Big Society* [Online]. London: House of Commons Library Number 5883. Available from: www.parliament.uk/commons-library

Hansard

HC Deb (1862–63) 4 May 1863 cc1067-1136W

HL Deb (1948–49) 22 June 1949 cc75-136W

HL Deb (1953–54) 22 July 1953 cc747-848W

HL Deb (1962–63) 5 February 1963 cc556-82W

HL Deb (2010) 2 December 2010 cc1618-1666W

References

[1] (Woodhouse, 2015).

[2] A valid question here would be 'what about heritage charities and museums?' Some might argue these are by definition conservative because they aim to hold assets such as land and cultural objects in perpetuity, and so fall foul of this principle. However, this misses the point. The distinction between progressive and conservative concerns relates to views about society. It can be argued that the preservation of assets for the benefit of future generations, when done in the right way, is a deeply *progressive* cause. For instance, the National Trust, which may at one time have seemed like the archetype of a conservative approach to philanthropy, now has a strong commitment to widening access to the land, property and objects it owns, and also a specific focus on engaging young people with nature; both of which exemplify a clearly progressive attitude.

[3] (Rodgers, 1949), 2.

[4] (Jones, 1969), 10.

[5] (Andrew, 1989), 22.

[6] *Ibid.*

[7] *Ibid.*

[8] *Ibid.*

[9] (Slack, 1995), 197.

[10] (Ben-Amos, 2008), 242–243.

[11] (Jordan, 1959), 146.

[12] (Jordan, 1961).

[13] (Slack, 1995), 41–42.

[14] *Ibid.*

[15] (Ben-Amos, 2008), 114.

[16] *Ibid.*

[17] (Jordan, 1959), 233.

[18] (Jordan, 1959), 163.

[19] (Jordan, 1959), 233.

[20] Quoted in (Jordan, 1959), 236.

[21] (Archer, 2002), 225.

[22] Quoted in (Jordan, 1959), 238.

[23] (Archer, 2002), 226.

[24] *Ibid.*

[25] *Ibid.*

[26] *Ibid.*

[27] (Andrew, 1989), 11.

[28] (Slack, 1995), 8.

[29] (Archer, 2002), 231.

[30] (Slack, 1995).

[31] *Ibid.*

[32] *Ibid.*

[33] (Fishman, 2008), 48.

[34] (Jordan, 1959), 113.

[35] The *Pemsel* case is covered in more detail in the section entitled *Philanthropy Beyond the State* in Chapter 4. In very brief terms, it was an 1891 court case in which the judge, Lord Macnaghten, outlined 'four heads of charity', which still constitutes the basis of much charity law today.

[36] (Harding, 2014), 9.

[37] (Jordan, 1959), 114.

[38] (Fishman, 2008), 41–43.

[39] (Fishman, 2008), 43.

[40] (Jones, 1969), 57.

[41] (Jones, 1969), 120.

[42] *Ibid.*

[43] *Ibid.*

[44] (Jones, 1969), 109.

[45] (Jones, 1969), 128.

[46] *Ibid.*

[47] (Jones, 1969), 139.

[48] Morice v Bishop of Durham [1805].

[49] (Owen, 1964), 177.

[50] *Ibid.*

[51] *Ibid.*

[52] (Owen, 1964), 207.

[53] (Jordan, 1959), 154.

[54] (Andrew, 1989), 19.

[55] (Cunningham, 2015), 21.

[56] (Roberts, 1998), 70.

[57] (Slack, 1995), 41.

[58] (Owen, 1964), 17–19.

[59] (Roberts, 1998), 68.

[60] (Owen, 1964), 33–34.

[61] (Roberts, 1998), 68.

[62] (Owen, 1964), 415–416.

[63] (The Victorianist, 2011).

[64] (*The Times*, 1869).

[65] (Healey E, 1984).

[66] (Owen, 1964), 419.

[67] *Ibid.*

[68] *Ibid.*

[69] *Ibid.*

[70] (Owen, 1964), 106.

[71] *Ibid.*

[72] *Ibid.*

[73] (Owen, 1964), 221.

[74] (*The Guardian*, 1885).

[75] (Owen, 1964), 216.

[76] www.family-action.org.uk

[77] See, for instance (Harlock, 2013).

[78] The existence of a membership body for social impact analysts (Social Value International) is testament to this fact.

[79] For a further discussion of the debate over appropriate demands for impact measurement in philanthropy, see (Davies, 2014c).

[80] (Fiennes and Reed, 2014).

[81] (Rodgers, 1949), 11.

[82] (Kirkman Gray, 1905), 285.

[83] More information on Booth's work, including digitised versions of his maps, can be found at: http://booth.lse.ac.uk/static/a/4.html

[84] (*The Gentleman Magazine*, 1790), 288.

[85] (*The Times*, 1857).

[86] (Rodgers, 1949), 62.

[87] (Rodgers, 1949), 67.

[88] (Rodgers, 1949), 88–89.

[89] (Rodgers, 1949), 87.

[90] (Owen, 1964), 3.

[91] (Slack, 1995), 42.

[92] (Innes, 1998), 37.

[93] (Owen, 1964), 11.

[94] (Prochaska, 1980), 22.

[95] (Owen, 1964), 92.

[96] (Prochaska, 1980), 22.

[97] *Ibid.*

[98] *Ibid.*

[99] (Owen, 1964), 92.

100 Or even, as argued by the outspoken philanthropist Gina Miller, that the Charity Commission should cap the amount that UK charities spend on administration. See (Pudelek, 2013).

101 In fact, some have argued that the evidence suggests that more effective charities actually spend *more* on administration costs than less good ones. See, for instance, (Fiennes, 2013).

102 The US fundraising expert Dan Pallotta gained wide attention in philanthropy circles for a TED talk he gave in 2013 on this issue (Pallotta, 2013), in which he argued that donors were doing themselves a disservice by sticking to the mistaken belief that administration costs were a meaningful measure of an organisation's effectiveness.

103 (Price, 1999), 67.

104 (Price, 1999), 192–193.

105 *Ibid.*

106 (McCarthy, 1989), xi.

107 (Kirkman Gray, 1908), 3.

108 (Slack, 1995), 6.

109 *Ibid.*

110 (Jones, 1969), 128.

111 *Ibid.*

112 *Ibid.*

113 *Ibid.*

114 (Jordan, 1959), 127.

115 (Slack, 1995), 41.

116 (Great Britain, Nathan Committee, 1952), §38.

117 (Roberts, 1998), 78.

118 (Owen, 1964), 211.

119 (Great Britain, Nathan Committee, 1952), §44.

120 (Thane, 2001).

121 *Ibid.*

122 (Owen, 1964), 119.

123 (Owen, 1964), 211.

124 (Owen, 1964), 502.

125 (Price, 1999), 193.

126 (*The Times,* 1856).

127 (Finlayson, 1994), 413.

128 (Prochaska, 1990), 388.

129 *Ibid.*

130 (Prochaska, 1980), 21.

131 (Prochaska, 1990), 358.

132 (Harrison, 1966), 353. The 'Mayhew' referred to in the quote is Henry Mayhew, a well-known Victorian social reformer and the co-founder of the satirical magazine *Punch*.

133 (Owen D, 1964), 457.

134 *Ibid.*

135 (Finlayson, 1994), 137.

136 (Prochaska, 1990), 389.

137 (Owen, 1964), 104.

138 It was the work of Charles Booth (mentioned on p40) that provided much of the impetus for this development.

139 (Owen, 1964), 511.

140 *Ibid.*

141 *Ibid.*

142 (Finlayson, 1994), 137.

143 (Finlayson, 1994), 165.

144 *Ibid.*

145 (Cunningham, 1998), 2.

146 (Archer, 2002), 244.

147 (Cunningham, 2013), 5.

148 (Owen, 1964), 55.

149 The Philanthropic Society became the Royal Philanthropic Society, and continued to work on addressing youth poverty issues for more than 200 years before going through a series of mergers with other organisations and eventually becoming Catch22, which remains one of the biggest charities operating in the UK at the date of writing.

150 (Owen, 1964), 120–121.

151 *Ibid.*

152 (Cunningham, 1998), 2.

153 *Ibid.*

154 (Great Britain, Nathan Committee, 1952), §39.

155 (Finlayson, 1994), 12.

[156] (Owen, 1964), 62.

[157] *Ibid.*

[158] *Ibid.*

[159] (Kirkman Gray, 1908), 4.

[160] (Cunningham, 2013), 19.

[161] (Finlayson, 1994), 198.

[162] *Ibid.*

[163] (Thane, 2011).

[164] Quoted in (Moore 1971), 35.

[165] (Cunningham, 2013), 18–19.

[166] *Ibid.*

[167] (Prochaska, 1990), 390.

[168] (Davis Smith J, 1995), 25.

[169] (Finlayson, 1994), 221.

[170] (Finlayson, 1994), 416.

[171] (Finlayson, 1994), 231.

[172] (Finlayson, 1994), 249.

[173] *Ibid.*

[174] (Davis Smith and Oppenheimer, 2005), 110.

[175] (Owen, 1964), 6.

[176] *Ibid.*

[177] Quoted in *Ibid.*

[178] (Obler, 1981), 17.

[179] (Thane, 2011).

[180] (Brenton, 1985), 21.

[181] (Prochaska, 1988), 84–85

[182] *Ibid.*

[183] Quoted in (Davis Smith and Oppenheimer, 2005), 110.

[184] (Finlayson, 1994), 420.

[185] *Ibid.*

[186] (Thane, 2011).

[187] *Ibid.*

[188] *Ibid.*

[189] (Great Britain, Nathan Committee, 1952), §49.

[190] *Ibid.*

[191] (Finlayson, 1994), 297.

[192] (Great Britain, Nathan Committee, 1952), §632.

[193] (Great Britain, Nathan Committee, 1952), §61.

[194] (Great Britain, Nathan Committee, 1952), §63.

[195] (Beveridge, 1948), 302.

[196] (Rodgers, 1949), 20.

[197] (Great Britain, Nathan Committee, 1952), §641.

[198] *Ibid.*

[199] (Finlayson, *1994)*, 403.

[200] *Ibid.*

[201] (Beveridge, 1948), 150–151.

[202] (Finlayson, 1994), 307.

[203] (Finlayson, 1994), 329.

[204] (Parker, 1975).

[205] (Finlayson, 1994), 307.

[206] (Deakin, 1995)

[207] (Finlayson 1994), 308.

[208] *Ibid.*

[209] (Finlayson, 1994), 318–319.

[210] *Ibid.*

[211] *Ibid.*

[212] (Davis Smith and Oppenheimer, 2005), 108.

[213] (Brenton, 1985), 135.

[214] *Ibid.*

[215] (Davis Smith and Oppenheimer, 2005), 113.

[216] (Brenton, 1985), 36.

[217] (Brenton, 1985), 140.

[218] (Finlayson, 1994), 359.

[219] *Ibid.*

[220] (Brenton, 1985), 141.

[221] (Deakin, 1995), 55.

[222] Quoted in (Brenton, 1985), 143.

[223] *Ibid.*

[224] For more on the history of public sector markets, see (Gash and Roos, 2012).

[225] (National Council for Voluntary Organisations, 2014).

[226] (Brenton, 1985), 145.

227 For more on notions of value in public service delivery, see (Davies, 2009).

228 (Great Britain, Parliament, House of Commons, 2012).

229 For further information on potential concerns about the Social Value Act, see (Davies, 2012).

230 (Harris, 1990), 114.

231 (Great Britain, Nathan Committee, 1952), §645.

232 E.g. (Hudson, 2010).

233 See, for instance, (Hillier and Cook, 2014).

234 (Innes, 1998), 47.

235 (Great Britain, Nathan Committee, 1952), §55.

236 (Thane, 2011).

237 *Ibid.*

238 *Ibid.*

239 For more background on Social Impact Bonds, see (Social Finance, 2014).

240 (Owen, 1964).

241 *Ibid.*

242 (Kirkman Gray, 1905), 229.

243 (New Philanthropy Capital, The Smith Institute and The Peabody Trust, 2013), 77.

244 (*Jewish Chronicle,* 13 March 1885).

245 (Dobkin Hall, 2006), 35.

246 *Ibid.*

247 (Sievers, 2010b), 384.

248 (Nasaw, 2006).

249 (Strom, 2010).

250 (Mider, 2014).

251 (Bloomberg *Businessweek*, 2014).

252 See, for example, (West, 2014).

253 See, for example, (Lieu, 2010).

254 (Page, Bartels and Seawright, 2013).

255 (Abrahamson, 2013), 32.

256 (Preston, 2013).

257 (Prochaska, 1980), 222.

258 (Price, 1999), 216.

259 (Prochaska, 1980), 227.

260 *Ibid.*

261 (Davis Smith and Oppenheimer, 2005), 112.

262 (Prochaska, 2006).

263 *Ibid.*

264 *Ibid.*

265 *Ibid.*

266 (Great Britain, Nathan Committee, 1952), §53.

267 Quoted in (Owen, 1964), 326–327.

268 (Owen, 1964), 132.

269 (Owen, 1964), 129.

270 (Owen, 1964), 130.

271 (Kirkman Gray, 1908), 11–12.

272 (Cunningham, 1998), 9.

273 (Finlayson, 1994), 405.

274 (Beveridge, 1948), 182.

275 *Bowman v Secular Society* (1917).

276 *Ibid.*

277 (Harding, 2014), 175.

278 *Ibid.*

279 *Bowman v Secular Society* (1917).

280 (Harding, 2014), 183.

281 *Ibid.*

282 (Harding, 2014), 175–6.

283 For instance, in 2014, the UK government's Minister for Civil Society, Brooks Newmark, caused uproar in the voluntary sector when, in his first major speech, he said that charities should 'stick to their knitting and stay out of politics' (*The Guardian*, 2014). Newmark was subsequently forced to backtrack on his comments.

284 (Great Britain, Parliament, House of Commons, 2014).

285 For further detail, see (Pickering, 2014).

286 See (Kindell and Reilly, 1997) for further detail.

287 See e.g. (Bowie and Lioz, 2012).

288 (Harding, 2014), 191.

289 (Charities Aid Foundation, 2015).

290 (Coutts, 2014).

291 See (Breeze, 2010) and (Bekkers and Wiepking, 2007).

292 Recent examples include the Dorfman Theatre at the National Theatre, the Dorothy and Michael Hintze Room at the National Gallery, the Blavatnik school of Government and the Oxford Martin School at Oxford University, The Dickson Poon School of Law at King's College London, and The Dyson Engineering Design Centre at Cambridge University.

293 For further discussion of this issue see e.g. (Eisenberg, 2013).

294 (Andreoni, 1990).

295 (Great Britain, Nathan Committee, 1952), §122.

296 (Great Britain, House of Commons Culture, Media and Sport Committee, 2011).

297 (Reich, 2011).

298 For instance, a gift to an individual, where there was no expectation of return, but also no benefit to wider society as a result of the gift.

299 42% of £1 million donations in the UK in 2012 went to higher education institutions (£570 million in total), while 7% (£95.4 million) went to arts, culture and humanities organisations. By way of contrast, the total grant for the Higher Education Funding Council for England (HEFCE) in 2012/13 was 0.8% of public sector Total Managed Expenditure (TME), while the entire budget of the Department for Culture, Media and Sport in the same year was only 0.06% of public sector TME. (Figures taken from Coutts, 2013, Higher Education Funding Council for England, 2014 and Great Britain, HM Treasury, 2013).

300 (Harding, 2014), 140.

301 (Kenny, 2014).

302 (Great Britain, HM Treasury, 2013).

303 (NHS England, 2013).

304 (Sullivan, 2014).

305 (Owen, 1964), 337.

306 (Livingston Booth and Brophy, 1999), 6.

307 (United States, US Senate, 1917), ch. 63, 1201(2).

308 Information taken from (Livingston Booth and Brophy, 1999) and (Owen, 1964).

309 (Charities Aid Foundation and National Council for Voluntary Organisations, 2012).

310 (Owen D, 1964), 331.

311 (Owen D, 1964), 332.

312 Ibid.

313 Ibid.

314 Ibid.

315 (The Times, 1863a).

316 Ibid.

317 Ibid.

318 (The Times, 1863b).

319 (Great Britain, HM Treasury and HMRC, 2012).

320 (BBC News, 2012).

321 CAF was heavily involved as one of the organisations leading the 'Give it Back George' campaign that opposed the Chancellor's proposal.

322 For a useful overview of this whole incident, see (Seely, 2013).

323 HC Deb (1862–63).

324 (The Times, 1863b).

325 HC Deb (1862–63). Sections in bold are the author's emphasis.

326 Cited in (Gousmett, 2009).

327 (Conservative Party, 2008).

328 (Ben Amos, 2008), 227.

329 (Ben Amos, 2008), 229.

330 Ibid.

331 (Archer, 2002), 237.

332 (Jordan, 1959), 216.

333 (Reproduced in Jordan, 1959), 217–18.

334 (The Times, 1850).

335 (Owen, 1964), 470.

336 Ibid.

337 (Finlayson, 1994), 54.

338 (Prochaska, 1980), 40.

339 (Prochaska, 1990), 366.

340 (Andrew, 1989), 83.

[341] (*The Spectator,* 1893).

[342] For instance, former New York Mayor Michael Bloomberg, who is himself a notable philanthropist, cites Carnegie as one of his role models. (Jack, 2013).

[343] (Nasaw, 2006).

[344] *Ibid.*

[345] (Sturges, 1996), 258.

[346] For more on the rise in influence of foundations in the US, see (Karl and Katz, 1981).

[347] (Davies, 2014).

[348] (Moore, 2004).

[349] (Moore, 2004), 68.

[350] *Ibid.*

[351] (Sturges, 1996), 262.

[352] (Partridge, 1973).

[353] (Sturges, 1996), 262.

[354] All taken from (Sturges P, 1996).

[355] (Bielenberg, 2003).

[356] (Howell, 1979).

[357] While there is a slower, long-term trend towards a higher proportion of created wealth in the UK, there has also been a much more dramatic shift in the last 25 years or so. The author of the *Sunday Times Rich List* has noted that in the first index in 1989, roughly two-thirds of entrants were there as a result of inherited wealth, but by contrast in the most recent index, roughly 80% of entrants had created their own wealth (Reuben, 2013).

[358] (Bishop and Green, 2010), 21.

[359] (Owen, 1964), 470.

[360] *Ibid.*

[361] Research from the University of Southampton, which analysed the explanatory letters of all the individuals who have signed the 'Giving Pledge', found that self-made billionaires were more likely to sign. (Sadeh, Tonin and Vlassopoulos, 2014).

[362] (Owen, 1964). 472–473.

[363] (Buffett, 2010).

[364] (Nasaw, 2006).

[365] (Karl, 1992), 32.

[366] (Quakers in the World, n.d. a).

[367] (Quakers in the World, n.d. b).

[368] Respectively, (Rowntree, J,1865) and (Rowntree, BS, 1908).

[369] These are the Joseph Rowntree Housing Trust, The Joseph Rowntree Foundation, The Joseph Rowntree Charitable Trust and the Joseph Rowntree Reform Trust.

[370] We should note that the sense of 'stewardship' here is different to that mentioned in the discussion of inherited v created wealth: there, the suggestion was that those who have inherited wealth view themselves as stewards of that wealth on behalf of their family and children. Here, however, the suggestion is that Protestant doctrine taught a notion of stewardship of wealth on behalf of society as a whole.

[371] Social contract theory is most closely associated with the names of Locke, Hobbes and Rousseau. For further information on the theory and related issues, see (Vallier and D'Agostino, 2014).

[372] (Jordan, 1959), 153–154. Emphasis is the author's.

[373] (Andrew, 1989), 18.

[374] *Ibid.*

[375] *Ibid.*

[376] E.g. In the US, *Forbes* magazine's 'America's 50 Top Givers'; In Asia, *Forbes Asia* magazine's '48 Heroes of Philanthropy'; and in the UK the *Sunday Times* '*Giving Lis*t' (produced in association with CAF).

[377] (Sellers, 2010).

[378] (Hu, 2014).

[379] (Arnold, 2014).

[380] E.g. (Wessel, 2011), (Sorkin, 2011).

[381] (Gentilucci, 2014a).

[382] E.g. (Chapman, 2012).

[383] Quoted in (Jordan, 1959), 187.

[384] (Andrew, 1989), 42.

[385] *Ibid.*

386 This is not the place for a full history of the Charity Commission, but some clarification is required. The system of Charity Commissioners was made more formal with the introduction of a permanent Board in the mid 19th century. The powers of these Commissioners were then incrementally increased until the Charities Act (1960) established the Charity Commission as an independent organisation. The powers of the Commission were regularly reviewed and enhanced, and in 2006 the updated Charities Act established the current Charity Commission for England and Wales. One further point to note is that prior to the introduction of devolved government in both Scotland and Northern Ireland, there was not really a question over jurisdiction; however, following devolution both countries established their own charity regulators (the Office of the Scottish Charity Regulator and the Charity Commission for Northern Ireland). In the course of the text, I have used 'Charity Commission' to refer to the organisation operating in England and Wales (and by extension Scotland and Northern Ireland prior to devolution) at the relevant point in history.

387 Quoted in (Jordan, 1959), 186.

388 Chuck Feeney, one of the world's biggest philanthropists, has long espoused a mantra of 'giving while living'. This is explored in detail in (Atlantic Philanthropies, 2010). Feeney himself used the majority of his wealth to establish the Atlantic Philanthropies foundation back in 1982, and remains heavily involved with its work.

389 (Gowen, 2013).

390 (Owen, 1964), 31.

391 (Owen, 1964), 48.

392 (Owen, 1964), 57.

393 (Owen, 1964), 480.

394 Ibid.

395 (The Times, 1880).

396 (Owen, 1964), 176.

397 (Andrew D, 1989), 17.

398 (Prochaska, 1980), 125.

399 (Owen, 1959), 149.

400 Ibid.

401 (Sturges P, 1996), 264.

402 (Owen D, 1964), 53.

403 Ibid.

404 (Gose and Gipple, 2012).

405 (Piff, Kraus, Keltner, Côté and Hayden Cheng, 2010).

406 Quoted in (Gose and Gipple, 2012).

407 (Macdonald, 2011).

408 (Owen, 1964), 431.

409 (Ross and Chapman C, 2013).

410 (The Times, 1911).

411 (Owen, 1964), 428.

412 (Owen, 1964), 136.

413 (Owen, 1964), 98.

414 Ibid.

415 (Owen, 1964), 228.

416 (Owen, 1964), 230.

417 (Owen, 1964), 231.

418 (Eaton, 2011).

419 (Thomas Cook, n.d.).

420 Quoted in (Harrison, 1966), 358.

421 Speech from 1883, quoted in (Himmelfarb, 1992).

422 (Jordan, 1959), 149.

423 (Finlayson, 1994), 51.

424 (Finlayson, 1994), 97.

425 Ibid.

426 Quoted in (Waddington, 2000), 30–31.

427 (Andrew,1989), 97.

428 Ibid.

429 (Owen, 1964), 97–98.

430 (Prochaska, 1990), 370.

431 Ibid.

432 (Finlayson, 1994), 51.

433 Ibid.

434 Quoted in (Finlayson, 1994), 130.

435 (Churchill, 1909), 363.

436 For more on this, see (Davies, 2014).

437 (Soskis, 2014).

438 (*The Guardian*, 1891).

439 (Kirkman Gray, 1908), ix.

440 (Kirkman Gray, 1908), 4.

441 (Owen, 1964), 162.

442 (Kirkman Gray, 1905), 288.

443 *Ibid.*

444 (Preston, 2012).

445 (Serrano, 2007).

446 (Miller, 2012)

447 Singer has produced a number of papers exploring the issues that underpin effective altruism, but the classic statement of the original idea is (Singer, 1972).

448 For more information, see www. centreforeffectivealtruism.org.

449 For a discussion of one instance of this controversy, see (Davies, 2013).

450 (de Tocqueville, 1835) 27–28.

451 (Owen, 1964), 221.

452 Quoted in (Finlayson, 1994), 135.

453 (Hobson, 1914), 296.

454 For instance, the American urban activist and church worker Robert Lupton has criticised what he terms 'toxic charity' for creating dependency amongst beneficiaries. See (Lupton, 2011).

455 For the classic statement of Malthus views, see (Malthus, 1798).

456 Quoted in (Owen, 1964), 167.

457 See (Abramitzky and Braggion, 2003).

458 For instance, by the outgoing CEO of the Charity Commission in 2014: see (Green, 2014).

459 (Owen, 1964), 167.

460 (Owen, 1964), 277

461 *Ibid.*

462 *Ibid.*

463 *Ibid.*

464 (Owen, 1964), 279.

465 www.trustforlondon.org.uk

466 (Beveridge, 1948), 356–380. Beveridge's analysis of charitable trusts builds on the work of the Charity Commissioner Arthur Hobhouse, who had first identified many of these 'horrors' in the 19th century. (Hobhouse, 1868).

467 Details taken from (Beveridge, 1948) and (Wilson, 1979).

468 (Beveridge, 1948), 358.

469 E.g. (nfpSynergy, 2014).

470 (Harrison, 1966), 363.

471 (IPSOS MORI, 2014).

472 A survey by ICM for CAF in 2011 found that members of the public estimated that charities spend 42p to raise every pound of income, and thought that an acceptable amount would be 26p for every pound. Data suggests, however, that the actual figure is closer to 12p for every pound. See (CAF, 2011).

473 (Owen, 1964), 474.

474 (Owen, 1964), 475.

475 (Resource Alliance and Rockefeller Foundation, 2012), 5.

476 (Bank of America and Center on Philanthropy at Indiana University, 2012), 47.

477 (Kasper and Marcoux, 2014).

478 (Owen, 1964), 402.

479 (*The Spectator,* 1886).

480 *Ibid.*

481 *Ibid.*

482 *Ibid.*

483 Quoted in (Owen, 1964), 408.

484 (Owen, 1964), 402.

485 Quoted in (Andrew, 1989), 21.

486 (Wilde, 1909), 3–4.

487 (Žižek, 2009).

488 (Harrison B, 1966), 370.

489 (Godwin, 1797), 800.

490 (Wilde, 1909), 9.

491 (Kirkman Gray, 1905), 269–270. The reference in the quote is to (Alcock, 1752).

492 (Prochaska, 1990), 375.

[493] (Owen, 1964), 481–482.

[494] (Prochaska, 1990), 375.

[495] (Owen, 1964), 481–482.

[496] (Prochaska, 1990), 375.

[497] (Rodgers, 1949), 8.

[498] (Prochaska,1980), 124.

[499] (Harrison, 1966), 360.

[500] Quoted in (Harrison, 1966), 367.

[501] (Nasaw, 2006).

[502] (Gentilucci, 2014b).

[503] (Owen, 1964), 397.

[504] *Ibid,*

[505] (Owen, 1964), 401.

[506] (*The Times*, 1857).

[507] (*The Times*, 1840).

[508] For instance (Chorley, 2014).

[509] For further details see (International Association for Scottish Philosophy, n.d.).

[510] Quoted in (Owen, 1964), 27.

[511] (Petrosino, Turpin-Petrosino, Hollis-Peel and Lavenberg, 2002).

[512] (Yu, 2014).

[513] (Owen, 1964), 324.

[514] (Owen, 1964), 325.

[515] (*The Times,* 1926).

[516] (Thomas Dolby Publisher, 1825), 111.

[517] (*The Times,* 1926).

[518] See (Gousmett, 2009).

[519] (Buffett, 2013).

[520] (Bernard Shaw, 1907).

[521] (*The Guardian,* 1997).

[522] *Ibid.*

[523] For a detailed discussion of the 'tainted money' affair and its relevance to modern debates about philanthropy see (Soskis, 2014).

[524] For further discussion of the ethical and practical issues facing charities confronted with a 'tainted donation' see (Davies, 2011).

[525] (Nasaw D, 2006).

[526] (Malkin, 2007).

[527] The 'Shared Value' concept, developed by Harvard academics Michael Porter and Mark Kramer, aims to take this notion even further by arguing for a new understanding that puts business success and social progress on an equal footing and contends that the two are mutually reinforcing. See (Porter and Kramer M, 2011). Some large companies such as Nestle have even started adopting a 'Shared Value' approach to their business: www.nestle.com/csv

[528] (Owen, 1964), 434.

[529] (Owen, 1964), 434–435.

[530] (Owen, 1964), 435.

[531] *Ibid.*

Picture credits

P16 – The *Selling of Indulgences*. Image taken from Chamberlain, A. (1913) *Hans Holbein the Younger, Vol. 1*. New York: Dodd, Mead and Company, facing page 199. Digitised as part of the Internet Archive project (www.archive.org). Original work is out of copyright.

P20 – Thomas Becon. Image taken from Simms, J. (1873) *A New Physiognomical Chart of Character*. Glasgow: Dunn & White, page 56. Digitised as part of the Internet Archive project (www.archive.org). Original work is out of copyright.

P21 – Thomas Sutton. Image from Wellcome Library, London. Reference number ICV No 5877. Made available by Wellcome Images (www.wellcomeimages. org) under a Creative Commons Attribution 4.0 International licence.

P22 – Charterhouse Hospital School. Image from Wellcome Library, London. Reference number ICV No 13311. Made available by Wellcome Images (www. wellcomeimages.org) under a Creative Commons Attribution 4.0 International licence.

P32 – Angela Burdett-Coutts. Image made available under a Creative Commons Attribution-NonCommercial-NoDerivs 3.0 Unported licence by the National Portrait Gallery. Image reference NPG 618.

P39 – John Howard. Image from Wellcome Library, London. Reference number ICV No 6927. Made available by Wellcome Images (www.wellcomeimages.org) under a Creative Commons Attribution 4.0 International licence.

P41 – Lazaretto at Genoa. Image taken from Howard, J. (1789) *An Account of the Principal Lazarettos in Europe*. Warrington: William Eyres, page 6. Made available by Wellcome Images (www.wellcomeimages. org) under a Creative Commons Attribution 4.0 International licence.

P42 – *The triumph of benevolence*. Made available under a Creative Commons Attribution-NonCommercial-NoDerivs 3.0 Unported licence by the National Portrait Gallery. Image reference NPG D13059.

P54 – William Rathbone. Image taken from Tooley, S. (1906) *A History of Nursing in the British Empire*. London: Bousefield, page 288. Made available by Wellcome Images (www.wellcomeimages.org) under a Creative Commons Attribution 4.0 International licence.

P55 – Florence Nightingale. Image taken from Duyckinick, E. (1872) *Portrait Gallery of Eminent Men and Women in Europe and America, vol II*. New York: Johnson, Wilson & Company, page 533. Digitised as part of the Internet Archive project (www.archive.org). Original work is out of copyright.

P56 – *Queen's Nurses.* Image from Wellcome Library, London. Reference number CMAC SA/QNI/X.38/1. Made available by Wellcome Images (www. wellcomeimages.org) under a Creative Commons Attribution 4.0 International licence.

P60 – General James Oglethorpe. Image taken from The Georgia Historical Society, (1913). *The Spanish official account of the attack on the colony of Georgia, in America, and of its defeat on St. Simons Island by General James Oglethorpe.* Savannah, GA: Georgia Historical Society. Digitised as part of the Internet Archive project (www.archive. org). Original work is out of copyright.

P61 – The Trustees of the colony of Georgia receiving the Indians. Image taken from Clark-Kennedy, A. (1929) *Stephen Hales, DD, FRS: an eighteenth century biography.* Cambridge [England]: Cambridge University Press, page 170. Made available by Wellcome Images (www. wellcomeimages.org) under a Creative Commons Attribution 4.0 International licence.

P64 – Salvation Army poster. Accessed via Wikimedia Commons. This image is in the public domain because it is a mechanical scan or photocopy of a public domain original. The original is in the public domain because it is an artistic work other than a photograph or engraving (e.g. a painting) which was created by the United Kingdom Government prior to 1966.

P66 – Statue of Aneurin Bevan, by Robert Thomas. Queen Street, Cardiff, UK. Image accessed via Flickr. Taken by user DncnH and made available under a Creative Commons Attribution 2.0 Generic licence.

P67 William Beveridge. Made available under a Creative Commons Attribution-NonCommercial-NoDerivs 3.0 Unported licence by the National Portrait Gallery. Image reference NPG x2936.

P83 – Peabody Square Model Dwellings. Accessed via Wikimedia Commons. Unknown author. This is a faithful photographic reproduction of a two-dimensional work of art. The work of art itself is in the public domain because the author died more than 70 years ago.

P92 – The Anti-Slavery Society Convention. Made available under a Creative Commons Attribution-NonCommercial-NoDerivs 3.0 Unported licence by the National Portrait Gallery. Image reference NPG 618.

P93 – Wedgwood Anti-Slavery medallion. Image is certified as public domain.

P112 – William Gladstone. Made available under a Creative Commons Attribution-NonCommercial-NoDerivs 3.0 Unported licence by the National Portrait Gallery. Image reference NPG 3378.

P113 – Benjamin Disraeli. Image is certified as public domain.

P120 – 'A Word to Grand Stand Specialists'. Image taken from *Puck,* v. 53, no. 1370 (1903 June 3), centrefold. Made available by US Library of Congress, reproduction number LC-DIG-ppmsca-25747. No known rights restrictions.

P121 – Sir Francis Walsingham. Made available by Wellcome Images (www. wellcomeimages.org) under a Creative Commons Attribution 4.0 International licence.

P123 – Caricature of Michael Thomas Bass. Image taken from the City College of New York Art Collection on www.Flickr.com. Made available under a Creative Commons Attribution-NonCommercial-NoDerivs 2.0 Generic licence.

P124 – 'A Christmas Sermon'. Image taken from *Puck,* v. 48, no. 1242 (1900 December 26), centrefold. Made available by US Library of Congress, reproduction number LC-DIG-ppmsca-25485. No known rights restrictions.

P126 – Caricature of Sir Andrew Barclay Walker. Image taken from the City College of New York Art Collection on www.Flickr.com. Made available under a Creative Commons Attribution-NonCommercial-NoDerivs 2.0 Generic licence.

P127a – The Walker Art Gallery. Made available under a Creative Commons Attribution-NonCommercial-NoDerivs 3.0 Unported licence by the National Portrait Gallery. Image reference NPG 3378.

P127b – Caricature of Lord Iveagh (Edward Guinness). Image taken from the City College of New York Art Collection on www. Flickr.com. Made available under a Creative Commons Attribution-NonCommercial-NoDerivs 2.0 Generic licence.

P130 – Maurice de Hirsch. Accessed via Wikimedia Commons. Photograph taken by Remi Jouan and published under a Creative Commons Attribution-ShareAlike 3.0 Unported licence. This is a faithful photographic reproduction of a two-dimensional work of art. The work of art itself is in the public domain because the author died more than 100 years ago.

P132 – Elizabeth Fry. Made available under a Creative Commons Attribution-NonCommercial-NoDerivs 3.0 Unported licence by the National Portrait Gallery. Image reference. NPG D46118.

P133 – Advertisement for Fry's 'Five Boys' milk chocolate. Accessed via Wikimedia Commons. Image is a flatbed scan of an original from Jarrold & Sons (eds.) Pictures in Colour of the Isle of Wight. London: Jarrold & Sons, Ltd. This image is in the public domain because its copyright has expired and its author is anonymous.

P134 – Joseph Rowntree. Image taken from Shaw, A. (1906) The American Monthly Review of Reviews: An International Magazine, Vol. XXXIII, January–June 1906, page 768. Digitised as part of the Internet Archive project (www.archive.org). Original work is out of copyright.

P135 – JS Fry and Sons Manufactory. Image taken from Nicholls, J. and Taylor, J. (1882) Bristol Past and Present. Bristol: Arrowsmith, page 243. Digitised as part of the Internet Archive project (www.archive.org). Original work is out of copyright.

P140 – 'The Crabbed Millionaire's Puzzle'. Image taken from Puck, v. 50, no. 1275 (1901 August 7), centrefold. Made available by US Library of Congress, reproduction number LC-DIG-ppmsca-25553. No known rights restrictions.

P147 – Thomas Coram. Made available by Wellcome Images (www.wellcomeimages.org) under a Creative Commons Attribution 4.0 International licence. Image ref ICV No 147.1.

P149 – John Passmore Edwards. Made available under a Creative Commons Attribution-NonCommercial-NoDerivs 3.0 Unported licence by the National Portrait Gallery. Image reference NPG 3958.

P152 – Thomas John Barnardo. Made available by Wellcome Images (www.wellcomeimages.org) under a Creative Commons Attribution 4.0 International licence. Image ref ICV No 26451.

P153 – Thomas Cook. Accessed via Wikimedia Commons. Published under a Creative Commons Attribution-ShareAlike 3.0 Unported licence.

P154 – Friezes on the front of the Thomas Cook Building in Leicester. Image published by NotFromUtrecht at Wikimedia Commons under a Creative Commons Attribution-ShareAlike 3.0 Unported licence.

P165 – Alexis de Tocqueville. Accessed via Wikimedia Commons. This image has been certified as in the public domain.

P166 – Thomas Robert Malthus. Accessed via Wikimedia Commons. This is a faithful photographic reproduction of a two-dimensional, public domain work of art. The work of art itself is in the public domain because the author died more than 100 years ago.

P170 – The Brown Institution, Vauxhall. Image taken from Illustrated London News, 24 February, 1872. Accessed via Wikimedia Commons. Image is a scan of the original, which is out of copyright.

P175 – Samuel Morley. Image taken from Hodder, E. (1888) The Life of Samuel Morley. New York: A.D.F. Randolph & Co. Frontispiece. Digitised as part of the Internet Archive project (www.archive.org). Original work is out of copyright.

P176 – Caricature of Samuel Morley. Image taken from the City College of New York Art Collection on www.Flickr.com. Made available under a Creative Commons Attribution-NonCommercial-NoDerivs 2.0 Generic licence.

P181 – 'A Christmas Reminder'. Image taken from Puck, v. 50, no. 1294 (1901 December 18), centerefold. Made available by US Library of Congress, reproduction number LC-DIG-ppmsca-25591. No known rights restrictions.

P183 – Thomas Holloway. Image taken from Illustrated London News, 5 January, 1884. Accessed via Wikimedia Commons. This image is in the public domain because its copyright has expired and its author is anonymous.

P185 –Royal Holloway College. Image taken by Don Cload for www.geograph.org.uk and made available under a Creative Commons Attribution-ShareAlike 2.0 Generic licence.

P187 – 'The Gospel according to "Saint John"'. Image taken from *Puck*, v. 57, no. 1470 (1905 May 3), cover. Made available by US Library of Congress, reproductiown number LC-DIG-ppmsca-25951. No known rights restrictions.

P189 – 'An Object Lesson'. Image taken from *Puck,* v. 49, no. 1268 (1901 June 19), centrefold. Made available by US Library of Congress, reproduction number LC-DIG-ppmsca-25539. No known rights restrictions.

P193 – 'A phase of our tax system – the greater the service, the heavier the tax'. Image taken from *Puck,* v. 69, no. 1774 (1911 March 1), centrefold. Made available by US Library of Congress, reproduction number LC-DIG-ppmsca-27715. No known rights restrictions.

P195 – George Bernard Shaw. Made available under a Creative Commons Attribution-NonCommercial-NoDerivs 3.0 Unported licence by the National Portrait Gallery. Image reference NPG x81843.

P197 – George Cadbury. Image taken from Stead, H. (1909) *How Old Age Pensions Began to Be.* London: Methuen & Co. Plate facing page 75. Made available by Wellcome Images (www.wellcomeimages. org) under a Creative Commons Attribution 4.0 International licence.

P198 – Cadbury's Cocoa advert. Image from The Gardner's Chronicle (1874).*The Gardeners' chronicle : a weekly illustrated journal of horticulture and allied subjects, Vol X –Third Series* (1874), page 135. Digitised as part of the Internet Archive project (www.archive.org). Original work is out of copyright.

P199 – Suggestion box. Taken from Head, B. (1903) *The Food of the Gods: A popular account of cocoa.* London: R Brimley Johnson, page 62. Digitised as part of the Internet Archive project (www.archive.org). Original work is out of copyright.